Plato
GORGIAS

The Focus Philosophical Library

Plato's Sophist • E. Brann, P. Kalkavage, E. Salem • 1996
Plato's Parmenides • Albert Keith Whitaker • 1996
Plato's Symposium • Avi Sharon • 1998
Plato's Phaedo • E. Brann, P. Kalkavage, E. Salem • 1998
Empire and the Ends of Politics • S. D. Collins and D. Stauffer • 1999
Four Island Utopias • D Clay, A. Purvis • 1999
Plato's Timaeus • P. Kalkavage • 2001
Aristotle's Nicomachean Ethics • Joe Sachs • 2002
Hegel's The Philosophy of Right • Alan White • 2002
Socrates and Alcibiades: Four Texts • David M. Johnson • 2003
Plato's Phaedrus • Stephen Scully • 2003
Plato's Meno • George Anastaplo and Laurence Berns • 2004
Spinoza's Theologico-Political Treatise • Martin Yaffe • 2004
Plato's Theaetetus • Joe Sachs • 2004
Aristotle: Poetics • Joe Sachs • 2005

Plato
GORGIAS

Translated by

James A. Arieti
and
Roger M. Barrus

Focus Publishing
R. Pullins Company
PO Box 369
Newburyport, MA 01950
www.pullins.com

Cover image: A conversation between philosophers (also known as The School of Plato). Mosaic, from Pompeii, 1st CE. Photo: Erich Lessing / Art Resources, NY. Museo Archeologico Nazionale, Naples, Italy.

ISBN 10: 1-58510-243-1
ISBN 978-1-58510-243-3

Printed in the United States of America
10   9   8   7   6   5   4   3   2   1

1006TS

CONTENTS

For my son Samuel Abraham and my daughter Ruth Sophia.

(J.A.A.)

For my children Dana Janelle, Corinne Suzanne, Arianne Kathleen, Tyler Walsh, and Caitlin Paige.

(R.M.B.)

optima haereditas a patribus traditur liberis omnique patrimonio praestantior gloria virtutis rerumque gestarum. (Cicero, *de officiis*)

Preface

One of the older English meanings of *translation* is the conveyance of a person from earth to heaven without death. It is, alas, beyond the power of academic translators, even in our modern computer age, to accomplish *that* task, but, in a sense, those who undertake to translate Plato do try, within the laws of physics, to transcend the constraints of place and time in order to transport the words of a man who lived two and a half thousand years ago in the tranquil air of the Aegean to our world, where the atmosphere is tempest-tossed with an infinity of electronic digits. The transport of Plato's thought and the metamorphosing of his language into our idiom is to take his soul, as it were, to a different realm, not of heaven, but where the great thinker may continue to exert his influence upon the living. While it is, to be sure, an imperfect transport, it is nevertheless the only one available to mere human beings.

In preparing this translation, we have tried to produce a rendering as faithful as possible to the best Greek edition. We have also tried to be true to Plato's spirit as we understand it. Where consistency of translation is possible, we have worked hard to be consistent. When, however, the connotative range of a word in Greek would not allow for a consistent translation in English without damage to an understanding, we have used a different word, and, where the substitution was of an important word, we have indicated the change in the footnotes. We have tried, as far as English will allow, to catch some of the word-play of Plato's Greek—his puns, his quips, his parodies. Where this has been impossible for us to do in English but where the playfulness is important to the meaning, we again have written a footnote. We are aware that having to read a footnote to understand a text is a handicap, but we hope that the passage of two and a half thousand years will mitigate the blame that attends this practice.

Two features that exist in the Greek language but not in English are a class of words called "particles" and the use of personal pronouns as subjects only for emphasis.

Particles are words—not easily translated into English—that suggest tone of voice.[1] Greek writers often used several even is a short sentence. Homer, for example (*Iliad* 1.101) has four in a sentence of nine words. The difference in English between a sentence without particles and one with them may be seen in the following two versions of an answer to the question "What are you doing tonight?":

1) I am going to the movies tonight.

2) Well, actually, if you really want to know, I thought I would damn well go to the movies.

In sentence (2), the words "well," "actually," and "damn well" are particles. Denniston remarks that once a student has learned the subtleties of particles, the difference between reading a page of Plato and one of Thucydides is the difference between reading a score by Beethoven and one by Bach.[2]

In Greek, as in such modern languages as Spanish and Italian, the form of the verb alone shows the person of the subject, and so no pronoun is needed to indicate that the subject is *I* or *he* or *we* or *you* or *they*.[3] When the pronoun *is* used it bears a special emphasis. We have indicated the emphatic use of the personal pronoun as subject by italicizing it. This artifice, imperfect as it is, has allowed us to convey an actual feature of the Greek without the addition of cumbersome excessive verbiage.

Another feature of conversational Greek, one present to a lesser degree in English, is the omission of words that the speaker or writer feels are easily to be inferred from what has been expressed. While a speaker often knows what he intends, it is not always apparent to a listener. Who of us, indeed, has found himself expecting his interlocutor to understand something we have said when it has actually been ambiguous or obscure? We have indicated where we have filled out the thought by a liberal use of bracketed words and phrases. Filling in what is missing from the text is necessary in English to render complete sentences that make sense. Most other translations have simply inserted the understood words as if they appeared in the Greek. We

---

1 The subject of particles is very complex and is treated with a fitness of distinctions worthy of the ancient rhetoricians by J.D. Denniston in his large book *Greek Particles* (Oxford: The Clarendon Press, 1954).

2 Denniston makes this observation on p. xxxix of *Greek Particles* (op. cit previous note). This discussion of Greek particles is borrowed from James A. Arieti and John M. Crossett, *Longinus: On the Sublime* (New York and Toronto: The Edwin Mellen Press, 1985) 115.

3 In English or French, however, where the form or pronunciation of the verb hardly changes (e.g., I run, you run, we run, you (plural) run, they run), it would be impossible to know the subject without the pronoun's being stated. In English the pronoun is a marker of the person of the verb becomes emphatic only by an extra expression (e.g., "It is I who am running").

have endeavored to indicate where we have filled out the thought. We think that the reader will be compensated in accuracy for the initial adjustment needed to read the text.

Just as there are no two words in a language that share exactly the same meaning, so there is for many words no exact one to one meaning across languages. It should be obvious that words for complex matters will be difficult to translate (see, for example, "resentment" in the Glossary). It is, alas, equally true for many words that seem simple. Consider *run* in English, which enjoys fifteen entries as a verb and eleven as a noun, with many sub-entries in *Webster's Seventh New Collegiate Dictionary*.[4] For some of the most significant terms we have explained our interpretation in the notes and the Glossary. As Aristotle observes in the *Ethics*, different subjects permit different degrees of precision. As he observes, we do not expect rhetorical proofs from a geometrician nor geometrical proofs from a rhetorician. Reading a translation, alas, is, as Don Quixote says, like looking at the back of a tapestry. Preparing a translation is the doomed task of trying to make the back of the tapestry as much like the front as possible.

Our work has benefited from the contributions of others. We should like first to acknowledge Kristin Hall, who read our translation of the *Gorgias* with exacting care and offered numerous excellent suggestions. We should like to acknowledge and thank the readers and editors of Focus Books, whose advice has resulted in a volume much better than it would otherwise have been. We wish to express our gratitude to Hampden-Sydney College for its support through summer grants and a sabbatical leave. Finally, we should like to recognize our wives, Barbara Arieti and Diane Barrus, for their support and patience.

James A. Arieti

Roger M. Barrus

July 2006

---

4   Even numbers are subject to varying interpretations. *xxxi* does not convey the same meaning as *31* (e.g., the instruction to see p. xxxi as distinct from p. 31 will take one to a very different part of a book).

INTRODUCTION

Of the dialogues in Plato's corpus, the *Gorgias* most clearly shows why Athens executed Socrates. The *Republic,* to be sure, portrays a robustly nasty exchange between Thrasymachus and Socrates, but after the opening book, the dialogue devolves into a long and sometimes irritatingly congenial conversation, in which Socrates' new interlocutors Glaukon and Adeimantus rarely raise any challenging objections to the startling conclusions that Socrates draws but with apparently incessant compliance affirm them all. And the *Meno,* while it portrays an energetic and outspoken title interlocutor, shows a conversational partner who is stupid and easily confounded and who, like the *Republic's* Thrasymachus, as a non-Athenian constitutes no real threat to Socrates. In the *Gorgias,* however, in successive encounters, we observe Socrates dueling with three successively more challenging arguers, the final and most significant of whom is Callicles, an Athenian, who directly threatens Socrates and whose grim predictions accurately foretell Socrates' failure to gain acquittal at his future trial. Callicles may very well lose his theoretical arguments with Socrates, but his practical perspicacity is affirmed. Every reader knows that Socrates, for all his dialectical expertise, will end up dead and is prompted to ask, "How profits a man philosophy, if it cost him his life?"

Though the *Gorgias* is often seen as a battleground between rhetoric and dialectic,[1] a reading of the dialogue as a play—a work of philosophical drama—shows a different while perhaps complementary meaning. In the course of the drama we witness an initially likeable and charming Callicles transformed through conversation with Socrates into an angry, sullen, belligerent man who asserts principles incompatible with civilized life. It is said in the dialogue that the truest politician is the one who can make his citizens better (521d–e), and many readers of the *Gorgias* have believed

---

1   E.g., P. Friedländer, *Plato,* translated by H. Meyerhoff (Princeton and London: Princeton University Press, 1969) vol. 2, 244–45. Or, as W. Jaeger puts it (*Paideia: The Ideals of Greek Culture,* translated by G. Highet (New York: Oxford University Press, 1962) vol. 2, 133), between "the philosophy of power and the philosophy of culture."

1

Socrates when he claims to be the only true politician because he is the only one who makes his fellow citizens better. Yet, if we look at the drama of the dialogue, what do we see? We seem to see not the improvement of a single citizen, but just the opposite! Socrates' first two interlocutors, Gorgias and Polus, who are not Athenian citizens, remain mostly unaffected from their encounter with Socrates: Gorgias seems unmoved and aloof, Polus bewildered and unconvinced. Callicles, the Athenian interlocutor, *is* moved by his encounter. But he is moved to sullenness, anger, contempt, and withdrawal. By his encounter with Socrates, we seem to observe Callicles actually being transformed into a less virtuous person![2]

Of Socrates' three interlocutors, Gorgias and his disciple Polus represent those rhetoricians who do not care for the meaning but only for the form of what they say. They represent the position of Gorgias in his *Encomium on Helen* (13), in which he says that a speech delights and persuades an audience by the brilliance of its composition, not by its accuracy. This view is manifest in the dialogue in the discussion of who would be elected a town's doctor, as Gorgias insists that a rhetorician would persuade the voters to vote for him while a candidate trained in medicine but unskilled in the technical skill of persuasion—rhetoric—would fail. Socrates avers that this frightening outcome will occur if the voters are ignorant. The reader, however, is tempted to agree with both Gorgias and Socrates: we all *know* that most voters are ignorant—a group that of course does not include us.

In Socrates' subsequent conversation, Gorgias' disciple Polus asserts that a tyrant—the man who has the freedom and the power to do anything he wants—is the happiest man in his country. Socrates retorts that a tyrant is the least powerful person in his country; he has *no* power, and, in fact, is the least happy of human beings. When Polus says that no one will believe such absurd assertions, Socrates says that he does not care at all for the views of the multitude but for the views of Polus alone, and he will be satisfied when he has persuaded only Polus. As readers we observe how Socrates ties Polus in philosophical knots and forces agreement out of him. In the climax of this conversation, Socrates compels Polus to agree that we should punish only our friends for their wrongdoing; our enemies we should let go scot-free to continue their wrongdoing so that they will rot from the continued degradation of their souls. And yet. . . is Polus *persuaded*? Is the *reader* persuaded? Was Plato himself persuaded? Would anyone who is even partly sane wish to live in a state where not only is justice *not* equal, but

---

2   And, as if to support the idea that Socrates is *not* the true statesman he claims to be, Plato has Socrates himself raise the specter of Alcibiades, certainly not a model of one who has become better through acquaintance with Socrates. On Alcibiades, see the translation of *Gorgias*, note 78.

where justice requires one's hated wrongdoers to go free and one's beloved wrongdoers to pay the severest penalties?

In the first major dialectical exchange, Socrates succeeds in coercing a contradiction from Gorgias the rhetorician. In his defense of his art, Gorgias has said that it is possible to misuse an education in rhetoric, just as it is possible to misuse an education in bodybuilding (456e), and, he added, it is not right to blame teachers for their students' misuse of learning. But when Gorgias is led to agree that the person who knows what justice is will be just and will act justly—and hence *not* misuse justice—he has evidently contradicted himself. As all with even a slight knowledge of philosophy know, any contradiction whatsoever is fatal to an argument. Polus, Gorgias' student of rhetoric and himself a rhetorician, enters the discussion at this point, accusing Socrates of bad taste, of making a philosophical mountain out of an anthill of a contradiction. If a little inconsistency is squeezed out of Gorgias, a complete renunciation of his passionately proclaimed views is Polus' fate. Not only will Polus admit that tyrants are miserable and more miserable in proportion to the failure of their crimes to be punished, but he is driven to admit that if rhetoric has any use at all, it is to persuade oneself and one's kin to seek punishment for their wrongdoing and to try everything to see to it that one's enemies escape all punishment and continue their crimes. This is quite a comic reversal.[3]

Socrates' conquest of Gorgias because of an inconsistency about rhetoric was too much for Polus and forced him into the action; Socrates' conclusions about who should be punished prove too much for Callicles and force *him* into the action. In what seems a rational question, Callicles, Gorgias' host and in whose house the dialogue takes place,[4] asks Socrates whether he is serious, for if he is, says Callicles, all human life would be turned upside down.

Instead of answering directly, Socrates launches into a long speech that is quite nasty in its apparently unprovoked criticism of Callicles. He and Callicles each have two loves: Socrates loves both Alcibiades and philosophy;

---

3   Aristotle discusses reversal (*peripeteia*) in tragedy in *Poetics* 1152a22–52b8. An example would be Jocasta's attempt to calm her husband Oedipus, an attempt that actually agitates and alarms him. Unfortunately Aristotle's discussion of comedy has been lost, but surely it included the subject of peripety, perhaps involving a situation that looks as though it will result in disaster but ends in triumph.

4   Callias, a rich man well known for entertaining visiting dignitaries, is described by Plutarch (*Dion* 17) as having hosted Dion of Syracuse, a disciple of Plato whom Plato "turned him toward philosophy." Perhaps Plato was thinking of Callias, as well as of others, when he created and named Callicles. Just as Plato has conflated the chronology (see p. 13), perhaps he has also conflated the *personae dramatis*. On Callicles as an amalgam of Cleon and Critias, see note 5 and p. 15.

Callicles loves both the Athenian demos and a man named Demos.[5] While his own love of philosophy has made him constant in his views, Callicles' love of the Athenian demos has made Callicles fickle in his. In addition, says Socrates, Callicles is forever uttering absurdities because of his love of Demos. Socrates' speech has an immediate negative effect on Callicles. He changes from the friendly, witty person we observed in the opening scene, the solicitous host who made special arrangements for Socrates to meet Gorgias. In a long reply to Socrates, Callicles' tone shifts wildly, from angry to critical to conciliatory to insulting to threatening. He accuses Socrates of demagoguery and Polus of being too full of a sense of shame to state his views candidly. Callicles asserts two major points in his tirade. The first concerns the nature of justice and its relationship to the famous fifth-century debate on nature and convention.[6] Here Callicles argues that *by nature* justice is the raw use of power to get what one wants and that *by convention* the weak make laws to turn justice into a namby-pamby do-gooder naiveté. *Stronger* and *better*, he says, refer to the same people. His second major point is an attack on philosophy as a serious pursuit for adults. A little philosophy is fine in one's youth, for it shows that one has been well educated; but to take philosophy seriously into maturity renders one pathetic in the real-life world of the polis. To make this point, Callicles refers to a scene from a lost play of Euripides, *Antiope,* in which Antiope's sons Zethus and Amphion represent the differing values of the contemplative and practical lives. Callicles' thesis derives considerable force from all readers' knowledge that in fact Socrates failed in court to secure acquittal.

In the ensuing argument, Socrates prevails over Callicles with astounding speed. Callicles had declared that law is the mechanism of the weak to keep the powerful in check, but now he is forced to admit that when the poor are united they are powerful and hence, by Callicles' own statements, the better. Though Callicles tries to bob and weave his way out of his contradictions by changing the precise meaning of his terms, changing, for example, *stronger* to *better* and *better* to *worthier* and *more intelligent,* Socrates toys with him, taking his comments literally in a way to catch Callicles in contradiction. Callicles reacts with silence, anger, and sullenness.

One of the features of the rhetorical movement, as it was introduced by Gorgias in the latter half of the fifth century B.C.E., was the claim that it could be persuasive about the most unlikely propositions. Some of the

---

5   In Aristophanes' *Knights,* Paphlagon, a stand-in for Cleon, a type of tyrannical man, also has a lover named Demos. As Callicles will also be presented as a type of tyrannical man, perhaps it is a commonplace or *topos* to claim a lover of Demos to be a tyrant. On *demos* see Glossary.

6   See below, pp. 8-11.

philosophers known as *Presocratics*, who dealt primarily with questions of cosmology and physics, put forth a number of pronouncements that were contrary to what appeared self-evident. For example, there was Thales' claim that everything was made of water, Heraclitus' that everything was in constant flux, Parmenides' that everything was a single unchanging unity, Democritus' that everything was made of invisible atoms, and so on. Most of these claims were asserted without any supporting argument; others, like those of Parmenides, were argued with awesome logical force. Teachers of rhetoric were not to be outdone, and Gorgias himself was famous for his praise of Helen, the notoriously wanton woman whose adulterous behavior resulted in the Trojan War. In Plato's *Gorgias* it is none other than Socrates himself who argues conspicuously outrageous claims, like those discussed above about letting go one's enemies who have committed crimes and prosecuting only one's friends and relatives. One must always be alert to Plato's sense of humor: the real Gorgias was able to let Helen off the hook; Socrates has *all* one's enemies, no matter how viciously depraved they are, let off the hook for their crimes. He has out-Gorgiased Gorgias![7]

What, then, is the *Gorgias* about? On one level, it is about rejecting extremes. Gorgias and Polus represent the extreme of those rhetoricians who care not for the meaning but wholly for the form of what they say. They represent the position of the real Gorgias in the *Defense of Helen* (13), when he says that a speech delights and persuades an audience by the brilliance of its composition, not by its accuracy. Callicles represents the extreme position of one who cares only for the utility of rhetoric, for the power it can get one. He represents the person concerned not with abstract reflection or contemplation but with the life of action. Socrates too represents an extreme view: his care is only for the world of the soul, for goodness and virtue abstracted from life, for the cloistered and isolated world of contemplation, and for logical consistency regardless of the effect it may have on his interlocutors.[8] He may

---

7   James A. Arieti has argued that something similar takes place in the dramatically linked *Republic* and *Timaeus*, that where Socrates draws a similitude between the human soul and the polis in his long speech in the *Republic,* Timaeus, capping Socrates' conceit, draws a similitude between the human body and the entire *universe* in the dialogue that bears his name (*Interpreting Plato: The Dialogues as Drama* [Savage, MD: Rowman & Littlefield, 1991] 23).

8   Plato presents the choice of lives as between a life of philosophy and a life of political involvement, or as it is often formulated, between a life of contemplation and a life of action. This distinction is very ancient in Greek thought, appearing even in Homer's *Iliad,* when Phoenix, Achilles' tutor, explains how Achilles' father charged him with making Achilles "a speaker of words and a doer of deeds," a man combining both types of lives. The difficulty of choosing the superior way of life is manifest half a millennium later in Aristotle's *Nicomachaean Ethics,* where the philosopher at times seems to consider the happiest life one of active virtue, at other times, one of contemplation.

come out best in the philosophical debate, but does he actually achieve a victory if it makes his victims despise philosophy? In the *Gorgias* we see the rejection of these extremes—the excessively contemplative Socrates and the deficiently contemplative rhetoricians. Socrates' arguments, seductive and appealing while they are being aired, are not suitable for the world of active living. No one could run a civil society by allowing criminals to go free so that they would receive punishment from the continued corruption of their souls. The positions of Callicles and the rhetoricians are not beneficial either, for they make no attempt to improve the moral health of the citizenry. Plato is showing that each extreme is inadequate for a good life. Socrates' extreme of pure contemplation regardless of the consequences and Callicles' extreme of actions unsupported by moral reflection are both inadequate. What is left—in its unstated dramatic implications—is a life that embraces the mean, a life of political involvement modulated by ethical reflection.

On another level, perhaps, the dialogue is a mockery of the schools of rhetoric, which cannot contend with Socrates' dialectic in a sustained way. Yes, rhetoricians may be able to persuade a crowd of people, but they cannot hold their own against a lone Socrates' persistent questioning. At yet another level, perhaps, the dialogue is about politics and politicians. What does it mean to be a true politician? Is it a person who makes his fellow citizens better or one who makes them better off? And is *better* the same as being *better off*? But if being *better* means being wiser and more virtuous rather than possessing bigger docks and more lavish cities, have there actually been any such politicians—people who have made their citizens wiser and more virtuous? Can Plato's point be that if one really cares for his soul (and its condition in the afterlife, if there is such a thing), one should avoid politics altogether and become a philosopher? Can the author of the *Laws* and the *Republic* be making *this* point?

Can it be that Plato is making all of these points and none of them, that by making a series of outrageously paradoxical claims that seem both plausible as they are made but absurd after reflection, he is actually drawing us, the readers, into the arguments? How can a reader not say to himself, over and over again as the dialogue continues, "Stop, Gorgias, Polus, Callicles; what you *should* have replied to Socrates is . . ." or "Hold on there, Socrates, aren't you pulling a fast one now?" And the reader laments that he was not there at Callicles' house to set the discussion straight. Plato thus would not be writing the kind of philosophy that purports to supply answers; he would be producing an inspirational spirited challenge to a philosophical debate.

The greatest of the Platonic dialogues—the *Phaedo*, Book One of the *Republic*, the *Meno*, the *Crito*, the *Protagoras*, and the *Gorgias*—produce this inspirational effect on the reader. Far from being lulled into a somnolent stupor, he finds his blood rushing, feels his spirit rising, and cannot wait to join the fracas. For two and a half thousand years Plato's dialogues have been provoking people to join the philosophical fray. To be sure, a great many readers (including the authors of this very book!) have assumed that they alone had unlocked the secret meaning that had eluded others, even though Plato warns against doing so. In the "Seventh Letter," if it be genuine, he explicitly says that he has never published his thought in the form of a treatise (342c–d):

> There neither is nor will there be any treatise of mine concerning these things; you see, it is not capable of being put into words, as are other things that are learned; instead, as a result of much being together concerning the matter itself and from much living together, suddenly, just as light kindled from a spark that has leapt out, having come to be in the soul, it itself nourished itself instantaneously.

A commentator from late antiquity, Olympiodorus, tells the story that just before dying Plato saw himself become a swan, and, leaping from tree to tree, defied the attempts of hunters to catch him. Olympiodorus interpreted the dream as a prediction that later interpreters of Plato's doctrines would not be able to hunt down his ideas and catch them.[9] Perhaps Plato's underlying purpose was to inspire the hunt.

Background of the *Gorgias:* The Sophistic Movement and Rhetoric

One feature of the Greek mind of the classical age was a conscious effort to understand the world by reason. In the sixth century B.C.E., this effort was directed generally at questions of cosmology and physics by those whom the history of philosophy later called Presocratics. For the most part, the questions had no immediate practical value for human life. After the Persian Wars, when it was observed how the power of human reason in a small Greek force could overwhelm the irrational management of vastly larger forces, the Greek world fell in love, so to speak, with the possibilities of reason and began consciously to apply logic to many areas of human life, with a goal of practical success. Among the individuals who sought and taught the means for worldly success were the Sophists and the rhetoricians.

In a monarchy or aristocracy based on blood, there was little need for persuasive skills; a chief could give orders and expect them to be obeyed. He did not have to persuade others that he should be the leader. After the

---

9   The anecdote is found in Alice Swift Riginos, *Platonica: The Anecdotes concerning the Life and Writings of Plato* (Leiden: E.J. Brill, 1926) 24–25.

Persian Wars, in poleis with democratic constitutions, political skills were essential. Celebrity-sophists traveled throughout the Greek world, lecturing about the means for achieving success. The greatest and most teachable of these means was "to be good at speaking." This phrase—"to be good at speaking"—carries the same ambiguity in Greek as it does in English, an ambiguity that goes to the heart of the problem of sophistry. "To be good at speaking" implies, on the one hand, an ability to manipulate the truth so as to persuade cunningly by appeals to emotion, displays of eloquence and verbal pyrotechnics, deception, and other forms of bamboozlement. On the other hand, "to be good at speaking" also implies a desire to speak the truth plainly, without ornament, and without emotional appeals intended to distract or confuse. Very early on it became clear that a successful rhetorical ploy was to *seem* to be a plain speaker while subtly manipulating the hearers. Aristotle makes the Machiavellian observation that it is necessary for a speaker to conceal his art and to *seem* to be natural: men suspect artifice in speech the way they suspect doctored wine and think that the speaker is trying to trick them.

Convention and Nature

Among the questions the sophists raised was one that has come to be known as "the problem of convention and nature" (in Greek, the problem of *nomos* and *physis*). The problem is still with us, and sometimes is referred to by the variant name of "the problem of nurture and nature." It is manifested in various ways.

One way concerns whether the reality that we understand around us is created by our minds or whether our minds understand reality as it actually is. Protagoras began one of his controversial works claiming that "Man is the measure of all things, of the things that are that they are, and of the things that are not that they are not."[10] The statement probably means that in the human world human beings determine the various standards and limits. Plato, however, has Socrates take Protagoras' statement to mean a total and pervasive relativism, where every individual person establishes his own standards of everything at every moment, and in Plato's *Protagoras,* a conversation takes place in which Socrates argues Protagoras into a complete reversal of his original position on the question of whether virtue can be taught.[11]

Another manifestation of the problem of nature and convention reflects the discovery by the early thinkers that some of the rules governing the human mind and the whole universe are fundamentally the same. For

---

10   Quoted in Diogenes Laertius 9.51.
11   In the amusing dialogue, Protagoras starts by arguing the orthodox Platonic view that virtue can be taught; by the end he argues that virtue can *not* be taught.

example, the Pythagoreans had claimed that the same rules about number that govern nature also govern human life. Some sophists, however, saw the morality of human beings as radically different in different places. If justice meant obedience to the laws of the political community in which one lived as a citizen, and if the laws were different in various poleis, then what was just in one polis was not just in another. Other sophists inquired into whether there was an underlying universal justice for all humans beings that arose out of their nature as human beings. Antiphon (fl. 5th cent. B.C.E.), claimed in this revolutionary spirit that Greeks and barbarians (i.e., non-Greeks) have the same nature:

> This can be seen from the natural needs of all men. They can all satisfy them in the same way, and in these matters there is no distinction between Greeks and barbarians. We all breathe the same air through mouth and nose, and all eat with our hands.

To live in a state one had to obey the laws made by human beings or at least "appear" to obey them. But the laws of *nature* had to be obeyed no matter what.

Closely related is the problem of civilization and the polis.[12] Is human social organization a result of nature or is it somehow a defiance of nature? Does civilization arise from an agreement of people to live together for common benefits like protection and culture? And if it does, is such an agreement natural? And if it is natural, what kind of political community most conforms to human nature? Is there a state in which human beings can best fulfill their nature? Are states living organisms, subject to diseases, as living organisms are, and, if so, do the diseases follow a natural progression, and can they be prevented or cured? Or is the notion of the state as an organism a metaphor that, when taken literally, presents more problems than insights? These are a few of the questions that were asked by the sophists and are pursued by the writers of the fifth and fourth centuries.[13]

---

12   On "polis," see the Glossary.

13   The question of the origin of civilization seems to have been a favorite of Protagoras, at least as portrayed in the *Protagoras* of Plato, who, even if he cannot be trusted to present Protagoras' views fairly, perhaps reflects Protagoras' interest in the question (Plato, *Protagoras* 322 b-c). The origin of the state is the focus of Herodotus' story of Deioces (Herodotus, *History of the Persian Wars* 1.96–101). The question of the best regime figures in the discussion of the Persian conspirators (Herodotus, *History of the Persian Wars* 3.80–88) and prominently in Aristotle (*Politics*, books 3 and 4). The question of the state as an organism is the model for Plato in the *Republic* and of Menenius Agrippa's speech in Livy (*History of Rome* 2.32). The question of disease as a metaphor for what ails the state is pervasive in Thucydides. See Charles Norris Cochrane, *Thucydides and the Science of History* (New York: Russell & Russell, 1965).

Fundamental to the work of the sophists and their claim to educate men for political life, indeed, fundamental to education generally, is the question of whether virtue can be taught, and if so, in what meaningful sense. Perhaps it is self-evident that masonry and archery are skills that can be passed on to other human beings. What about goodness? Parents hope to train their children to be good people, yet their hope is frequently disappointed as apparently good parents have bad children. If virtue can be taught, virtue would seem a kind of knowledge, like the knowledge of shooting an arrow, and would seem to be subject to rules. And yet why is it so much easier to teach archery than goodness? In the *Gorgias*, Gorgias claims to be able to teach aspiring rhetoricians virtue if they do not already know it, and this claim is what traps him in a contradiction. The question of the teachability of virtue is the focus of Plato's dialogues *Meno* and *Protagoras*.

Closely related to the question of whether virtue can be taught is the question of whether the faculty of speaking well can be taught. The very existence in antiquity of a plethora of manuals on rhetoric, articulating myriads of subtle distinctions, suggests that rhetorical technique *can* be taught. Yet there always remains the question of whether a knowledge of techniques can be translated into creative skill and real eloquence. One might know very well what a metaphor is and even be able to analyze metaphors with great acumen without being able to invent a single one, just as one might be a fine critic of opera without being to carry a tune or play a musical instrument. But if a knowledge of technique will not produce good speakers, why should one spend hard-earned money paying a Protagoras or a Gorgias for lessons? Is it enough to study with a good teacher? Or is it sufficient to have talent, and, if so, why expensive lessons?[14]

The Presocratics, who claimed that everything was made of water or air or atoms, recognized that the form in which we see things does not constitute their underlying reality. In the same way, the sophists were aware that what *seems* to be a good argument might not in actual fact be so. Yet persuasion works by convincing someone that a proposition is true, that is, by making a proposition *appear* to be true, whether it is true or not. The art of persuasion—rhetoric—did not claim to use perfect arguments to achieve its goals. Aristotle, who perhaps wrote the best book on rhetoric and may have taught rhetoric in Plato's Academy, said that rhetoric is the counterpart of dialectic or logic,[15] and he defined the basic instrument of

---

14   Whether poetical skill is a gift of the gods is the subject of Plato's *Ion*. For a balanced discussion of the question of the place of nature and technique in writing, see chapter 2 of Longinus' *On the Sublime*.

15   Aristotle, *Rhetoric* 254 a1. "Counterpart" is the usual translation of the Greek word *antistrophos*. For other possibilities, see George A. Kennedy, *Aristotle: On Rhetoric: A Theory of Civic Discourse* (New York: Oxford University Press, 1991) 28–29 n.

rhetoric, the enthymeme, as a rhetorical syllogism, that is, a syllogism in which the premises are merely probable (*Rhetoric* 1356 a37–b26). Rhetoric uses language to work on the emotions. One of the perennial charges against rhetoric is that it makes the worse argument *appear* the better. This is a serious charge, for it makes rhetoric guilty of deliberate fraud, and to teach others to be skilled at fraud would be like teaching them to be skilled at swindling.

Perhaps it is clear why Plato seems to have made war on both rhetoric and the sophistic movement. Truth does not allow for seeming. Appearing to be good is not the same as actually being good. When rhetoricians boasted that for practical purposes an appearance of knowledge was even better than real knowledge because it had the same effect on the audience without the effort involved in acquiring knowledge, and that when rhetorical skill was present in a speaker he was more persuasive than a person with knowledge, this boast seemed to demean the value of truth. That manipulating arguments so as to appear wise was itself a skill that required a clever use of the faculty of reason was no redeeming feature for Plato, for whom goodness and cleverness are not the same.

The Peloponnesian War

For Athenians like Plato, who came to adulthood in the last years of the fifth century, the dominating event of their lives was the long and devastating war with Sparta. If Plato knew anyone at all who had personally heard Themistocles, the Athenian hero of the Persian Wars, that person would have been a very old man when Plato knew him and a very young man in Themistocles' era. Pericles had died before Plato was born, and, in an era long before Movietone News, Plato would have learned of him primarily through the distorted memory of his opinionated fellow citizens. Alcibiades, Socrates' youthful companion, was a generation older than Plato and had died far away in Persia by the time Plato was in his early twenties. And so when Plato writes of these individuals, he is writing on the basis of other peoples' memories of them, and when he has Socrates say that neither Pericles nor any other politician made his fellow citizens better, he does so with the objectifying distance that comes from time measured in generations.

The Persian Wars, beginning in about 498 B.C.E. with the Athenian burning of Sardis, ended in 479 B.C.E., about twenty years later. Most of that time was spent in elaborate preparations and expeditions, and the actual fighting took place in a few battles, each lasting only a few hours. After the war, for the next fifty years, the history of Greece was, in effect, the history of Athens and her relations with the other poleis of Greece. A lesser power when the Persian Wars started, Athens displayed such heroism and virtue in the war, especially in the sea-battles, that she came out of the war joining Sparta as what we would call one of the two great "super-powers." Almost from the day that peace with Persia came, Athens and Sparta were engaged in a "cold war"—again to use a modern expression. That cold war was broken intermittently by confrontations and even by battles; but the actual hot war did not begin until fifty years later, in 430.

The rise of Athens, her growing power, was—according to Thucydides— the cause of the war, for the growing power produced fear in Sparta and compelled her to go to war. Athens, powerful because of her leadership in the war against Persia, was afforded the leadership of a group called the Delian League, formed as a defensive alliance against further invasions by Persia. The League's headquarters was located on neutral ground, the island of Delos, sacred to Apollo. It was the job of each member of the league to contribute ships to a common navy; but each member also had the right to contribute money to a common treasury, out of which ships could be purchased. As one might expect, many city-states preferred paying money to working, and so the treasury was built up. Athens, as the leader, was primarily in charge of expenditures. As the polis in charge, she found her power increasing, and as the bureaucratic administration of the treasury became more and more to depend on Athens, Athens found it more and more convenient to have the treasury located at Athens. One day the other members of the league discovered that the transfer had been made and that the Athenian Empire was a reality.

In the war with Sparta Pericles persuaded Athens to adopt a defensive policy, believing that Athens could sustain herself because of her access to the sea, even if Sparta ravaged her countryside. The defensive policy brought the agricultural population outside Athens within the city's walls and perhaps created the conditions for the great plague, spread by contagion, that wiped out a large number of the polis' population, including Pericles. After Pericles' death, Athens was ruled by others, who undertook all sorts of offensive operations, some of them startlingly successful. But her most ambitious operation, launched in 415, about fifteen years after the start of the conflict, an attempt to conquer Sicily, ended in disaster. Even so, Athens continued fighting, squandering numerous opportunities both for victory and for settling with Sparta peacefully. In the end, at the Battle of Aegospotami, far from Athens on the eastern side of the Aegean up the Hellespont, the Athenian navy was destroyed and, hope gone, Athens soon surrendered. Though Athens could expect the same brutal treatment she had often imposed on others—destruction and slavery—Sparta was surprisingly mild, imposing disarmament and a government friendly to Sparta.

The three-hour or so continuous conversation in Plato's *Gorgias* takes place, it seems, over the greater course of the thirty-year war. This impossibility occurs because radically inconsistent temporal allusions abound.[16] While a reference to Pericles' recent death would set the dialogue in 429 or 428, Diodorus Siculus (fl. 50 B.C.E.), a much later ancient historian, would set the dialogue in 427, when Gorgias first visited Athens (Diodorus, 12.53). A reference to Archelaus' seizure of the tyranny of Macedonia would set the dialogue no earlier than 413. Quotations from Euripides' tragedy *Antiope,* would set the dialogue in 411 or 408, and a possible allusion to a trial of Athenian generals after the Battle of Arginusae, would set the dialogue in 405. It was evidently not important to Plato to place the conversation at any fixed particular moment, and perhaps he wished his audience to assume the entire period of the war, with the events that he pointedly mentions as the background. The topics argued about would then be understood not as airy academic speculation in an ivoried penthouse suite of the Academy but as vital questions being asked even as the life and death struggle was raging in the previous generation. The shift from a genial conversation about the profession of a visiting celebrity to the emotionally ferocious debate about the meaning of life reflects Plato's attempt to infuse the dialogue with the passions that one might have in the stress of a seemingly endless war.

And yet it somehow happens that this diffuse and uncertain chronology allows the immediacy of a real crisis to evaporate. The crisis of greatest significance in the *Gorgias* is the one that will not take place until after the dramatic date, whatever it is, has passed—the trial and execution of Socrates. That crisis, and Socrates' failure to overcome it, is predicted by Callicles (486a–b) and acknowledged by Socrates (511b). And it is this crisis, which every reader is aware of, that gives grim real-world credibility to Callicles' pronouncements even as they are philosophically undermined by Socrates. And it is this disjunction between the reality we know will happen and the ethical conclusions that we would like to be true but suspect will never inform the actions of human beings that gives the dialogue its bitterness and force.

Finally, though we can never be sure of the dating of the dialogues beyond certain very wide parameters, it is virtually certain that Plato is writing after the execution of Socrates. He would then be writing years after

---

16   For a chronological listing of these, see E.R. Dodds, *Plato, Gorgias: A Revised Text with Introduction and Commentary* (Oxford: Oxford University Press. 1966) 17–18. Henceforth this edition will be referred to simply as "Dodds." As all who work on Plato's dialogues, and particularly on the *Gorgias,* we are greatly in Dodds' debt. His edition is a model of critical acumen, literary insight, and philosophical good sense. On the occasions when we have ventured to disagree with him, we have done so with much trepidation.

the defeat of Athens in her war against Sparta. And thus it would be not only Callicles' prophetic words that ring true but also those of the dialogue's Socrates. When Sparta imposed terms on Athens after Athens surrendered, in addition to the disarming of Athens there was the establishment of an oligarchical regime friendly to Sparta.[17] The dominant person in this regime was Critias, who used his position to murder his rivals and opponents with impunity and then steal their wealth.[18] Critias' success, however, was short-lived, as the democratic leader Thrasybulus led a successful rebellion in the Piraeus, in which Critias was killed (*Hellenica* 2.3.11-13). The takeover of Athens by men like the rapacious and cruel Critias[19] shows that the position taken by Callicles is not only repugnant philosophically and antithetical to civilized life but is also, for all the bluster of its adherents, not assured of real-world success.[20] Moreover, in further validation of Socrates' remarks, it is equally clear that the so-called great Athenians of the past, Themistocles and Pericles, had provided no long-term benefit to Athens. They all failed to develop a citizenry that could prepare for its own long-term good or even long-term political supremacy.

The Cast

Of the five speaking roles in the *Gorgias,* four represent real human beings attested in other sources. In addition to Socrates, of course, these are Chaerephon, Gorgias, and Polus. Callicles is probably invented by Plato for the dialogue and constitutes an amalgam of those having his "realistic" point of view.[21] In order of appearance, the characters of the dialogue are:

Callicles

The first to speak is Callicles, Gorgias' host during a visit to Athens and the person, in the drama as Plato has arranged it, instrumental in affording Socrates the opportunity to meet the famous visitor. During

---

17   This may be the sort of "group-tyranny" (or junta) often mentioned in the dialogue.

18   For details on the brutality of this regime, known as the Thirty, and on Critias' involvement in the assassination of the more moderate colleague Theramenes, see Xenophon, *Hellenica* 2.3-4. For a further ancient assessment of Critias, see Philostratus, *Lives of the Sophists* 1.16

19   On the possibility that Callicles is a stand-in for Critias, see below, p. 15.

20   The debacle of Critias, who was a relative, perhaps an uncle, of Plato's, was instrumental in persuading Plato to stay out of the politics of Athens ("*Seventh Letter*" 324d).

21   There is a long debate over the historical status of Callicles. Dodds thinks Callicles to have been a real human being, claiming (p. 12) that Plato does not introduce fictional characters. But surely his Diotima, in the *Symposium,* is a fictional character. Dodds thinks that details, like Callicles' deme and relations with Demos, would be superfluous in a fictional character. But, we think, such details are just what lend verisimilitude to a character. On Demos, see above, note 5.

Socrates' discussion with Polus (458d), when Polus wants to stop talking, Callicles interjects his desire that the discussion continue, and, a little later, when Polus has concluded his discussion with Socrates, asks Chaerephon whether Socrates has been serious. The last and most forceful of Socrates' interlocutors, he expresses his candid view that a little philosophy shows one's good breeding but too much renders a man impotent in the world of practical affairs. Justice for Callicles—justice according to nature—is the power to do whatever one wants, a power that finds its fulfillment in the life of a tyrant, and to be a tyrant is the highest aspiration of a real man. Callicles' views were probably common in the Athens of Plato's youth and are expressed, as well as in other places, in Thucydides' *Melian Dialogue* (e.g., 5.105). They may have represented the actual views of Critias, for whom Callicles is possibly a fictitious stand-in. In addition, Critias, who seems to have been a follower of Gorgias (Cicero, *On Oratory* 2.23.93), was a playwright, and there survives a summary of his play *Rhadymanthus*. Given the substantial references to Rhadymanthus in Socrates' concluding speech, it seems possible that the allusions are designed to prompt this identification. One of the characters in another of Critias' plays, the *Perithus,* says, "A useful manner (*chrêstos tropos*) is more credible than law, for no orator can overcome it..." (fr. 11), a view consistent with those Callicles expresses (e.g., 483e–484a).

Socrates

Socrates was executed by Athens in 399, when he was seventy years old. He is said to have been a stonecutter and to have been married to a wife who complained that he was too often in the marketplace arguing with his talking companions.[22]

The attempt to find "the historical Socrates," like the attempts to find the historical Jesus or the historical Homer, is surely futile. Antiquity has left us accounts of Socrates besides those in Plato: Xenophon's *Memorabilia, Symposium, Oeconomicus,* and *Apology*; Aristophanes' *Clouds;* and some fragments of Aeschines' *Alcibiades.* But, for most people, Plato's picture has won the day.

Plato shows Socrates in pursuit of definitions of such words as *justice, love, friendship, virtue, courage,* and *piety,* and the dialogues about these words are among the most accessible and stimulating of all the dialogues. Everyone, after all, thinks he knows the meaning of these simple words, and yet only a few questions expose the complex difficulties of finding definitions that at once capture the way the words are used, cover their

---

22   Shakespeare called Socrates' wife Xanthippe "curst and shrewd" (*The Taming of the Shrew* 1.2.70). The ancient source for Xanthippe's bad reputation seems to be Xenophon, *Symposium,* 15.

connotations, and lack self-contradiction. It must have been amusing for young men to stand around watching Socrates argue with people who, though supremely confident of their knowledge, were quickly deflated by a few simple questions. And we see this in the *Gorgias*, where such pleasure is taken that the non-interlocutors insist that the suffering interlocutors continue the conversation. In the *Gorgias*, and throughout the dialogues, we observe people who affirm a proposition with great heat and certitude but after a few Socratic questions abandon their original position altogether.

For the majority of Plato's readers, the most inspiring quality of the Socrates represented in the dialogues is the enactment of his courage to pursue truth no matter the cost. What gives substantial historical meaning to his life was his decision to die rather than to abandon his post as philosopher of Athens. If he had accepted banishment, like Protagoras and Anaxagoras, or had fled, like Aristotle, who declined to "allow Athens to sin twice against philosophy,"[23] he would not serve as the martyr to philosophy—the upright thinker who valued truth and justice above everything else. Plato portrays Socrates throughout the dialogues as willing to stand up to bullies like Thrasymachus and Callicles and Meno, who praise the tyrannical life over the virtuous life and threaten Socrates personally. And Plato shows him as completely unintimidated by such famous intellects as Protagoras, Parmenides, Gorgias, and Aristophanes, with whom he more than holds his own.[24]

It seems safe to assert that in life Socrates was a polarizing figure. Athenians must have been sufficiently annoyed with him or with his political allies to execute him. At the same time, whether or not Plato's picture of Socrates is true, even in part, the real Socrates was inspirational to many who knew him. And he has continued to be a source of inspiration throughout Western history. Dante placed him among the virtuous pagans; Erasmus invoked him in his prayers, saying, "Holy Socrates, pray for us." And for those who begin their study of philosophy with a Platonic dialogue, he continues to inspire.

Chaerephon

In addition to his appearance here in the *Gorgias*, Chaerephon is mentioned by Socrates in Plato's *Apology* as the friend who went to the oracle at Delphi to ask whether anyone was wiser than Socrates. The

---

23   Aelian, *Historical Miscellany* 3.36; also Diogenes Laertius, *Life of Aristotle* 5.9.

24   It needs to be repeated that he meets these individuals in the *dialogues,* Plato's plays about Socrates. It is probable that all these encounters were invented by Plato for the sake of a dramatic conversation.

Delphic response, that no one was wiser, bewildered Socrates, for he had no sense of being wise at all. To learn what the oracle meant, he went about questioning others, who, he claims to have discovered, though they boasted wide knowledge turned out not actually to possess it. From this discovery Socrates concluded that he was wiser than others because *he*, at least, knew what he did not know. Thus Chaerephon is portrayed as the catalyst of Socrates' life's work. His name comes up also in several plays of Aristophanes (*Clouds, Wasps, Birds*) and in the work of other comic playwrights as a sort of Socratic "groupie."

Gorgias

Gorgias, a rhetorician from Leontini, in Sicily, was one of the sensational successes in the latter part of the fifth century B.C.E. He lived an exceedingly long life, the exact span of which was in dispute among the ancients but not that it was at least one hundred years. He was famous for a prose that exploited all the vices of which the highly inflective and highly syntactic Greek language was capable, including its natural tendency towards assonance, rhyme, balanced contrasting clauses, and subtle distinctions in similar words. Larue Van Hook attempted to convey a sense of the Gorgianic style in an English translation of *The Encomium of Helen,* one paragraph of which is quoted here:

> But if by violence she [Helen] was defeated and unlawfully she was treated and to her injustice was meted, clearly her violator as a terrifier was importunate, while she, translated and violated, was unfortunate. Therefore, the barbarian who verbally, legally, actually attempted the barbarous attempt, should meet with verbal accusation, legal reprobation, and actual condemnation. For Helen, who was violated, and from her fatherland separated, and from her friends segregated, should justly meet with commiseration rather than with defamation. For he was the victor and she was the victim. It is just, therefore, to sympathize with the latter and anathematize the former.[25]

Though contemporary taste finds this repetitive razzle-dazzle rather tiresome, the Greeks found it enchanting. Gorgias had many imitators of his pyrotechnics, and Plato occasionally makes fun of them, as indeed he does in the *Gorgias*.[26]

---

25   Larue Van Hook, *Greek Life and Thought: A Portrayal of Greek Civilization* (New York: Columbia University Press, 1948), 165–166.

26   See, for example, the parody of Polus at 448c and the various jingles we point out in the footnotes (e.g., 520c, 521d).

Gorgias is perhaps the example par excellence of the person who does not care much for the content of what he says but only for the form. The works of Gorgias that survive, the *Encomium of Helen* and the *Palamedes*, show a writer aiming at cleverness rather than at profundity. And so it is not surprising that when Plato has him contradict himself in his argument, he does not seem to care much. He is emotionally uninvolved in the argument because, as Reginald Bunthorne says in Gilbert and Sullivan's *Patience*, "the meaning doesn't matter if it's only idle chatter of a transcendental kind." Despite this shallowness, Gorgias found an eager market for his skills and did not suffer the grim fate of many a philosopher.

Polus

Polus, like Gorgias, was from Sicily. In the dialogue, he bears to Gorgias the same relationship that Chaerephon does to Socrates—idolizing disciple or "groupie." Plato mentions him as a collector of maxims and phrases in a catalogue of professional rhetoric-teachers in the *Phaedrus* (267b–c). In Greek, his name—*polus*—generally means *foal*, but sometimes the word refers to other young animals, including puppies, and Socrates jokes about this meaning (e.g., *Gorgias* 463d). In the *Gorgias*, Polus take the argument more earnestly than his teacher, and he becomes genuinely upset over what he sees as Socrates' trapping Gorgias into minor inconsistencies that are irrelevant to the thrust of the argument.

Plato and the Academy

The sophists in the generation before Plato—such men as Gorgias, Hippias, Protagoras, and Prodicus—traveled from city to city, perhaps in a way comparable to the lecture-tours that Thackeray, Arnold, and Wilde made to the United States in the nineteenth century. We can get some sense of the excitement and respect they produced by looking at the opening pages of Plato's dialogues *Protagoras* and *Gorgias*. On these "tours" they gave "courses"—as we would now call them—of varying depth, length, and price.

In the next generation, Plato and his rival Isocrates, in addition to being native Athenians, had strong notions of dignity, and they changed the procedure radically: now the "teachers" stayed put and the "pupils" came to them, from the rest of the Greek world and beyond. The implications of the change were enormous, for out of this decision came the need, ultimately, for buildings, classrooms, equipment, libraries—in short, the rise of that kind of institution that resembles, in many ways, our own institutions of higher learning. Yet we can be sure that these later developments were far from the actuality of Plato's first visit to a public park to set about the work of his educational "program." Though archaeological work is still going on, it would seem reasonable to assume that what Diogenes Laertius (3.5,6) says is true—that at first Plato used for his place of instruction the public groves and gymnasium of the Academy, an area of about 492 yards by 328, situated northwest of Athens about a mile and a quarter from the agora, the center of town, apparently walled in as early as the end of the sixth century B.C.E. We find a picture of how a visiting sophist could use such public facilities in the dialogue *Eryxias*, attributed to Plato: here the scene is the Lyceum (presumably a spot similar to the Academy). The sophist Prodicus seems to have been giving a "talk" of some kind before an audience that was seated (*Eryxias* 397D); a newcomer—what we would call a "heckler"—begins to challenge the sophist, and the debate between them becomes heated enough to impel the man in charge of the building (the gymnasiarch) to request that Prodicus leave, on the grounds that his theories were unsuited for the young (398E).

It is not possible, alas, to know with any certainty what was taught in the Academy. From the ancient evidence it seems likely that mathematics was taught as well as the relationship of mathematics to philosophy. We believe that rhetoric was also taught, perhaps even by Aristotle, and that at least some of the principles of Plato's rhetorical instruction can be inferred from the *Gorgias*.[27]

Plato's Academy would not have been the only place people could go for an education in rhetoric, and many of the issues involving such instruction lie in the background of the *Gorgias*. Among other schools were those of Alcidamas and Isocrates. Alcidamas, a student of Gorgias, is said to have been so devoted to his teacher that he succeeded Gorgias as the master of his school (Suda 388). And like Gorgias in the *Gorgias* (447c), Alcidamas is reported to have boasted of an ability to answer extemporaneously questions on any subject. He could not only answer any question, but could answer it eloquently and teach others to do so too.[28] Isocrates, another schoolmaster, was born in 436 B.C.E., just a few years before the Peloponnesian War, and died in 338, just two years before Alexander became king of Macedonia. Possessed of a weak voice himself, he wrote speeches for others to deliver and taught speechwriting. Among his students were many of the most celebrated writers and statesmen of the fourth century. Isocrates attacks the claim of those teachers of rhetoric who believe they can turn anyone whatsoever into a polished speaker. Isocrates believed that while art and technique are important, they achieve their perfection only when applied by a person of

---

27   See Appendix B.

28   L. Van Hook, "Alcidamas Versus Isocrates: The Spoken Versus the Written Word," *The Classical Weekly* 12(1919) 89.

natural ability.[29] If a student had a promising nature, technique and practice could develop his skills greatly. In the *Phaedrus,* Plato has his Socrates give Isocrates what must be a very backhanded compliment. Praising his literary endeavors as greater than those of all who went before, Socrates predicts that *if* Isocrates devoted himself to philosophy instead of speechwriting he would achieve still greater success. Since *Plato* is casting this remark about his own contemporary into the distant past, it looks very much as though he is expressing disappointment at the course his rival *did* take. Given that human nature has not changed since ancient times, we can imagine that the competition among the various schools must have been very intense.[30]

The Text

A relatively large number of texts of Plato's *Gorgias* survive from the Middle Ages in the great libraries of the world.[31] According to E. R. Dodds, only two, known as B and T, had been carefully arranged when he began work on his edition of the *Gorgias.*[32] In preparing his edition of the Greek text, which is, with few exceptions, the text we have used for this translation, Dodds undertook to arrange two other manuscripts, those known as W and F, and to consider readings from four other manuscripts that had their own proponents. As he says, the work of preparing a text based on the collation of all the manuscripts is a task still to be done. This, certainly, will be a massive job, and even when it is completed, one is not likely to be reading the actual text that Plato wrote.

The causes of the uncertain state of the manuscripts are the same that plague all ancient works. And when one compares the condition of a sacred text like the Bible, which had to be copied word for word with such strict accuracy that if a section had one error the entire section had to be recopied, and looks at the critical apparatus that accompany the scholarly editions— and these contain only a small selection of the variants—one can imagine the situation of non-sacred texts. Fallible copyists, who may or may not have been paying close attention to their labors, might easily have added, omitted, or scrambled words. Brumbaugh and Wells point out a particularly striking

---

29   See *Longinus,* op. cit., 11-15.

30   Isocrates retaliated, of course, and it is generally agreed that the first three chapters of his *Helen* are aimed at Plato.

31   The sixty-seven known ones are catalogued by library in Robert S. Brumbaugh and Rulon Wells, *The Plato Manuscripts: A New Index* (New Haven and London: Yale University Press, 1968) 87–89.

32   Dodds 35.

example of such a copying error: the omission of a *sigma*—converting *hekaston* to *hekaton*—increases the "geometrical number" in *Republic* 546b by a factor of 100, from x^2y to $100x^2y$, with significant consequences for the understanding of Plato's argument.[33] Further, some copyists tried to correct the text they had before them, but in some cases their interpretations introduced meaningful changes in Plato's original. Thus, for example, Plato's intentional ambiguity or humor may well have been "corrected" into clarity and seriousness. Finally, for anyone who has seen the actual manuscripts or their facsimiles, pity is the immediate emotion he feels for the copyists, who, without good lighting or corrective lenses or even magnifying glasses, had to decipher some very poor penmanship on faded and over-erased pages. In short, the text that survives for us to translate is far from perfect.

In antiquity, the *Gorgias* was one of the most read dialogues of Plato. Unfortunately, this ancient popularity was not entirely healthy for the condition of the text. Ancient authors such as Plutarch, Aelius Aristides, Iamblichus, Eusebius, and Stobaeus and ancient commentators such as Olympiodorus and the scholiasts frequently refer to the text, quoting some bits and pieces and paraphrasing others, and glossing various words and allusions. The citations of these and other authors have themselves undergone the difficulties of the manuscript tradition as well as having the additional problems that arise because they were cited by a flawed memory or were modified intentionally for a special purpose.

---

33   Brumbaugh and Wells, 4–5.

Gorgias

Gorgias	Chaerephon
Callicles	Polus
Socrates	

Callicles: War and battle—that's the way, Socrates, they say,   447a
to participate in [these]!

Socrates: Oh? Have we arrived, as the saying goes, too late
for a feast? [1]   ḑoᵐᵉ

Callicles: And, in fact, too late for a very urbane feast. Gorgias,
you see, has given us a display [2] of many fine things just a
little while earlier.

---

1   The dramatic opening presupposes that Gorgias has just completed a dazzling oratorical display, no doubt one in which he showed off his signature razzle-dazzle effects. (For a sample in English, see Introduction, p. 17.) Callicles here is evidently paraphrasing a proverb about the "merits" of arriving late for a battle—and is thus tactfully receiving a late-arriving Socrates. Socrates replies with a self-deprecating remark: he has understood Callicles' noting of the late arrival and charmingly substitutes "feast" for "war and battle"—he's arrived late not for a conflict but for a feast, and so the loss is his. Both fighting and feasting foreshadow the *Gorgias*. What starts out as a "feast of words," one that gives Callicles pleasure, will end as a battle, one that Callicles will evidently wish to have avoided altogether. Perhaps it was a characteristic of Socrates to arrive late, one that his friends readily forgave. In the *Symposium* he arrives late for dinner at the poet Agathon's house and is nevertheless received with cordiality (*Symposium* 175c). Readers should note that, as in drama, no stage directions are given in Platonic dialogues and it is left to the readers to infer what is going on. Making such inferences is one of the challenges, and delights, of reading Plato.

2   The Greek word translated as "display" contains the root of one of the three varieties of speeches distinguished in early rhetorical theory. The three varieties are forensic, ① which deals with the truth of what happened in the past—a variety for the courtroom; deliberative, which deals with what is best to do concerning a decision for what might ② happen in the future—a variety for legislative assemblies; and epideictic, speeches ③ primarily of praise and blame—the variety for patriotic occasions and funerals. Gorgias has been giving an epideictic speech. In epideictic, as Aristotle points out (*Rhetoric* 1417b), the facts are taken on trust. For example, when we hear a funeral oration we do not press the issue of whether the deceased person really deserves all the good things said about him. Philosophy, of course, prefers *proofs*, and of proofs, what are known as demonstrative or logical proofs are best. Most subjects do not lend themselves to the precision of syllogistic reasoning, and one of the themes in this and many other Platonic dialogues is the difficulty of applying the precision of rigorous logic to the fuzziness of human life. In the present passage, Socrates seems to be suggesting that he is not interested in set epideictic speeches, Gorgias' forte, but wants instead to engage in conversation.

23

Socrates: Well, Callicles, it's this Chaerephon here who's to blame for my lateness, forcing us to wear out[3] time in the marketplace.

447b   **Chaerephon:** No matter, Socrates—I'll also provide the cure. You see, Gorgias is my friend, so he'll put on a display for us now, if it seems best, or later, if you wish.

Callicles: What's this, Chaerephon? Does Socrates have his heart set on hearing Gorgias?

Chaerephon: In fact, it's for this very thing that we're here.

Callicles: Then, when you wish, won't you visit me at my house? You see, Gorgias is staying with me and will give you a display.

447c   **Socrates:** Well spoken, Callicles. But would he be willing to engage in dialectic[4] with us? You see, I wish to find out from him what is the power of the man's technical skill,[5] and what it is that he proclaims and teaches. And, as for the rest of his display, let him do it later, as *you* say.

Callicles: There's nothing like asking him, Socrates. You see, Gorgias had this as one part of his display. As a matter of fact, he was just now asking anyone of the people present inside to ask anything he wished, and he said he'd give an answer to everything.

Socrates: Excellent! Chaerephon, go ahead, ask him.

Chaerephon: What shall I ask?

447d   **Socrates:** Ask him who he is.

---

3   We have translated the verb "wear out" literally to preserve the image. While it might also be translated more idiomatically as "waste," the metaphor would be lost. Writers are very often conscious of the etymological meanings of the words they use, and Plato seems particularly conscious of the verbal opportunities in etymologies; a term that means "rub away" or "wear out," moreover, seems appropriate for a professional stonecutter like Socrates.

4   On the verb translated as "engaging in dialectic," see Glossary.

5   The Greek word for "technical skill" is *techne*, which refers to a skill that requires specialized knowledge of a set of rules and procedures. Lyre-playing, medicine, and horsemanship would be examples of such *technes*. See below, 500e–501a, where Socrates describes what it is to be a "technical skill." The word can also be translated as "art," but we have consistently translated it "technical skill" to remind the reader that it must include specialized knowledge, as "art" in contemporary English would not. See also the Glossary.

Chaerephon: What do you mean?

Socrates: For example, if someone happened to be a craftsman of shoes, he would answer, I suppose, that he was a shoemaker. Or don't you understand what I'm saying?

Chaerephon: I do understand and I shall ask. Tell me, Gorgias, is this Callicles saying the truth when he says that you declare that you will answer whatever someone asks you?

Gorgias: He is saying the truth, Chaerephon. You see, I too was just now declaring these very things, and I [also] say that no one has asked me a new thing in many years.   448a

Chaerephon: Then, Gorgias, I suppose, you might answer easily.

Gorgias: It's for you to test this, Chaerephon.

Polus: By Zeus, but if you wish, Chaerephon, of course make [the test] of me. You see, Gorgias seems to me to be answered out—he's just talked about a lot of things.

Chaerephon: What's this, Polus? Do you think *you* can answer more excellently than Gorgias?

Polus: What does it matter—if for *you*, in fact, I've answered   448b
well enough?

Chaerephon: It doesn't matter. But since *you'd* like to answer, answer.

Polus: Ask away.

Chaerephon: I'll ask, then. If Gorgias happened to be one who knew the technical skill of his brother Herodicus, what would we justly name him? Wouldn't it be the name that we called Herodicus?

Polus: Yes, of course.

Chaerephon: Then, in saying that he was a physician we would be speaking excellently.

Polus: Yes.

Chaerephon: And if, of course, he were experienced in the technical skill in which Aristophon, the son of Aglaophon, or his brother is experienced, what would we rightly call him?

448c   **Polus:** It is clear that we would call him a painter.

Chaerephon: And now, since [Gorgias] is one who has knowledge of some technical skill, what name—calling him rightly—would we call him?

Polus: Chaerephon, many technical skills have been discovered experientially among men by experience. Experience, you see, makes life proceed by technical skill, inexperience by chance. And of each of these various men have various shares variously, and of the best things the best men have a share, and Gorgias is among these best and has a share of the most beautiful of the technical skills.

repetition

448d   **Socrates:** Gorgias, Polus appears excellently prepared, of course, for speeches. But, you see, he is not doing what he promised Chaerephon.

Gorgias: In what way, precisely, Socrates?

Socrates: He doesn't seem to me at all to have answered what was asked.

Gorgias: But *you* ask him, if you'd like.

Socrates: No, [I'd rather not,] if of course you yourself are willing to answer. But it would be more pleasant if you [answered]. You see, it's clear to me from the things Polus said that he has cared more for what's called rhetoric than for engaging in dialectic.

448e   **Polus:** What do you mean, Socrates?

Socrates: That, Polus, when Chaerephon was asking what technical skill Gorgias had knowledge of, though you gave a speech of praise about his technical skill as though someone had given a speech of blame about it, you did not answer what the [skill] is.[6]

Polus: Did I not answer that it was the most beautiful?

Socrates: You surely did. But no one is asking about the quality of Gorgias' technical skill, but what it is and what it is necessary to call Gorgias. Just as in the examples that
449a   Chaerephon gave you before you answered him excellently

---

6   These words—praise and blame—refer to the subject matter of epideictic oratory (see note 2).

and briefly, so now say what his technical skill is and what it is necessary for us to call Gorgias. But, better, Gorgias, tell us yourself what it is necessary to call you, as a man having knowledge of what technical skill?

Gorgias: Of rhetoric, Socrates.

Socrates: Then it is necessary to call you a rhetor?

claim of fame

Gorgias: A good one, in fact, Socrates— if you wish to call me what I, in fact, "boast to be," as Homer says.[7]

Socrates: But I do wish [to call you one].

Gorgias: Call me one, indeed.

Socrates: And aren't we to say that you have the power of making others rhetors too?   449b

Gorgias: I do in fact declare these things, not only here but also elsewhere.

Socrates: And so would you be willing, Gorgias, in just the way we're now engaging in dialectic, to continue to the end—asking one thing, answering another? And as for this windiness of words such as Polus began to use, [would you be willing] to put it off till later? But don't be false to what you promise, but be willing to answer briefly what is asked.

Gorgias: There are some compelling reasons to give speeches at length.[8] But I shall try to answer in as brief a form as possible. You see, this is one of the claims I make, too— that no one else is able to say the same things in a briefer form than I.   449c

---

7   See *Iliad* 6.211; 14.113. Actually, it is the characters Glaukos and Diomedes who utter these words, each when talking about his glorious ancestors. Gorgias' use of these words—to those who remember Homer's line—calls attention to several matters: first, it stresses how Gorgias, in contrast to the Homeric warriors, derives glory simply from words (i.e., he is no "doer of deeds"); second, it suggests that Gorgias' excellence derives from his own talents, not from his pedigree—a sentiment suitable to the democratic Athens that he is visiting; and third, it shows how even a word or two, wholly out of context, might be quoted, perhaps as an affectation, by such a rhetorician as Gorgias.

8   Here and elsewhere Gorgias uses circumlocutions where briefer forms are possible. Perhaps Plato is parodying a feature of Gorgias' style. For example, here Gorgias could have said, "to give long speeches" instead of "to give speeches at length."

Socrates: There's need for this, Gorgias. And make a display for me of this very thing, of brevity; prolixity we'll put off for later.

Gorgias: But I shall do so, and you will say that you've never heard a more minimeloquent[9] man.

449d **Socrates:** Come, indeed. You see, you say that you are one who knows the technical skill of rhetoric and who knows how to make another a rhetor too. What, of the things that are, does rhetoric happen to be about? For example, weaving is about the making of clothes, isn't it?

Gorgias: Yes.

Socrates: And isn't music about the making of tunes?

Gorgias: Yes.

Socrates: By Hera![10] Gorgias, I am, in fact, marveling at your answers—how you are answering as briefly as possible.

Gorgias: You see, Socrates, I think I am doing this very suitably.

Socrates: You *are* speaking well. Come, answer me in the same way about rhetoric. About what part of reality is it a knowledge?

449e **Gorgias:** About words.

Socrates: What sort of words, Gorgias? Are they the words that show the sick what kind of life they need to lead to become healthy?

Gorgias: No.

Socrates: So rhetoric is not about all words?

Gorgias: No, indeed.

---

9   In Greek, the word for *very brief* is very long, a joke we have tried to imitate by our invention of "minimeloquent."

10   Oaths in ancient literature are not casually sprinkled into conversation as they might be by modern college students, soldiers, or rappers, but seem actually to show a sincere or, as here, sarcastic emotional response. Aristotle, in the *Rhetoric* (1375a) classifies oaths as one of the five kinds of proof that are "without technique." And a little later (1377a) he gives the four divisions of the category "oaths." Dodds cites Olympiodorus, who allegorizes the present oath fantastically. Socrates swears by the dog at 461b and again at 482b. He also utters oaths at 466c, 470e, 489e, and 516d.

Socrates: But, of course, it does make people powerful at speaking?

Gorgias: Yes.

Socrates: About the things they say *and* about the things they think?

Gorgias: How not?

Socrates: Does the [technical skill] of medicine, which we've just now been speaking about, make people powerful at thinking and speaking about the sick? 450a

Gorgias: Necessarily.

Socrates: *Medicine*, too, as it seems, is about words.

Gorgias: Yes.

Socrates: Words about illnesses, of course.

Gorgias: Very much so.

Socrates: And isn't *gymnastics* also about words, those about the good and bad conditions of bodies?

Gorgias: Of course.

Socrates: And, indeed, the other technical skills, too, Gorgias, are the same. Each of them is about those words that happen to be the subject of the technical skill? 450b

Gorgias: It appears so.

Socrates: Then, why don't you call the other technical skills *rhetorics*, since they are about words, if you call rhetoric *that which is about words*.

Gorgias: Because, Socrates, while the whole knowledge concerning the other technical skills deals, as it were, with the [skill's] hands-on actions and suchlike, the knowledge of rhetoric is not such a hands-on thing, but the whole action and authority [of rhetoric] is through words. On account of these things, *I* think I am right in saying that the rhetorical technical skill is about words— to put it rightly, as *I* say. 450c

Socrates: Well, then, do I understand the sort of thing you wish to call rhetoric? But I shall quickly know what you mean more clearly. But answer: we have technical skills, don't we?

Gorgias: Yes.

Socrates: Of all the technical skills, there are some, I think, that require mostly action and need few words, and there are some that need no word at all, but the [practice of the whole] technical skill might be accomplished even in silence, such as painting and sculpture and many others.

450d   You seem to me to be saying that rhetoric is not one of these technical skills. Or aren't you?

Gorgias: And so you understand very well, Socrates.

Socrates: But of course there are others of the technical skills that accomplish all they do through speech, and they need either no work at all, so to speak, or very little work, such as number theory and arithmetic[11] and geometry and, of course, draughts[12] and many other technical skills. Of these, some have words in just about equal [proportion] to actions, but many have more words than actions, and

450e   their whole action and authority is through words. And you seem to me to be saying that rhetoric is one of such [skills].

Gorgias: That's the truth.

Socrates: But I don't think you'd wish at all to call any of these *rhetoric,* even though, to use your phrasing, it is "through speech" that rhetoric has its authority, and someone, if he wished to be pesky in his arguments, might ask, "Gorgias, are you saying that number theory is rhetoric?" But I

---

11   English derivatives are misleading here: *arithmetiké* deals with numbers abstractly and we have translated it as "number theory"; *logistiké* with computations, and we have translated it as "arithmetic." Arithmetic deals with actual calculations, but number theory deals with the numbers abstracted from any calculations.

12   The game of draughts, a board game in which the board has thirty-six squares, seems to have been a game that, like chess, involved skill in moves. According to Allan Bloom, the game of draughts is frequently used by Plato to represent philosophical dialectic. "In dialectic," Bloom explains, "premises—like pieces—are set down and are changed in relation to the moves of one's partners. The game can be played over, and one's moves can be improved on the basis of experience with the opponent's moves. It is a friendly combat and an amusement for its own sake" (Bloom, *The Republic of Plato* [New York: Basic Books, 1968] 443).

don't think you are saying that either number theory or geometry is rhetoric.

Gorgias: You are thinking rightly, you see, and you are taking me justly.   451a

Socrates: Come now and *you* complete the answer to the question I asked. Since rhetoric happens to be one of the technical skills that use speech for the most part (and there happen to be other such ones), try to say what *is* the authority that rhetoric has through words. Here's an example of what I mean: Let's say someone were to ask me, about any of the technical skills of which I was speaking, "Socrates, what *is* the technical skill of number   451b theory?" I would say to him, as *you* were just saying, that it is one of the [skills] having its authority through speech. And if he should ask me further, "One of the [skills] having authority about what?" I would say that it is one of the [skills] about the even and odd—about all things that pertain to each. And if he should ask again, "What technical skill do you call arithmetic?" I would say that it is the one having authority over the whole matter in speech. And if he should ask further, "The [skill] having authority about what?" I would say, as those who write laws in the demos[13] say, that while in other things number   451c theory and arithmetic are the same—you see, they are about the same thing, the even and the odd—they differ in this, that arithmetic looks at the odd and even, how they treat quantities with respect to themselves and to each other. And if someone should ask about astronomy (as I am saying that this same [skill] of astronomy also has authority in all its matters by speech), "What are astronomy's words about?" I would say that they were words about the motion of the stars and sun and moon, how their speeds relate to one another.

Gorgias: *You* would, of course, be speaking rightly.

---

13   We have elected to transliterate *demos* into English, a procedure we have also followed in the case of *polis* (see note 16). See Glossary.

451d   **Socrates:** Now it's *your* turn, Gorgias. Rhetoric happens to be one of the [skills] managing and having authority over all its things by speech. Isn't it?

Gorgias: These statements are so.

Socrates: Tell me, of these [skills], what is rhetoric about? What is this thing, of the things that are, that the words that rhetoric uses are concerned with?

Gorgias: About the greatest and best of human matters, Socrates.

451e   **Socrates:** But, Gorgias, you are saying a thing that goes in different directions and is not at all clear. I think, you see, you've heard men in drinking parties singing this ditty, in which the singers count up first how being healthy is best, second is being beautiful, and third, as the one who made the ditty says, being wealthy without having used deceit.

Gorgias: I have heard [the ditty.] But for what purpose are you saying this?

452a   **Socrates:** Because just then, if the craftsmen—the physician and the trainer and the money-maker—of these things on which the maker of the ditty bestowed praise were present, first the physician would say, "Socrates, Gorgias is deceiving you! You see, his technical skill is not about the greatest good for human beings, but mine is!" So if *I* asked him: "Who are *you* who say these things?" perhaps he would say, "I am a physician." And I'd say, "Is the work of *your* technical skill the greatest good?" Perhaps he would say "How not? What is a greater good

452b   to human beings than health?" And if, in turn after him, the trainer would say, "I myself would wonder, Socrates, if Gorgias could display a greater good from his technical skill than *I* could show from mine," I in turn would reply to him, "Who are *you*, Sir, and what is *your* work?" He would reply, "A trainer, and my work is to make human beings beautiful and strong in their bodies." And after the trainer, the moneymaker, altogether looking down

452c   his nose at them, as *I* think, would say, "Come on, see, Socrates, whether there appears to you a greater good than the wealth that Gorgias or any one else has in his possession." And so we would say to him, "What? Are *you* a craftsman of [wealth]?" He would say that he was. "Who are you?" we would ask. "A moneymaker," he would reply. And we shall say, "And so? Do *you* judge that wealth is the greatest good for human beings?" "How not?" he'll reply. And we would say, "Well, in fact, this Gorgias goes in a different direction and says that the technical skill in *his* possession is responsible for a greater good than *yours*." And so it is clear that after this, the moneymaker would ask, "And *what* is this good? Let Gorgias answer." Come 452d on, then, Gorgias, after thinking it over, and having been asked by those craftsmen and by me, answer what is this thing *you* say to be the greatest good for human beings and of which you say you are a craftsman.

Gorgias: What is, in truth, the greatest good and also the thing responsible,[14] on the one hand, for freedom among human beings themselves, and, on the other, for ruling over others[15] in one's own individual polis.[16]

Socrates: And so what is this thing you are speaking of?

Gorgias: *I* am speaking, of course, [of the ability] to persuade 452e by means of words jurors in the jury room, councilors in the council chamber, and assemblymen in the assembly, and [of the ability to persuade] in every other meeting— any meeting that deals with the *polis*. And listen, because of this power you will have the physician as your slave, and the trainer [as your slave] too. And *that* moneymaker, why, he'll be shown to be making all that money for somebody other than himself—for *you*, [the one] who has the power of speaking and persuading the multitude.

---

14 The Greek word for "the thing responsible" is *aitia*, a word that very often carries the negative implication of "blame" but can also be used in a neutral or good sense as "being responsible" for what has occurred. The word is often translated as "cause," a translation that dryly deprives it of its moral connotations.

15 Dodds cites Thucydides 3.45.6 as a parallel for this view and says that it probably represents Gorgias' authentic view. He also cites *Meno* 73c-d for Gorgias' definition of the special excellence (*areté*) of a man as being a capacity for leadership.

16 *Polis*, which we have elected to transliterate, is usually translated "city-state" or simply as "city," but these translations do not convey a sense of the richness of the term, which embraced the entire spiritual, cultural, and material life of those who lived in *poleis*. For more on this term, see Glossary.

Socrates: Now you seem to me, Gorgias, to have shown most
453a   nearly what you think the rhetorical technical skill to be,
and, if *I* have any understanding at all, you are saying
that rhetoric is the craftsman[17] of persuasion,[18] and that
all its activities end up, in a nutshell, in this. Or can you
say that rhetoric has the power to do more than produce
persuasion in the hearers, in their soul?[19]

Gorgias: No, I'm not, Socrates. But you seem to me to have
defined it sufficiently. You see, in a nutshell, this is
rhetoric.

Socrates: Hear what I have to say, Gorgias. Know well—you
453b   see, *I've* persuaded myself of this—that if there's anyone
who talks with someone else wanting to know just what
it is that the argument is about, I am one of these people,
and I think I am right in saying that you are, too.

Gorgias: Well, then, what, Socrates?

Socrates: *I'll* tell you now. As for the persuasion from rhetoric,
whatever it is and whatever subjects it is about, know well
that I just don't clearly *know* what *you* are saying, though
of course I *suspect* I *think* I know what you are saying,
about them. But my suspecting what you think is no less
reason to ask, and so I'll ask what *you* say is the persuasion
453c   that comes from rhetoric and what subjects it is about. For
what purpose shall I ask you and not say myself, though
I suspect what you will say? Not for your sake, but for
the sake of the argument,[20] in order that it go forward as

---

17   The term "craftsman" is *demiourgos* in Greek, a word that literally means "worker of the
people." It is most famously used by Plato in the *Timaeus,* where the Demiurge fashions
the universe. Its most usual meaning in the Greek of this time is "craftsman," and it is so
rendered in this translation. Since Gorgias has just been speaking of rhetoric in the polis,
the word may very well retain some of its root sense here.

18   On "persuasion" see Glossary.

19   This, the first use of "soul" in the dialogue, marks a turning point to the serious discussion
of education.

20   The word that we have translated as "argument" is the Greek word *logos. Logos* presents a
difficulty to translators because it covers a range of meanings. The word basically refers to
that faculty that separates and distinguishes human beings from beasts. In the singular it
means *word* or *argument* and in the plural it refers to speeches and writings. As Isocrates
observes in his *Nicocles* (5.9), we use the same *logos* in reasoning with ourselves that we
use in persuading others. This double nature of *logos* also causes the modern translator
difficulty in rendering the Greek word into a modern language.

much as it can and make clear to us what is argued about. Consider whether I seem right to question you further. If, for example, I happened to be asking you about which one of the painters Zeuxis was, if you said that he painted living things, would I justly ask you what sort of living things he painted and where he painted them?[21]

Gorgias: Yes, of course.

Socrates: And wouldn't I be right for this reason—that there · are various painters who paint various living things? 453d

Gorgias: Yes.

Socrates: But, of course, if nobody other than Zeuxis painted, [the question] would have been excellently answered by you?

Gorgias: Well, how not?

Socrates: Come on, then, and tell me about rhetoric. Does rhetoric alone produce persuasion, or do the other technical skills also? I'm saying something like this: whoever teaches a subject, doesn't he persuade about what he teaches?

Gorgias: Not only that, Socrates, but he persuades most of all.

Socrates: Let's talk again about these technical skills that we've been just now talking about. Doesn't number theory—and the numerically theoretical person—teach us about as much as there is to know about number? 453e

Gorgias: Yes, of course.

Socrates: And so he persuades also?

Gorgias: Yes.

Socrates: Is the numerically theoretical man also a craftsman of persuasion?

Gorgias: It appears so.

---

21 Our translation reflects the ms. reading of the Greek word for "where." We think that "where" refers to the surface (walls, pots, wax) upon which the painting is rendered (not the location of the studio). Those who painted murals were considered a quite different kind of craftsmen from those who painted pots. We suspect that in the case of painters, the medium was fully part of the job description.

Socrates: If someone asks what sort of persuasion [it is] and about what, we'll answer him, I suppose, that it is the sort that teaches about the even and the odd, as much as there is to know about them; and concerning all the other technical skills that we were now speaking of, we shall be able to show that they are craftsmen of persuasion, of what kind of [persuasion] they are, and about what subjects. No?

454a

Gorgias: Yes.

Socrates: Then rhetoric is not the lone craftsman of persuasion.

Gorgias: You are saying the truth.

Socrates: Since it is not the only [skill] that works this work [of persuasion], but others do, too, as in the example about the painter, wouldn't we justly also ask of the one saying [that rhetoric is the craftsman of persuasion]: "Rhetoric is the technical skill of what sort of persuasion and of persuasion about what?" Or does this further questioning not seem right to you?

454b

Gorgias: To me, of course, [it seems right].

Socrates: Answer, then, Gorgias, since in fact it seems so to you.

Gorgias: I tell you, Socrates, that rhetoric is [the sort of] the persuasion that is in courtrooms and in other crowds, as I was also just saying, and it is about the things that are just and unjust.

Socrates: I also was suspecting that you were saying that this was the persuasion and that [rhetoric] was about these things, Gorgias. But so you won't wonder if a bit later I might further ask some such thing—which [though] it seems to be clear I *will* ask about further. You see, what I was saying, it's for the sake of progressing through the argument in an orderly way that I ask, not for your sake—but so we don't get used to guessing and snatching ahead of time what is said from each other, but so you may progress through your own [thoughts] as you wish, according to your underlying view.

454c

Gorgias: You seem to me to be acting rightly, Socrates.

Socrates: Come, indeed, let us look into this. Do you call "to have learned" something?

Gorgias: I do.

Socrates: And what? "To have believed"?

Gorgias: *I* do, of course. 454d

Socrates: Do "to have learned" and "to have believed" seem to you to be the same thing, and do also the processes of learning and believing, or [do they seem to be] something different?

Gorgias: *I*, of course, Socrates, think they are different.

Socrates: You see, you think well. And you may know it from this. You see, if someone would ask you, "Gorgias, is there a false belief and a true one?" you would say there was, as *I* think.

Gorgias: Yes.

Socrates: And what [about this]? Is there a true and a false knowledge?

Gorgias: By no means.

Socrates: Then it is clear that they are not the same.[22]

Gorgias: You say the truth.

Socrates: But both those who have learned *and* those who have believed have been persuaded. 454e

Gorgias: This is so.

Socrates: Do you wish, then, that we establish that there are two "looks"[23] of persuasion, the one that provides belief

---

22 There is an equivocation in the Greek, for Socrates is saying that "to have learned" (*memathkenai*) is not the same as "to have believed" (*pepisteukenai*). But now Socrates is acting as though "to have learned" is the same as "to possess knowledge"(*episteme*). The implication is that one cannot have learned something false.

23 This is the word *eidos* in Greek. It comes from the verb "to see" and comes to mean *species,* a word that derives from one of the Latin words for seeing. An object has a "look" that distinguishes it from other things, and when enough of the objects have the same look, they make a "species." The word *eidos,* like *idea,* is used for Platonic "forms." We have chosen here to use the non-technical meaning of the word. Though in the drama of the dialogue Socrates is not, of course, speaking as a Platonist member of the Academy (for one thing, it did not yet exist), it is possible that the more technical meaning, as "form," might very well have been in the minds of Plato's audience at the Academy.

without knowing, the other that provides knowledge?[24]

Gorgias: Yes, of course.

Socrates: And so does rhetoric produce persuasion in courtrooms and other crowded places about the things that are just and unjust? And from it does there come about believing without knowing, or from it [does there come about] knowing?

Gorgias: It's clear, I do suppose, that from it comes believing.

455a   **Socrates:** Rhetoric, as it seems, is a craftsman of a *believing* persuasion and not of a *teaching* persuasion about the just and the unjust.

Gorgias: Yes.

Socrates: Then the rhetor is not a teacher in courtrooms and other crowded places about the just and the unjust things, but only a creator of belief. You see, I do suppose that he wouldn't have the power to teach very much about such great matters in a short time.[25]

Gorgias: Clearly not.

Socrates: Come, let's see just what *we* are saying about
455b   rhetoric. You see, *I* myself don't have the power to wholly comprehend[26] what I am saying. When there is a

---

24   The word we have translated as "knowledge" is *episteme* in Greek, from which comes "epistemology," a field of philosophy devoted to understanding knowledge and knowing. The use of the word "knowledge" is remarkably consistent down to the first century C.E.: an apprehension that cannot be tripped up, that is strong and sure, and that cannot be faulted by argument. It is certain and demonstrable by logic. The ancient rhetorical theoreticians never found such certainty of knowledge as was found in such areas of ancient philosophy as logic and mathematics, although they kept on trying, and the failure to find such an intellectual basis of rhetoric prevented rhetoric from ever attaining the status of philosophy.

25   Socrates here still is assuming that teaching produces knowledge (that is always true) and not mere belief (that might be either true or false). As Dodds points out, of Aristotle's three branches of rhetoric, the forensic, the deliberative, and the epideictic, here only the forensic seems to be considered. Hence the limitation imposed by time, for a water-clock, the *clepsydra*, was used to limit the duration of speeches in the courtroom. Socrates, of course, in the *Apology*, makes the same claim, when he says that he could not refute the old charges against him in one day. On the different types of rhetoric, see note 2.

26   We have split the infinitive here intentionally to emphasize the force of the compound verb translated "comprehend."

meeting about the choice of physicians in a polis or about shipbuilders or about some other tribe of craftsman, isn't it the case, of course, that [in these situations] the rhetorical man will not join in the counsel? You see, it is clear that in each of these choices it is necessary to choose the most skilled. Nor when [it is a matter of deciding] about the construction of walls or the equipping of harbors or dockyards [will the rhetorical men be consulted] but the architects; nor again will there be a council-meeting about choosing generals or some tactic against an enemy or some seizure of lands, but the *generals* will then consult together, not the rhetorical men. Or what do you say, Gorgias, about such things? You see, since you yourself say that the rhetor makes other people rhetorical, it is good to learn the matters of your technical skill from you. Consider that I too am out to promote your [work]. You see, perhaps someone of those who are inside is wishing to become your student, as I perceive some, maybe even quite a few, who are perhaps ashamed to ask you further questions. So when you are questioned further by me, consider that you are questioned further by them also. "What shall we have, Gorgias, if we pass time with you? About what things shall we be able to give counsel to the polis? Will it be only of a just and unjust thing or also of the things that Socrates was speaking about?" And so try to answer them.

455c

455d

Gorgias: But *I* shall try to strip the veil from the whole power of rhetoric [and make it] clear to you, Socrates. In fact, you yourself have led the way excellently. You know, I do suppose, that these dockyards and walls of the Athenians and the equipping of harbors have come about from the counsel of Themistocles, and other things [have come about] from [the counsel of] Pericles but not from [the counsel of the] craftsmen.

455e

Socrates: This *is* said, Gorgias, about Themistocles. And I myself heard Pericles when he gave counsel about the middle wall.[27]

456a   **Gorgias:** And, of course, when there's a decision to be made about the things *you've* just now spoken of, Socrates, you see that the rhetors are the ones counseling and that they are the victors in judgments about these things.

Socrates: And it's [because I've been] wondering at these things, Gorgias, that I've long been asking what the power of rhetoric is. You see, to me, in fact, as I look for the answer, it appears in its greatness to be some magical power.[28]

Gorgias: If you knew everything, of course, Socrates, [you'd know] how, so to speak, rhetoric brings together all powers
456b   under it! And I'll give you a great piece of evidence. You see, I've often gone with my brother and other physicians to the house of someone who was sick who was not willing to drink his medicine or to undergo surgery or cautery from the physician, and though the physician didn't have the power to persuade him, *I* persuaded him, and by no other technical skill than by rhetoric. And I say that a rhetorical man and a physician, upon going into any polis you wished, if there were a need to compete by means of a speech in an assembly hall or in some other

---

27   After the Persian Wars Themistocles secured the port of Athens, the Piraeus, by constructing two walls, one that went to the north of the harbor and one that extended south to Phalerum so that most of the land facing the Bay of Phalerum was protected. The weakness of this arrangement lay in the vulnerability to enemy attack of some unprotected shore. Pericles, at some time when Socrates would have been old enough to hear him, succeeded in persuading the Athenians to construct a third wall just south of the north wall and running parallel to it, forming a protected corridor from the Piraeus to Athens, and this was the wall known as the "middle wall." The south wall to Phalerum soon fell into disrepair and it is not entirely certain today what its boundaries were.

28   The term we have translated as "magical power" is from the Greek word *daimon,* a word very difficult to translate. In Plato's *Symposium* (202e), a *daimon* is explained as an intermediary between the human and divine, and a man who is wise in these matters is described (*Symposium* 203a) as *daimonic* (the very word used here). Daimons are mentioned also in Plato's *Republic* (392a, 427b, and 617d) and *Laws* (713d and 717b). In antiquity, *daimons* could be either good or bad. In the *Apology* (31d), Plato has Socrates claim to have his own *daimon* that warns him when not to engage in some activity (like politics). Our English word derived from *daimon,* "demon," is only bad.

meeting where it was necessary to choose a physician,
the physician would by no means come to the fore, but   456c
the one having the power to speak would be chosen, if he
so wished. And if he were competing against any other
craftsman whatsoever, the rhetorical man would persuade
[the others] that he himself should be chosen rather than
anyone else whatsoever. You see, there is not one, not any of
the other craftsmen, who would speak more persuasively
in a crowd on any subject than the rhetorical man. So great
and of such a character is the power of the technical skill.
Let me tell you, Socrates, it is necessary to use rhetoric
as [one uses skills] in every other competition. You see,   456d
in another competition it is not necessary to use [your
skill] against all people for this purpose—just because
you have learned to box and to kickbox[29] and to fight with
weapons—to prevail over your friends and enemies; no, it
is not necessary to clobber[30] or stab or kill your friends for
the [simple] purpose [of prevailing over them]. And, by
Zeus, if some guy wanders over to a wrestling club and,
having his body in good shape, becomes a boxer, and then
clobbers his father and his mother and someone else of
his household or friends, why, it's not necessary for this
reason to hate his trainers and those who taught him to   456e
fight with weapons and to throw *them* out of the poleis.
You see, those people have given these [things] to him to
use justly against his enemies and unjust people, in self-
defense, not in aggression, but *they*, having turned [these   457a
things] around, don't use their strength and technical
skill rightly. And so the ones who've taught [him] aren't
evil, nor is the technical skill responsible or evil for this
reason, but, I think, those not using it rightly [are the

---

29   We have translated the activity called *pankration* as "kickboxing," which seems to come
      closest to the ancient sport that combined boxing and wrestling with kicking, twisting
      and strangling. The sport allowed kicking one's opponent in the stomach and breaking
      his bones.

30   Gorgias is being rhetorical with his climax—starting with a minor, perhaps mildly
      humorous, kind of injury and working his way up to killing. "Clobber" reflects Gorgias'
      half-heartedness in taking seriously the idea that rhetoric can do wrong. Gorgias' failure
      to reflect on this issue is the core of Socrates' refutation of him that concludes in 460e-
      461b.

ones responsible and evil]. Indeed, this is the argument also about rhetoric. You see, the rhetor has the power to speak against everyone about everything, so as to be more persuasive among the multitudes—to put it briefly—about anything he may wish. But it is not at all necessary for this reason that he deprive physicians of their reputation—just because he has the power to do so—nor [deprive] any other craftsmen [of their reputation], but [it is necessary that he] use rhetoric justly, as in any competition. And, I think, if someone has become a rhetorical man and then with this power and this technical skill commits an unjust act, it is not necessary to hate the one who has taught him and throw the teacher out of the poleis. Although *that* man gave it to him to use for a just purpose, *he* uses it in the opposite way. It is just to hate the one not using it rightly and to throw him out and to kill him, but not the one who's taught him.

Socrates:[31] I think, Gorgias, that *you* also have experience of many arguments and that you have seen in them something like this— that [the people arguing] are not able easily to converse about the things they have taken in hand, formulating definitions and learning from and teaching one another, and so they break up their sessions, but if they go their separate ways about something and one says that the other does not speak rightly or clearly, they become difficult, and in a grudging way they each think that the other is speaking [about some matter concerning] themselves out of a love of victory and not seeking what lies before them in the argument; and some people, in fact, end up departing on the most shameful terms, being reviled and both saying and hearing such things [about one another] that even those who are around are annoyed at themselves because they had thought it would be good to become listeners of such men. Why am I saying these things? Because *you* seem

457b

457c

457d

457e

handwritten margin notes: because he can talk about anything. So the rhetor must use his power justly

handwritten margin note: pride

---

31   In this speech Socrates is suggesting many of the rules for engaging in dialectical arguments. Some are implied by being the opposites of the faults that are listed. See Appendix B.

to me now to be saying things that don't entirely follow
and do not harmonize with what you said at first about
rhetoric. And so I'm afraid of refuting you, lest you take it
as obvious that I am someone who is speaking as a lover
of victory, not *on* the subject, but *against* you. And so,   458a
if *you* too are one of those men such as *I*, *I* would gladly
question you thoroughly, but if you're not, I would leave
you alone. And of what sort of men am *I*? [One] of those
who would gladly be refuted if I should say something
not true, and [one] of those who would gladly refute if
someone else should say something not true, and no more
ungladly being refuted than refuting. You see, I think it a
greater good [to be refuted], by as much as it is a greater
good for oneself to be released from the greatest evil than
to release another. You see, I think there is no evil so great
for a human being as having a false opinion concerning   458b
the things our argument happens now to be about. And
so, if *you* say that you are such a man, let us converse; but
if it seems to you to be necessary to let it go, let's let it go
already and break up the discussion.

Gorgias: But, in fact, *I* say that I myself am also such a man,
Socrates, as *you* have described yourself to be. Perhaps,
however, it would be necessary to give thought to the
situation of those who are present. You see, *I* was making
a display of many things to those who were present long
before you and Chaerephon came, and now perhaps we
shall stretch things out [too] far, should we converse. And   458c
so it is necessary to look at the situation of these people,
lest we prevent some of them who wish from doing
something else.

Chaerephon:[32] Gorgias and Socrates, listen yourselves to
the din of these men who wish to listen, if you should

---

32   It is surely not particularly courteous for Chaerephon to interrupt here, for he is one
of the people who arrived late. It seems that he cannot help himself, for he is a lover
of argument. That Callicles reaffirms Chaerephon's statement, thus covering for
Chaerephon's impetuosity, is a sign of Callicles' politeness. Perhaps the fact that
Chaerephon is Gorgias' friend mitigates the interruption somewhat, but Gorgias seems
explicitly (by using the plural *you*) to have included Chaerephon as one who came late,
making him outside the group who might be annoyed to stay longer.

say anything. And so for me myself, may there never be so great a business such that doing something else would become more important a job than [hearing] such arguments and such things being spoken.

458d   **Callicles:** By the gods, Chaerephon, indeed, I myself have already been present in many arguments, and I don't know if I have ever taken such delight as now; so, for me, should you wish to converse for the whole day, good health to you![33]

Socrates: Well, Callicles, as far as I'm concerned, nothing stops [us], if Gorgias is willing.

Gorgias: Socrates, after this, it does indeed become a shame for me, of course, to be unwilling [to continue], having myself declared that I would answer whatever anyone wished. But if it seems best to these [who are present], engage in dialectic and ask what you wish.

458e

Socrates: Indeed, Gorgias, hear what I am wondering at in what you've said. You see, perhaps, though *you* are speaking rightly, *I* do not rightly understand. Do you say that you can make someone rhetorical if he should wish to learn from you?

Gorgias: Yes.

Socrates: [And don't you say that you can make him] persuasive in a crowd about all things, not teaching [the crowd] but persuading it?

459a

Gorgias: Yes, by all means.

Socrates: And you were saying just now that even concerning a matter of health a rhetor will be more persuasive than a physician?

---

33   Callicles will be Socrates' interlocutor in the second half of the dialogue. Perhaps it is significant that his principle for wishing the conversation to continue is his delight in the conversation, not what he is learning from it. Is his statement of delight a hint that he operates according to the pleasure principle—that the good and the pleasant are identical—or is it a gesture of a charming host? When *he* argues with Socrates, he will sullenly and bitterly try to disengage from the conversation himself, and Gorgias will step in to urge him to continue (see Introduction, p. 4). When one has finished reading the dialogue and has become familiar with Callicles, one might look back over this passage and ask just what it has been that has delighted Callicles about Socrates' conversation with Gorgias.

Gorgias: Well, I was also speaking about [his being persuasive] in a crowd, of course.

Socrates: And isn't this "in a crowd" among those who don't know? You see, I don't suppose, of course, that among those who do know he will be more persuasive.

Gorgias: You're saying the truth.

Socrates: If indeed he will be more persuasive than a physician, won't he be more persuasive than the one who knows?

Gorgias: Yes, of course.   459b

Socrates: Though, of course, not being a physician, eh?

Gorgias: Yes.

Socrates: And the not-physician, I do suppose, is not a knower of the things of which a physician is a knower.

Gorgias: It is clear.

Socrates: Then, when the rhetor is more persuasive than the physician, the one not knowing will be more persuasive than the one who knows, among the ones who are not knowing. Does this make sense, or is something else [the case]?

Gorgias: This does make sense, of course.

Socrates: Isn't it the same for the rhetor and rhetoric concerning all the other technical skills? With respect to these matters it is not at all necessary for rhetoric to know anything, but it is [necessary] for it to have found   459c
some mechanism of persuasion so that it may appear to those who do not know to know more than those who do know.

Gorgias: Socrates, doesn't rhetoric become a big facilitator, [for one] who has not learned the other technical skills but only this one, of not being considered less than the craftsmen?

Socrates: Whether the rhetor is considered inferior or is not considered inferior to the others on account of this fact, we'll examine right away, if there be something [in it] for our argument; but now let us first examine this: does the   459d
rhetorical man happen to be the same in relation to the

just and the unjust and the shameful and the fine and the good and the bad as he is to the healthy and to the other things which the other technical skills are concerned with, [and is it] that a man not knowing these things—what is good or what is bad or what is fine or what is shameful or just or unjust—devises persuasion about these things so as—[though he is] a man not knowing—to *seem,* among those who do not know, to be a man who knows

459e   rather than [actually being] a man who does know? Or is it necessary to know [these things] and is it necessary for him, when he has obtained knowledge of these things ahead of time, to come to you intending to learn rhetoric? And if he hasn't [obtained knowledge of them], will *you,* as a teacher of rhetoric, teach the one who's come to you none of these things—you see, it's not your job—or will you make him *seem* to know these things among the many when he doesn't know them and *seem* to be good when he's not good? Or will you be entirely unable to teach him rhetoric, if he doesn't know the truth about these things ahead of time? Or how do these things stand, Gorgias?

460a   And, by Zeus, as you were just saying, strip the veil away,[34] and tell us what the power of rhetoric is.

Gorgias: But *I* think, Socrates, that, should he happen not to know, he'll learn these things from me.

Socrates: Hold on right there! You see, you are speaking well. If *you* will make someone a rhetorical man, it is, of course, necessary that he know the just and unjust things either before or after learning from you.

460b   **Gorgias:** Yes, of course.

Socrates: What then? Is the man who has learned the building trades a builder, or not?

Gorgias: Yes.

---

34   Dodds says that in repeating this "pompous" word that Gorgias had used in 455d7, Socrates is speaking "without malice." We wonder whether it might instead show Socrates' sarcasm. In a sense, there is always a veil between a dramatic work and its audience: how can *we* know the motive of a fictitious character in a fictitious situation?

Socrates: And isn't the one who's learned music a musical man?[35]

Gorgias: Yes.

Socrates: And [the one who's learned] the matters of healing, a healer? And, according to the same argument, [in] the other matters too—is the one who has learned each of these [skills] that which the knowledge has made him?

Gorgias: Yes, of course.

Socrates: And so, according to this argument, the one who has learned just things is just?

Gorgias: Entirely, I do suppose.

Socrates: And the just man, I suppose, does just things?

Gorgias: Yes.

Socrates: Isn't it therefore necessary for the rhetorical man to   460c
be just and for him to wish to do just things?

Gorgias: It appears so, of course.

Socrates: Never will the just man wish, in fact, to be unjust.

Gorgias: Necessarily.

Socrates: And from the argument it is necessary that the rhetorical man be just.

Gorgias: Yes.

Socrates: Then the rhetorical man will *never* wish to be unjust.

Gorgias: It doesn't appear so, of course.

Socrates: And so do you remember saying a little earlier that it is necessary not to indict the trainers and to kick them   460d
out of the poleis, if a boxer should use his boxing skill to commit an injustice? And similarly, in the same way, if the rhetor should use rhetoric unjustly, [it is necessary] not to indict the one who's taught him and to drive *him* out of the polis, but [it is necessary] to indict the one who *is* committing the injustice and not using rhetoric rightly? Were these things said or not?

---

35   The term "musical" refers to a person who is skilled in *musiké*, the work of all the nine muses—poetry, dancing, lyric and epic poetry, as well as what is now called music.

Gorgias: They were said.

460e   **Socrates:** And now, of course, this same rhetorical man appears never to have committed an injustice. No?

Gorgias: It does appear so.

Socrates: And also in our first words, of course, Gorgias, it was said that rhetoric was about words[36]—not those [concerning] the even and odd, but those [concerning] the just and unjust. Yes?

Gorgias: Yes.

Socrates: Let me tell you, then: when *you* were saying these things, *I* understood that rhetoric—a thing that always makes speeches about justice—would never be an unjust business. But since you were saying a little later that the

461a   rhetor might use rhetoric unjustly, [I was] wondering and thinking that the things said [now] did not sing the same tune [as what was said before, and] I spoke those words, that if you thought it a gain to be refuted, as *I* do, it would be a worthy thing to engage in dialectic, but if not, to say farewell. And while we were carrying on our examination further, you yourself, indeed, see that again it is agreed that it is impossible for the rhetorical man to use rhetoric unjustly and to wish to be unjust. And so, by the dog,[37]

461b   Gorgias, where these matters stand is not [a matter] to look through sufficiently in a brief meeting.

Polus: What, Socrates? Do *you* believe what you're now saying about rhetoric? Or do you think—because Gorgias was ashamed not to agree with you that a rhetorical man didn't know about the just and the fine and the good, and [because he was ashamed to admit] that if a man not knowing these

---

36   Perhaps the infelicitous repetition of "words" is a deliberate attempt by Socrates to show both the ambiguities inherent in the term "words" and also how unconcerned he is with rhetorical eloquence.

37   In addition to its use here, this oath appears at 466c and, in it fullest form, at 482b, where Socrates says, "by the dog of the Egyptians." The reference is to Anubis, the dog-headed god of Egypt. Anubis was a lieutenant of Osiris in the underworld, and his job was to weigh the hearts of the dead against truth. It is thus appropriate for Socrates to use this oath when he is emphasizing truth (see, for the details of this interpretation of the oath, Russell Blackwood, John Crossett, and Herbert Long, "Gorgias 482b," *Classical Journal*, 57 [1962] 318-19).

things should come to him, he would himself teach that
man; then, from this agreement, perhaps some opposite
[claim] came into the conversation—this indeed is what   461c
makes you glad, when you are yourself leading people to
such questions—since who do you think would admit
that he himself did not know the just things and would
not teach [them to] others.[38] But to drag the arguments to
such [conclusions] is a really redneck thing to do![39]

Socrates: But, most fine Polus, it is for this set purpose that
we obtain companions and sons, in order that when we
ourselves become older [and] fall into error, you, the
younger men, being at hand, might correct our life both
in our deeds and in our words. And now if Gorgias and *I*   461d
are falling into error in our words, *you*, being at hand, set
us right—and you are just [to do so]—and *I* am willing, if,
of what we've agreed, something does not seem to you to
have been excellently agreed on, to replay it as *you* would
wish, if you watch out for only one thing for me.

Polus: What is this [one thing] you are speaking about?

Socrates: If you might check your prolixity, Polus, which you
undertook to use at first.

Polus: What? It is not permissible for me to say as much as I
want?

Socrates: You would suffer terribly, best [of men], if, upon   461e
arriving in Athens, where there is, of all Greece, the most
freedom of speaking, *you* alone would thereupon be
unlucky in this. But look at my side: if you should make
long speeches and not wish to answer what is asked, would
I not in turn suffer terribly—unless it will be permissible   462a
for me to go away and not to listen to you? But if you care
at all for the argument that's been made and you wish to
correct it, as I've now said—replaying whatever seems best
to you, taking turns asking and being asked, as Gorgias

---

38   The syntax in this speech here is out of control, showing how agitated Socrates'
      conversation with Gorgias has made Polus.

39   The term we have translated as "redneck" derives from a word for rural countryside and
      carries connotations of roughness and boorishness. The rustic boor or redneck is one of
      the types described by Theophrastus in *Characters* I (4).

and *I* were doing— [come, then,] refute and be refuted. You see, you are saying, I do suppose, that *you* also know whatever Gorgias knows. Or aren't you [saying this]?

Polus: *I* [am], of course.

Socrates: Won't *you* also, as a man who knows how to answer, bid that anyone ask you whatever he wishes at any time?

Polus: Yes, by all means.

462b   **Socrates:** And now, indeed, do whichever of these you wish: ask or answer.

Polus: But I shall do this. Answer me, Socrates: since Gorgias seems to you to be in perplexity about rhetoric, what do *you* say it is?

Socrates: Are you asking, then, what *technical skill* I say it is?

Polus: Of course I am.

Socrates: None at all, Polus, it seems to me—if, of course, the truth's to be told to you.

Polus: But what does rhetoric seem to you to be?

462c   **Socrates:** A thing that *you* yourself said made [rhetoric] a technical skill in the bit of prose *I* recently came to know.[40]

Polus: What is this thing you are speaking of?

Socrates: *I*, in fact, [say that] it is an experience.[41]

Polus: Rhetoric seems to you to be an experience?

---

40   The sentence is not entirely clear as the text has come down to us. The word we have translated as "bit of prose" is used in Plato's time to mean "written speech" or "book" and the verb we have translated as "came to know" can also mean "read." As we have interpreted the sentence, Socrates is referring to Polus' speech, delivered in a conspicuously Gorgianic style, back in 448c, where Polus credited experience with having created rhetoric. It is possible, however, as some commentators have understood the sentence, that Socrates is claiming to have recently read a treatise on rhetoric written by Polus. In the *Phaedrus* (267c), Plato's Socrates does refer to Polus' "shrines of duplications, maxims, and similes," but he does not mention any learned writing on rhetorical theory.

41   Socrates calls rhetoric an "experience" as distinct from a technical skill or other positive part of learning. Some would translate "experience" here as "knack," but to do so loses the surely deliberate echo of Polus' introductory speech (448e), when, imitating the style of Gorgias, he told Chaerephon, "many technical skills have been discovered experientially among men by experience. Experience, you see, makes life proceed by technical skill, inexperience by chance."

Socrates: To me, of course, it does— unless *you* say it is something else.

Polus: An experience of what?

Socrates: [An experience] of producing some delight and pleasure.

Polus: Doesn't rhetoric seem to you to be a fine thing, being able to produce delight in people?

Socrates: What, Polus, have you already learned from me what I say it is, so that you ask me next whether it doesn't seem to me to be a fine thing? 462d

Polus: Well, haven't I learned that you say it is some experience?

Socrates: Please, since you honor the act of producing delight, give me a smidgen of delight.

Polus: Of course I will.

Socrates: Ask me now whatever technical skill cooking seems to me to be.

Polus: Indeed, I do ask. What technical skill is cooking?

Socrates: None at all, Polus. "But what is it?" Ask that.

Polus: I do indeed ask [that].

Socrates: Some experience. "Of what?" Ask that.

Polus: I do indeed ask [that].

Socrates: [An experience] of producing delight and pleasure, Polus.

Polus: Then cooking and rhetoric are the same thing? 462e

Socrates: By no means, of course, but they are a part of the same pursuit.

Polus: Of what part of this pursuit?

Socrates: Wouldn't it be rather redneck[42] to say the truth? I hesitate for Gorgias' sake, lest he think I am making fun of his pursuit. But whether this is the rhetoric that Gorgias pursues, *I* don't know—you see, from our recent 463a

---

42 This repeats Polus' word from 461c3. As we took Socrates' echo of Gorgias in 460a to have been sarcastic, so here we think the echo of Polus to be sarcastic.

what Gorgias

argument nothing became clear to us about what he thought it was—but the thing that *I* call rhetoric is a part of a matter [that has] nothing [to do] with the fine things [at all].

Gorgias: Of what matter, Socrates? Tell us, [and] don't be ashamed at all as far as I am concerned.

Socrates: Well, then, I'll tell you, Gorgias; it does not seem to me to be a pursuit of a *technical skill,* but of a soul good at guessing and courageous and naturally clever at schmoozing with people; and, in a nutshell, *I* call it 463b *pandering.*[43] And there seem to me to be many various parts of the pursuit, and one is cooking, which seems to be a technical skill but according to my argument is not a technical skill but an experience and a pastime. And of [pandering] *I* call rhetoric a part and of course grooming and sophistry[44]—these four parts for four [different] things. And so if Polus wishes to find this out, let him 463c find it out! You see, he has not yet found out the part of pandering *I* say rhetoric to be, but it's escaped him that I haven't yet answered, and he further asks whether I don't think it a fine thing.[45] But *I* won't answer him whether I think rhetoric is a fine thing or a shameful thing until I first answer what it is. You see, it isn't right, Polus. But if you wish to find out, ask what sort of part of pandering I say that rhetoric is.

---

43   This word is usually translated as "flattery," a term that in contemporary English is insufficiently opprobrious. See Glossary.

44   "Sophistry" is the activity engaged in by sophists, traveling professors who taught techniques of persuasion and discussed various moral questions. Among the most famous sophists were Protagoras, who questioned whether morality is natural or conventional, absolute or relative, and is most known for the statement that "man is the measure of all things, the things that are, that they are, and the things that are not, that they are not"; Hippias, who held the view that there are universal laws for all societies; and Gorgias. All three are the title characters in Platonic dialogues. Plato seems to have been hostile to the sophists, and because of his profound status in western culture, his view has prevailed. Despite Plato, the sophists are worth serious study, for they both raised the fundamental issues involving social life and paved the way for liberal education and democratic governance by their commitment to the view that virtue and statesmanship could be taught.

45   Socrates here seems not to be addressing Polus but rather Gorgias and the crowd that is standing around listening to the conversation.

Polus: I shall ask indeed. And answer what sort of part.

Socrates: Would you learn, then, when I answer? Well,   463d
rhetoric, according to my argument, is a phantom of a
part of statecraft.

Polus: What then [follows]? Do you say that it is a fine or a
shameful thing?

Socrates: A shameful thing, of course—you see, *I* call bad
things shameful—since it's necessary to answer you as
though you already knew what *I* am saying.

Gorgias: By Zeus, Socrates, but *I* myself don't follow what you
are saying.   haha

Socrates: Fittingly, of course, Gorgias. You see, I'm not yet   463e
saying anything at all clearly. And this Polus, like a young
polo-pony,[46] is young and in a hurry.

Gorgias: But leave him [be], and tell me how you are saying
that rhetoric is a phantom of a part of statecraft.[47]

Socrates: But *I* will try to explain what, in fact, rhetoric
appears to me to be. But if [what I say] doesn't happen to
be [so], this Polus here will refute me. You call, I suppose,   464a
something a body and something a soul?

Gorgias: How not?

Socrates: And you think that there is some well-being of each
of these?

Gorgias: Of course I do.

Socrates: What? [Do you say that there] is a specious but not
actual well-being [of each]? I'm saying something like
this: many people think their bodies are well—people
whom one might not easily perceive as being not well—
but a physician and one of the body trainers [might].

Gorgias: You are saying the truth.

---

46   This is an attempt to capture the pun that is in the Greek: "This Colt"—the literal
meaning of 'Polus'—"is young and in a hurry."

47   "Statecraft" is our translation of the word *politiké*, from which we derive our word
"politics." But the Greek word refers not to campaigning (in the modern sense of
"politics") but to the technical skill of governance or of managing a polis—a sense
suggested by "statecraft".

Socrates: I am saying that something like this exists in a body and in a soul that makes the body and the soul *seem* to be 464b   well, but they are rather nothing [of the sort].

Gorgias: These things are [so].

Socrates: Come, indeed, if I have the power, I'll make a display[48] for you more clearly of what I am saying. I say that for the two things, body and soul, there are two technical skills: the [skill] for the soul I call statecraft, but I don't have a name like that for the [skill] for the body, and I [also] say that there are two parts of what is in reality one stewardship of the body—physical exercise and medicine. And for statecraft, in place of physical exercise [I say that there is] lawgiving and [I say that] the counterpart to 464c   medicine is justice.[49] Indeed, they have much in common with one another, inasmuch as they are in reality about the same thing [—a condition of health—] each [pair] of them, medicine with physical exercise and justice with lawgiving; nevertheless, they differ a bit from one another. Indeed, since there are these four things and since they are always acting as stewards for what is best—some for the body, others for the soul— the craft of pandering, in perceiving [them]—not *knowing*, I say, but guessing— [and] dividing itself four ways and secretly putting on the 464d   costume of each of the parts—pretends to be that whose costume she has put on. And she doesn't consider at all what is best but is always hunting mindlessness by means of what is most pleasant and snaring [it], so as to seem to be worthy of the greatest [esteem]. And therefore cooking puts on the costume of medicine and pretends to know the best foods for the body, so that if it were necessary among children to distinguish between a cook and a physician—

---

48   Socrates uses the term for making an epideictic speech (see note 2)—and does so appropriately—since he will be praising medicine and justice and blaming cookery and rhetoric.

49   The therapy or caring of the body comes in two kinds: preventive and curative. Law-making is preventive: laws tell people what to do and what not to do ahead of time so that they will live rightly—live lives as healthy citizens. Jurisprudence attends to people who have broken the law and restores them to justice—or to being healthy citizens. Thus law and medicine are analogous in both having preventive and curative qualities.

or in the same way among mindless men, who are like children—[and to determine] which one understood about the useful foods and the bad foods, the physician or the cook, the physician would die from hunger. And I call this pandering, and I say it is shameful to be such, Polus— you see, I am saying this to you—because [the practice of pandering] guesses at what is pleasant without [regard for what is] best. And I don't call [pandering] a technical skill but an experience, because it has no argument—none at all—for what [the pandering] produces—for the nature [of the results that it produces]—so that it is unable to talk about the causality of each thing.[50] And I do not call a thing that [does not have] an argument a technical skill. If you differ from [me] about these things, I am willing to uphold my argument.

464e

465a

And so, as I say, cooking is the pandering that lurks beneath medicine, and, in the same way, make-up is the pandering [that lurks beneath] physical training and is an evil-doer—deceitful and ill-bred and slavish, and deceiving in its poses and colors and smoothness and apparel so as to make the ones attracted by an alien beauty careless of their own [natural] beauty [that is properly acquired] through physical exercise. Therefore, so that I not make a long speech, I wish to speak to you as the geometers do—perhaps, you already might follow—that what make-up is to physical training, this is what cooking is to medicine; nay, rather this, that what make-up is to physical training, this is what sophistry is to lawgiving: and what cooking is to medicine, this is what rhetoric is to justice. With respect to what I am saying, however, [these things], on the one hand, differ by nature[51] in this way, but [on the other hand], inasmuch as these things are akin, sophists and rhetors are confused on these [subjects] and about the same things, and neither do they know what to do with themselves nor do other people know

465b

465c

---

50 This sentence is notoriously vexed; we have interpreted as best we can.

51 "By nature" is a buzzword in the sophistic movement of the late fifth century B.C.E., and Socrates' use of the term will be picked up later by Callicles (482e–483b). On "nature" see Glossary.

465d   what to do with *them*. You see, if the soul did not stand over the body, but [if the body stood over] itself, and [if] cooking and medicine were not thoroughly seen by [the soul] and distinguished, but the body itself judged what it calculated to be for its own delights, [then] the [view] of Anaxagoras would count for much, dear Polus—you see, *you* are experienced in these matters—[and] all things would be mixed together in this [and] the things having to do with medicine and health and cooking [would be] unseparated. [52]

465e   And so you have heard what *I* am saying rhetoric is: [it is] a counterpart in the soul of cooking, as that thing—cooking—is in the body. Perhaps, therefore, I have acted in a way that's out-of-place[53] because [while] not allowing you to speak long speeches I myself have stretched out a long speech. And therefore it's a worthwhile thing to forgive me; you see, when I was speaking briefly you weren't understanding, nor were you able to use the answer I answered to you, but you needed a thorough

466a   explanation. And so, if *I* too, when you are answering, won't be able to use [your answer], *you* stretch out your speech too, but if I can use it, let me. You see, it [would be] right. And now, if you are able to use this answer at all, use it.

Polus: And so, what are you saying? *Pandering* is what rhetoric seems to you to be?

---

52   Anaxagoras, who lived in the middle of the fifth century, believed that in the beginning all matter, which consisted of infinitely many fundamental forms, was mixed together. Order was brought into being by something he called *Nous,* "Mind" or "Intelligence." Unfortunately, Anaxagoras failed to explain exactly how Mind acted. Anaxagoras is said to have been a friend of Pericles, and he is said to have been brought to trial by Pericles' political enemy Cleon on a charge of impiety for having described the sun as a red-hot rock. Though Pericles defended Anaxagoras at his trial, he was fined and banished. It is likely, we think, that Plato's audience would have been familiar with this history and would be thinking of Anaxagoras as a philosophical martyr, as the Socrates of the dialogue was to become.

53   The Greek is *atopos,* often less literally translated as "strange." Underlying the term is the idea that things have a proper place. "Out-of-place" is a term that Plato seems fond of and often uses of Socrates (e.g., *Gorgias* 494d, *Symposium* 221d). Perhaps Plato is suggesting that Socrates is out-of-place in *this* world of practical affairs and that his proper place is in the world of ideas. Also, on this word, see Glossary.

Socrates: *I* said that it is a *part* of pandering. But don't you recall, Polus, though being so young? What will you do when you're older?

Polus: And so do good rhetors seem to you to be thought of as trivial[54] panderers in their poleis?

Socrates: Are you asking this question as a question or are   466b you speaking the beginning of some speech?[55] *sarcastic*

Polus: *I,* of course, am asking [it as a question].

Socrates: To *me,* in fact, rhetors don't seem to be thought of at all.

Polus: How "not thought of"? Don't they have the power to do what is the greatest thing in their poleis?

Socrates: Not, of course, if you are saying that to have power is something good to the one who has [the] power.

Polus: But I *do* say so, of course.

Socrates: Let me tell you that to me rhetors seem to have the least power of the people in the polis.

Polus: What? As though tyrants don't kill [any person] whom   466c they please, and take away [his] money, and throw out of the poleis [any person] whom it seems good [to them to throw out]?

Socrates: By the dog, Polus, I'm still of two minds concerning each of the things you're saying—whether [it's] you yourself [who] are saying these things and revealing your own opinion, or whether you're asking me.

---

54 The term that we have translated as "trivial" *(phaulos)* is a key term in Aristotle's discussion of comedy in the *Poetics* (49a31ff.), where it refers to the kind of person that comedy portrays. The term is contrasted with *spoudaios,* a term that signifies seriousness and virtue, qualities of the kind of person portrayed in epic and tragedy. Aristotle adds that the quality of being "trivial" is a kind of badness, not all badness, but the kind that involves the laughable and the ugly. Since comedy is the obverse of tragedy, the comic hero must have some goodness in him, otherwise we would not take delight in his prosperous outcome. In the *Nicomachaean Ethics* (1150a), Aristotle says that whatever is *phaulos* lacks the ability to originate action, while that which has intelligence can originate action. Hence, he says, a human being can be ten thousand times more evil than an animal. Perhaps because the person who is *phaulos* is reduced in his capacity for real injustice and harm, as well as for good, he is a proper subject of comedy. And for this reason Socrates' remarks about rhetors would be offensive to the rhetoric-loving Polus.

55 Socrates is parodying the style that Polus used earlier (448c): hence all this repetition.

Polus: But of course I am asking you.

Socrates: Well, friend, then are you asking me two things at the same time?

Polus: How [am I asking] two things?

466d
Socrates: Weren't you just saying something like this: "Don't rhetors kill [the people] whom they wish, like tyrants, and take their money, and drive out from the poleis [the person] whom it seems good [to them to drive out]?[56]

Polus: Of course I was.

Socrates: I'm telling you that these are two questions, and I of course shall answer to you about both. You see, Polus, *I* say that rhetors and tyrants have power about the smallest
466e
thing in their poleis, just as I was now indeed saying; you see, they don't do any of the things they want, so to speak, though they do what seems the best thing to them.

Polus: Isn't this therefore to have great power?

Socrates: No, of course, as Polus says.

Polus: *I* say that [it is] not [a great power]? Of course I say [that it is]!

Socrates: By the. . . ! No, *you* [are *not* saying that], in fact, since you say that to have great power is a good to the one who has it.

Polus: Well, I do say [*that*].

Socrates: Do you think it good, therefore, if someone should do the things that seem best to him, if he doesn't have a mind? And do you call *this* a great power?

Polus: *I* don't, of course.

Socrates: Then won't you refute me and show that rhetors *do* have a mind and [that they have] a [real] technical skill
467a
of rhetoric and not [just a] pandering? But if you let me

---

56   These shifts from Polus' singular person being killed, robbed, or driven out (466c) to a plural group of victims in Socrates' not quite verbatim repetition of the question and then the shift back to a singular victim at the end of Socrates' repetition are in the Greek text. Perhaps Socrates is first inclined to make the tyrant even more villainous than Polus had him by having the tyrant kill a plural number of people, but then decides to return to an accurate retelling of the question.

go unrefuted, then the rhetors who in the poleis do what seems best to them and the tyrants will not at all possess this [power] as a good, if power, as *you* say, is a good thing. But to do what seems best without sense—*you* also agree [that this power] is an evil thing. Or don't [you]?

Polus: *I* do, of course.

Socrates: How then could rhetors or tyrants have great power in the poleis, if Socrates has not been refuted by Polus that they *do* do what they wish?

Polus: This man . . .   467b

Socrates: I deny that they do what they wish. But, [go ahead,] refute me.

Polus: Weren't you just agreeing that they do what seems best to them—just before?

Socrates: Well, I *do* agree, even now.   *contrast*

Polus: And so aren't they doing what they wish?

Socrates: I don't say that.

Polus: While they are doing what seems best to them?

Socrates: [That's what] I say.

Polus: You're saying things shocking and in fact beyond nature, Socrates.

Socrates: Don't make accusations against[57] me, my Polus, my pal—in order that I might address you à la your style—but   467c
if you are able to question me, display how I am lying, but if not, you yourself answer.

Polus: But I want to answer, in order to know what you're saying.

Socrates: Do people, then, seem to you to wish that which they do each time they do something, or [to wish] that for the sake of which they do what they do? For example, those who drink the medicines they receive from their physicians, do they seem to you to wish to do what they are doing—drinking the medicine and experiencing its

---

57   Our translation reflects the reading of the manuscripts. Dodds accepts Naber's
emendation of the Greek to a term that would mean instead, "Don't belittle me."

pain—or do they wish to be healthy, which is why they are drinking the medicine?

467d   **Polus:** It is clear that [they wish] to be healthy.

Socrates: And those who travel[58] and those businessmen who are engaging in various business enterprises—it's not the travel they are doing that they wish—you see, who wants to travel and to undergo dangers and to have hassles?—but, I think, it's for this they travel— to be rich: you see, it's for the sake of being rich they travel.

Polus: Yes, of course.

Socrates: And so [do you say] anything else [or is it the same] also about everything? If someone does something for the sake of something, he wishes not that which he does, but
467e   that for the sake of which he does [what he does].

Polus: Yes.

Socrates: Does it follow that of the things that exist there is nothing that is neither good nor bad nor between them—[a thing] neither good nor bad?

Polus: It is very necessary, Socrates [that all things must be good, bad, or neither good nor bad].

Socrates: And don't you say that wisdom and health and wealth and other such things are good and that their opposites are bad?

Polus: Of course I do.

Socrates: And concerning the things that are neither bad nor good, don't you say this—that sometimes they share
468a   in the good, sometimes in the bad, and sometimes in neither—for example, sitting and walking and running and traveling, and further, for example, stones and wooden things and other such? Don't you say this? Or do you call some other kind of things neither good nor bad?

Polus: No, but these things.

Socrates: So when people do these things that are in between,

---

58   The traveling is specified here as "sailing," which in antiquity would have been fraught with peril.

do they do them for the sake of good things, or do they do good things for the sake of things in between?

Polus: I do suppose [they do] the things that are in between 468b for the sake of good things.

Socrates: And so it's pursuing the good that we walk when we walk, thinking it's better [to be walking], and, on the contrary, that we stand when we stand—[it's] for the sake of this, the good, no?

Polus: Yes.

Socrates: And we kill, if we kill someone, and we expel him and deprive him of money, thinking that it's better for us to do these things than not?

Polus: Yes, of course.

Socrates: Then, it is for the sake of the good [that] those who are doing these things do all of them?

Polus: I say so.

Socrates: And so, haven't we agreed that the things that we do for the sake of something are not the things we wish, but [what we wish is the good], for the sake of which we 468c do them?

Polus: Most definitely.

Socrates: Then we *don't* wish to slaughter [people] or to expel [them] from the poleis or to deprive [them] of money simply [to do so], but if these things be beneficial, we wish to do these things, and if they be harmful, we don't wish to do them. You see, it's the good things we wish, as *you* say, and it's not the neither-good-nor-bad nor the [strictly] bad [that we wish]. Well, do I seem to you to be saying true things, Polus, or not? Why don't you answer?

Polus: True things.

Socrates: And so, if we agree to these very things, if a person, 468d whether [he be] a tyrant or a rhetor, thinking it's better for himself, kills someone or expels him from a polis or deprives him of his money, but it actually happens to be worse [for him], he's [nevertheless] doing, I do suppose, what *seems* best to him? Well?

[handwritten margin notes: Contrast coming back b/w wishing and doing the best.]

Polus: Yes.

Socrates: And therefore [is he doing] also the things that he wishes, if indeed these things actually happen to be bad? Why don't you answer?

Polus: But to me he doesn't seem to be doing what he wishes.

468e **Socrates:** And so how is it that *such* a man has great power in this polis, if, by your agreement, it is a good to have great power?

Polus: It is not [possible].

Socrates: Then *I* was saying true things, when I said that it *is* possible for a person who does in a polis what seems best to him not to have great power and not to be doing what he wishes.

Polus: Indeed, Socrates, as though *you* wouldn't accept for yourself to be able to do what seems best to you in the polis rather than not, or be envious when you see someone either killing whom it seemed best to him [to kill] or taking his money or throwing him in jail.

Socrates: Are you speaking of [doing these things] justly or unjustly?

469a **Polus:** Either way he should be doing these things—isn't it enviable both ways?

Socrates: Watch your tongue, Polus.

Polus: *What?*

Socrates: Because one must not envy, but pity, the unenviable and the wretched.[59]

Polus: What? *That's* how it seems to you about the people *I'm* talking about?

Socrates: Well, how not?

Polus: And so whoever kills whom it seems best to him to kill, killing justly—*he* seems to you wretched and pitiable?

---

59   Perhaps Socrates is thinking of Pindar's verse that it "is better to be envied than pitied" (*Pythian* 1.85).

Socrates: To me, of course, [the one who kills justly] does not [seem wretched and pitiable] but, let me tell you, neither does he seem *enviable*.

Polus: Didn't you just say that he was wretched?

Socrates: The one killing unjustly, my companion, [is] of course [wretched] and, in fact, he is pitiable, as well; but the one [killing] justly is unenviable.   469b

Polus: Well, I suppose that the one dying unjustly is, of course, pitiable and wretched.

Socrates: Less than the one killing [him unjustly], Polus, and less than the one dying justly.

Polus: Yeah, right! How, Socrates?

Socrates: In this way: because the greatest of evils happens to be acting unjustly.

Polus: *This* is the greatest evil? Isn't being treated unjustly a greater [evil]?

Socrates: Not in the least, in fact.

Polus: Then *you* would rather be treated unjustly than to act unjustly?

Socrates: *I*, of course, would wish for neither. But if it were necessary either to act unjustly or to be treated unjustly,   469c
I would choose rather to be treated unjustly than to act   _as he
unjustly.   does by
                                                           drinking the hemlock.
Polus: Then *you* would not accept being a tyrant?

Socrates: Not, of course, if you say that being a tyrant is just what *I* say it is.

Polus: Of course I do say just what I've now been saying, that it's a license to do in the polis what seems best to [the tyrant], killing and throwing out and doing everything according to his own view.

Socrates: O happy one, when I am giving an argument, indeed, take hold of it. You see, if in a filled marketplace,   469d
I took a dagger under my arm and said to you, "Polus, some power and wondrous tyranny has just now come to me. You see, if it seem best to me that some one of these

men whom *you* see here should very immediately die,[60] he *will* necessarily die—he who it seems best [should die.] And if it seems best to me to smash the head of someone of these men, very immediately it necessarily *will* be smashed, and [if it seems best] that [someone's] cloak be torn to shreds, it *will* be torn—and so *I* have great power here in this polis." And so if I should show the dagger to a disbelieving you, perhaps you, upon seeing it, would say, "Socrates, in this way, *all* men would have great power, since in this way any house that seemed good to you [to burn] might be burned, and, of course, the dockyards of the Athenians, and their triremes, and all their ships both public and private." But this is not, then, to have great power, to do whatever seems best to one. Or does it seem so to you?

469e

Polus: No, indeed, it's not this way, of course.

470a   **Socrates:** Are you able therefore to say why you find fault with such power?

Polus: Of course I am.

Socrates: Why indeed? Speak.

Polus: Because it is necessary that the one who acts in that way will be punished.

Socrates: And is being punished not a bad thing?

Polus: Yes, of course it is.

Socrates: And so, wondrous one, doesn't having great power again appear to you a good thing, if acting beneficially follows for the one doing what seems [to him best], and this, as it seems, is to have great power; but if [acting beneficially does] not [follow], [it is] an evil thing and a small power? Let's also examine this: don't we agree that sometimes it is better to do these things—what we were now discussing—to kill and expel people and to deprive them of their money, and sometimes it isn't [better]?

470b

Polus: Yes, of course.

---

60   Socrates is perhaps humorously emphatic. A thing can no more be "very immediate" than "very unique."

Socrates: This indeed has been agreed, as it seems, by you and by me.

Polus: Yes.

Socrates: And so when do *you* say that it is better to do these things? Tell me where you would delimit the limit.

Polus: *You*, now, Socrates, answer this.

Socrates: *I* will tell you, Polus, if it's more pleasant for you   470c
to hear [it] from me. When, on the one hand, someone does these things justly, it's better; but when, on the other hand, he does them unjustly, it is worse.

Polus: It is a difficult thing, of course, to refute you, Socrates. But wouldn't even a child refute you [and show] that what you are saying is not true?

Socrates: And *I* shall owe the child much gratitude, and you equally, if you refute me and release [me] from [my] nonsense. But don't grow tired of helping a friend; but refute.

Polus: But, Socrates, it is not at all necessary to refute you by means of ancient matters. You see, the events of yesterday   470d
and the day before are sufficient to refute you and to show how many people acting unjustly *are* happy.

Socrates: What sort of things?

Polus: You do see, I suppose, Archelaus, the son of Perdiccas,[61] ruling over Macedonia?

Socrates: Even if I don't [*see* it], I of course *hear* about it.

Polus: Now does he seem happy to you, or does he seem wretched?

Socrates: I don't know, Polus; you see, I've not ever been with the man.

---

61   Perdiccas, who ruled Macedonia from the middle of the fifth century until his death in 413, was by turns an ally of Athens or an ally of the enemies of Athens, as circumstances changed. His son Archelaus ruled from 413-399, when he was assassinated, perhaps by two male lovers. Just as Plato's readers would know that Socrates had been executed, so they would know of Archelaus' miserable end. During his reign, Archelaus cooperated with Athens, supplying money and material for Athens' war effort.

470e   **Polus:** What? You'd know meeting him, but otherwise, on your own, you don't know that he is happy?

Socrates: By Zeus, indeed I do not!

Polus: Indeed, Socrates, it's clear that you'll say that you also don't know that the great king is happy?

Socrates: And of course I shall be saying the truth: you see, I don't know how he stands concerning education and justice.

Polus: What? Is all happiness in *this*?

Socrates: It is, of course, as *I* say, Polus. You see, I call the fine and good man and woman happy, but the unjust and wicked [I call] wretched.

471a   **Polus:** Then this Archelaus is, by your argument, wretched?

Socrates: If, in fact, my friend, [he is] unjust.

Polus: But indeed, how is he *not* unjust? In fact, nothing at all of the rule that he now holds belonged to him. He is the son of a woman who was a slave of Alcetus, Perdiccas' brother, and, according to what was just, he was Alcetus' slave, and if he wished to do just things, he would be a slave to Alcetus, and, by your argument, he would be a happy man. But now, wondrously, [look] how wretched he has become, since he has acted unjustly in the greatest

471b   things: first, in fact, he sent for his master and uncle, as though he would give back to him the rule that Perdiccas had deprived him of, and [then] having hosted him and having given him drink—him and his son Alexander (his cousin who was about his age)—he threw them into a wagon and took them out at night, slaughtered them, and made them both disappear. And having done these unjust things it escaped his notice that he had become

471c   most wretched, and he didn't care a bit! But a little later, Archelaus took [Alexander's] brother—a legitimate son of Perdiccas—a boy of seven, to whom the rule belonged according to what was just—and, not wishing to become happy by justly bringing him up and giving the rule back to him, threw him into a well and drowned him and went to [the boy's] mother Cleopatra and said that [the boy] had been pursuing a goose when he fell in [the well] and died. And let me tell you now, you see, inasmuch as he has done the greatest injustices of any in Macedonia, he is the most wretched of all Macedonians—but not the happiest—and perhaps there is someone of the Athenians—starting with you—who would accept becoming anyone else of the Macedonians rather than Archelaus.

471d

Socrates: At the beginning of the arguments, Polus, *I* in fact praised you because you seem to me to have been well educated in rhetoric though you have been careless about engaging in dialectic. And now is this the argument by which a child might refute me, and am *I* refuted by you, as *you* think, by this argument, when I say that the man who acts unjustly is not happy? Where [does this come from], my good man? In truth, I don't agree at all with any of the things *you* are saying!

ref. for essay

Polus: Well, you don't want to, since in fact what *I'm* saying *does* seem to you to be so.

471e

Socrates: Blessedly happy one,[62] you see, you are undertaking to refute me rhetorically, like those who think they refute in courtrooms. And there, you see, some do seem to refute others, when they provide many well-respected witnesses to the statements they state, but the one stating the opposite provides one [witness] or none. And this refutation is worth nothing at all as far as the truth is concerned. You see, sometimes one is undercut by many lying, false witnesses who *seem* [to be worth] something. And now about the things that *you* are saying, nearly all Athenians—and foreigners too—will say the same things as you, if you wish to provide witnesses against me, [to testify that] I am not saying true things; and they will testify for you, if you wish—Nicias, the son of Niceratus, and with him his brothers, whose tripods are standing in

very important to essay

472a

---

62   We have used "blessedly happy" for the Greek word *makarios* to distinguish it from "happy" for the word *eudaimon*. "Blessedly happy" is regularly used of the gods and of the virtuous dead who enjoy an afterlife in the Isles of the Blessedly Happy. "Happy" seems to be used for the state capable of being achieved by human effort, even if it is very rarely actually achieved.

I thought it might be suggesting that Polus is like a child... possible question.

472b

a row in the Dionysium, and, if you wish, Aristocrates, the son of Scellias, whose fine offering is at [the temple of the] Pythian, and, if you wish, [there is] the whole house of Pericles or any other family you might wish to choose from those here.[63] But *I*, being one man, won't agree with you; you see, *you* are not compelling me, but [in] providing many false witnesses against me you are undertaking to expel me from reality and from the truth. And if *I* don't provide you yourself as [the] one witness agreeing with the things I say, I think that nothing at all worthwhile will have been accomplished by me about the things about

472c

which we are having our argument. Nor do I think [that you will have done anything worthwhile] for yourself unless *I* myself, being one man alone, be a witness for you and you allow all these others to say goodbye. There is, therefore, a certain kind of refutation, as *you* think and many others too; but there is another kind too, as *I* for my part think. And so, tossing them alongside each other, let us examine whether they differ from one another at all. You see, it also happens that [the things] about which we are at odds are not at all small things, but they are something that is nearly the finest thing to know and the most shameful thing not to know. You see, the crowning point of these things is knowing or not knowing who

472d

is happy and who is not. Immediately, first, concerning the current argument, do *you* think that it is possible for a man acting unjustly and being unjust to be blessedly happy—if indeed you think that Archelaus is, on the one hand, unjust, but, on the other hand, happy. Aren't we to consider that your thinking is as I have described it?

Polus: Yes, of course.

---

63   These "witnesses," as Dodds points out, reflect the whole spectrum of Athenian politics—Nicias a moderate old-fashioned democrat, Aristocrates an oligarch (who came to oppose the more extreme members of the oligarchic party), and the house of Pericles new democrats. Thus Socrates' views are "out-of-place" with respect to his fellow citizens. In the *Crito,* in perhaps the saddest words of the entire Platonic corpus, Socrates acknowledges the loneliness of his whole attitude toward life when he says that few have ever agreed with him and few ever will agree with him that it is always wrong to requite evil with evil (*Crito* 49d).

↳ Elise with capital punishment.

Socrates: And *I* say it is impossible. *This* is one thing about which we are at odds. Let it be. When one acts unjustly, indeed, will he be happy if he should meet with justice and retribution?

Polus: Not in the least, of course, since, in that way, he would be most wretched.   *Sounds Like "Gyge's Ring"*

Socrates: But if the one acting unjustly should *not* happen   472e
upon justice, by your argument he will be happy?

Polus: I say so.

Socrates: But according to my opinion, of course, Polus, the one acting unjustly and the unjust man is entirely wretched—more wretched, let me tell you, if he does not pay a penalty nor, while doing wrong, meet with retribution, but he is less wretched if he pays a penalty and meets with justice from gods[64] and men.

Polus: Socrates, you are, of course, undertaking to say out-of-   473a
place things.

Socrates: I shall try, my companion, in fact, to make you also say the same things to me; you see, I think you are a friend. And so now these are the things that we differ on. *You*, too, examine this: *I* said, I suppose, in what we spoke of before, that to act unjustly is worse than being treated unjustly.

Polus: Yes, of course, [you did].

Socrates: And *you*, that [it is worse] to be treated unjustly.

Polus: Yes.

Socrates: And *I* said that those who act unjustly are wretched, and I was refuted by you.

Polus: Yes, by Zeus.

Socrates: As *you*, of course, think, Polus.   4737b

Polus: Thinking truly, of course.

---

64   This is the first mention of gods in the dialogue. Perhaps it is a foreshadowing of the myth at the end, where the gods see to it that justice is done, even if it must await the afterlife.

Socrates: Perhaps. But *you*, of course, [think] for your part that those who act unjustly are happy, if they don't pay a penalty.

Polus: Yes, of course, this follows.

Socrates: But *I* say they are most wretched, and those who pay a penalty are less [so]. Do you wish to refute this too?

Polus: But this is still more difficult to refute than that [which you said before], Socrates!

Socrates: No, indeed, Polus, it is impossible! You see, the truth is never refuted.

473c
Polus: What do you mean? If a person, acting unjustly, is captured while plotting a tyranny, and upon being captured, is tortured and castrated and his eyes are burned out— being tormented with every shape of many other great torments—and after he himself is tormented with many other great and multiform torments, and after he looks upon his children and wife [suffering in the same way], finally he is crucified and smeared with pitch and set aflame—*this* is the guy who will be happier than the one who escapes and becomes a tyrant and rules in the polis and lives his whole life doing whatever he wishes and is envied and thought happy by the citizens and the

473d
others—foreigners?[65] *These* are the things you say it is impossible to refute?

Socrates: You for your part are telling scary stories, noble Polus, and not refuting me. Just now you were calling a witness. But remind me of one small thing. Were you saying [that a person is happy] if [he is] *unjustly* plotting a tyranny?

Polus: Of course I was.

Socrates: Neither of these, let me tell you, will ever be particularly happy, neither the one working unjustly for a tyranny nor the one paying a penalty—you see, of two wretched people neither would be particularly happy.

473e
But I tell you, the one escaping and becoming a tyrant

---

65   Plato seems intentionally to make the end of Polus' impassioned speech fall flat, with the anticlimax in the words "and the others—foreigners."

is more wretched. What is this, Polus? You are laughing? Is this for your part another species of refutation, when someone says something—to laugh him down, but not to refute him? *haha,*

Polus: Don't you think you have been refuted, Socrates, when you say such things, which no human being would say? Then ask one of these [who are] here.

Socrates: Polus, I am not [one of] the politicians, and a year ago when my tribe held the chairmanship [of the assembly] and I was participating as a counselor, when it was necessary for me to put questions to a vote, I provided 474a laughter and I did not know how to put questions to a vote. And so now don't ask me to put the question to a vote of those who are here, but if you don't have a refutation better than these [arguments that you have been making] about what *I* was now saying, turn it over to me in turn to try to make the sort of refutation I think there needs to be. You see, *I* know how to provide *one* witness of what I'm saying, the one with whom I am having the argument, and I say farewell to the many; and I know how to put the question to a vote of *one* person, but with the many I don't engage in dialectic. And so, see whether you are willing 474b in turn to give a refutation by answering what's asked. You see, *I* myself think that indeed I and you and other people consider acting unjustly to be worse than being treated unjustly, and not paying a penalty to be worse than paying it.

Polus: And *I*, of course, [think] that neither I nor any other human being [believes this]. Come on, would *you* accept *he did,* being treated unjustly rather than acting unjustly? *remember*

Socrates: And *you* [would] too, of course, and [so would] everyone else.

Polus: Yeah, right! But neither *I* nor *you* nor anyone else [would]!

Socrates: So won't you answer? 474c

Polus: Yes, it follows that I will. You see, I desire to know whatever it is you'll say [next].

Socrates: Tell me, indeed, so you'll know, as if I were asking you from the start: does it seem to you, Polus, to be worse to act unjustly or to be treated unjustly?

Polus: To me, of course, to be treated unjustly.

Socrates: What indeed? Is it uglier to act unjustly or to be treated unjustly? Answer!

Polus: To act unjustly.

Socrates: And so it is also worse, if it is uglier.

Polus: Least of all, of course!

474d   **Socrates:** I understand: you don't seem to think that the beautiful and the good are the same, and that the bad and the ugly [are the same].

Polus: No, indeed.

Socrates: But what about this? Concerning all beautiful things, such as bodies and complexions and postures and voices and practices, without looking back at anything else, do you call each [of these] beautiful? First, for example, don't you say that beautiful bodies are beautiful according to the use for which each [body] is useful—[that they are beautiful] for this use—or [are they beautiful] according to some pleasure, if in the looking [at the beautiful bodies], the bodies make those who are looking rejoice? Do you have some [reason] apart from these for speaking about the beauty of a body?

474e   **Polus:** I don't.

Socrates: And for all other things [concerning the body], both postures and complexions, don't you declare the same—[that] they are beautiful on account of either some pleasure or benefit, or both?

Polus: Of course I do.

Socrates: And isn't it the same for voices and all the things that have to do with music?[66]

Polus: Yes.

---

66   On *music* see note 35.

Socrates: And, of course, with respect to the things, the fine things, that have to do with laws and practices, I don't suppose that they are fine—apart from being beneficial or pleasant or both.

Polus: No, to me, of course, they don't seem [to be].   475a

Socrates: And so, isn't the beauty of the things learned like this?

Polus: Yes, of course. And now you are, in fact, doing a beautiful job of making a definition, Socrates—defining the beautiful by both the pleasant and the good.

Socrates: And doesn't it follow that the ugly [is defined] by the opposite, by the painful and the evil?

Polus: Necessarily.

Socrates: Then, when of two fine things one is more beautiful, it's either in one or both of these qualities—either in pleasure or benefit or both—that the exceeding one is more beautiful.

Polus: Yes, of course.

Socrates: And, indeed, when of two ugly things one is uglier,   475b
it's either in pain or evil that the exceeding one will be uglier. Or isn't this necessary?

Polus: Yes.

Socrates: Come, indeed. How was it just now being said about acting unjustly and being treated unjustly? Weren't you saying that while it is worse to be treated unjustly, it is uglier to act unjustly?

Polus: I was saying [that].

Socrates: And so if it is uglier to act unjustly than to be treated unjustly, isn't it more painful and uglier as a thing exceeding in pain or in evil or in both? Isn't this also necessary?

Polus: Well, how isn't it [necessary]?

Socrates: First indeed, let us examine [the question]: is it that   475c
acting unjustly exceeds in pain being treated unjustly, and do those acting unjustly suffer more pain than those being treated unjustly?

Polus: By no means, Socrates, is this, in fact, [the case].

Socrates: Then [acting unjustly] does not, in fact, outdo [being treated unjustly] in pain.

Polus: Indeed, it does not.

Socrates: And so if [acting unjustly] does not [outdo the other in] pain, even more would it not exceed in both [pain and evil].

Polus: It appears [that it would] not.

Socrates: And so it remains [that acting unjustly exceeds being treated unjustly] by the other.

Polus: Yes.

Socrates: By evil.

Polus: It is likely.

Socrates: And so, as a thing exceeding in evil, acting unjustly would be worse than being treated unjustly.

Polus: Indeed, it is clear that [this is so].

475d   **Socrates:** And isn't it the case that earlier it was agreed with us by many people and by you that it was uglier to act unjustly than to be treated unjustly?

Polus: Yes.

Socrates: And now of course it has appeared worse.

Polus: It is likely.

Socrates: And so would you accept the worse and the more shameful rather than that which is less [so]? Don't hesitate to answer, Polus. It won't hurt, but nobly present [yourself] to the argument as though to a physician and answer; either assent or don't assent to the things I ask.

Polus: But I would not accept [the worse and more shameful], Socrates.

Socrates: Would anyone else of humankind?

Polus: It does not seem [so] to me by this argument, of course.

Socrates: Then it is true what *I* was saying, that neither *I* nor *you* nor anyone else of humankind would rather accept acting unjustly than being treated unjustly. You see, [acting unjustly] happens to be worse.

Polus: It appears so.

Socrates: And so, you see, Polus, that when the [one] refutation is placed alongside the [other] refutation, [it does] not seem at all like [it], but while all other people agree with you except me, *you* being only one person are sufficient   476a
for me, as you agree [with me] and are [my] witness, and *I* put the question to your vote alone and bid the others goodbye. And consider this to have been established in this way by us. Next, let us examine the second thing about   ✓
which we went off in different directions: [the proposition that] it is the greatest of evils for the one who acts unjustly to pay a penalty, as *you* were thinking, or [whether it is] a bigger [evil] not to pay a penalty, as *I* was thinking. Let us examine [the matter] in the following way: do you call it the same thing for the one acting unjustly to pay a penalty and to be disciplined justly?

Polus: Of course I do.

Socrates: And so, can you say that all just things are   476b
fine—insofar, of course, as they are just? Tell [us], after examining [the matter] thoroughly.

Polus: But it does seem so to me, Socrates.

Socrates: Look indeed also at this: if someone does something, is it necessary that there also be something passive [that is acted upon] by the one who is doing [that action]?

Polus: To me, of course, it seems [necessary].

Socrates: And is this [passive thing] experiencing what the doer does, and [is it experiencing] the sort of thing that   *repetition*
the doer does? I am saying something like this: if someone strikes a blow, is it necessary that something is struck a blow?

Polus: It is necessary.

Socrates: And if the one who strikes a blow strikes a blow violently or quickly, is the thing that is struck struck the   476c
blow in the same way?

Polus: Yes.

Socrates: Then what is struck a blow has an experience of the sort that the one striking the blow produces?

Polus: Yes, of course.

Socrates: And so if someone burns [something], is it necessary that something be burned?

Polus: Well, how not?

Socrates: And if of course he burns [something] violently and painfully, the thing burned is burned as the one doing the burning burns [it]?

Polus: Yes, of course.

Socrates: And if someone cuts something, the argument is the same. You see, something is cut.

Polus: Yes.

476d **Socrates:** And if of course the cut is big or deep or painful, as the cut is cut, the thing cut will be such as the cutter cuts.[67]

Polus: It appears so.

Socrates: In short, indeed, see whether you agree [with] what I've just been saying about everything, that exactly what the thing doing does, so the thing experiencing [what the thing doing does] experiences [it].

Polus: But I do agree.

Socrates: Since these things have been agreed, is paying the penalty experiencing something or doing something?

Polus: Of necessity it is experiencing [something].

Socrates: Isn't it [experiencing what is done] by the one doing [it]?

Polus: Well, how not? [It is] of course [experiencing what is done] by the one disciplining.

476e **Socrates:** And is the one [who is] disciplining rightly disciplining justly?

Polus: Yes.

---

67   These tongue-twisters are a parody of Polus' style.

Socrates: Is he doing just things or not?

Polus: [He is doing] just things.

Socrates: And isn't the one being disciplined experiencing just things in paying the penalty?

Polus: It appears so.

Socrates: And it was agreed, I suppose, that just things are fine things?

Polus: Yes, of course.

Socrates: Then of these people, the one does fine things and the other, the one who is being disciplined, experiences fine things.

Polus: Yes.

Socrates: And if [he experiences] fine things, [then he experiences] good things? And, you see, [these must be] either pleasant or beneficial things.   477a

Polus: [This is] necessary.

Socrates: Then, the one paying the penalty experiences good things?

Polus: It seems so.

Socrates: Then he is benefited?

Polus: Yes.

Socrates: Then, in what respect am *I* to understand the benefit? Does he become better in his soul, if he is justly disciplined?

Polus: Well, it seems.

Socrates: Then the one who pays the penalty is freed of the evil of his soul?

Polus: Yes.

Socrates: And so, then, is he freed from the greatest evil? Look   477b
at it in this way: concerning the condition of a person's money, do you see any other evil than poverty?

Polus: No, [nothing] but poverty.

Socrates: And what about the condition of [a person's] body? Would you say that weakness is an evil—and illness, and ugliness, and things like these?

Polus: *I* [would], of course.

Socrates: And in the soul, do you think that there is some wickedness?

Polus: Well, how not?

Socrates: And so wouldn't you call this injustice and ignorance and cowardice and things like these?

Polus: It follows, entirely.

477c   **Socrates:** And so, concerning money and body and soul, which are three things, haven't you said that there are three kinds of wickedness—poverty, illness, injustice?

Polus: Yes.

Socrates: And so which of these kinds of wickedness is the ugliest? Isn't it injustice and, in short, wickedness of the soul?

Polus: Of course, very much so.

Socrates: If it's indeed ugliest, is it also worst?

Polus: What's this you're saying, Socrates?

Socrates: This: according to what's been agreed to earlier, whatever provides the greatest ugliness—either the greatest pain or harm or both—is always the ugliest thing.

Polus: Very much so.

477d   **Socrates:** And hasn't it now indeed been agreed by us that injustice and every wickedness of soul are ugliest?

Polus: Well, [so] it has been agreed.

Socrates: Isn't it the most distressing and ugliest of these things because it exceeds in distress or in harm or in both?

Polus: It is necessary.

Socrates: And so more painful than being poor and worn out [by illness] is being unjust and wanton[68] and cowardly and ignorant?

---

68   "Wanton," from the Greek word *akolastos*, is our translation for the opposite of "self-restrained." It describes a person who lacks self-restraint when it comes to pleasures. The four classical virtues, whose vicious opposites are listed here by Socrates, are justice, self-restraint, courage, and wisdom. See the Glossary under "wantonness."

Polus: To me, of course, they don't seem so, Socrates, from these things [that we have just said].

Socrates: Then the rest of the soul's evil is [the] most ugly of all things because of some preternaturally great harm and exceedingly amazing evil, since it is not [exceedingly   477e great] in pain, as your argument goes.

Polus: It appears so.

Socrates: But, I suppose, in fact, the thing exceeding [in evil because of its] very great harm would be the greatest evil of [all] the things that are.

Polus: Yes.

Socrates: Then the injustice and the wantonness and the rest of the wickedness of the soul are the greatest evil of [all] the things that are.

how's that?

Polus: It appears so.

Socrates: And so what technical skill frees one from poverty? Is it not moneymaking?

Polus: Yes.

Socrates: What [frees one] from illness? Isn't it the medical [technical skill]?

Polus: Necessarily.   478a

Socrates: And what [technical skill frees one from] wickedness and injustice? If you don't easily see a way out, look at it in this way: where [do we go] and to what men do we take those worn out in their bodies?

Polus: To physicians, Socrates.

Socrates: And where do we take those who are unjust and intemperate?

Polus: Are you saying to the jurymen?[69]

Socrates: Isn't it to pay a penalty?

Polus: I say [so].

---

69   Athenian juries were quite different from ours, with jurors numbering from the hundreds to the thousands. Pericles introduced the practice of paying jurors, but the wage of two obols was somewhat less than what a laborer earned in a day.

Socrates: And then don't those who discipline rightly do their disciplining using some justice?

Polus: It is clear, indeed.

478b   **Socrates:** Then moneymaking frees one from poverty and medicine from illness, and justice from wantonness and injustice.

Polus: It appears [so].

Socrates: And so what do you say is the most beautiful of these things?

Polus: Of what things are you speaking?

Socrates: Of moneymaking, of medicine, of justice.

Polus: Justice is very different [from the other two technical skills], Socrates.

Socrates: Doesn't it in [its] turn make very much pleasure or benefit or both, if indeed it is a very beautiful thing?

478c   **Polus:** Yes.

Socrates: And so, then, isn't it pleasant to be treated by a physician, and don't those treated by a physician rejoice?

Polus: It doesn't seem so to me, of course.

Socrates: But it is beneficial, of course. No?

Polus: Yes.

Socrates: You see, [the person who is treated] is freed from a great evil, so that it is profitable [for him] to submit to pain[70] and to be healthy.

Polus: Well, how not?

Socrates: Would a person be happiest about his body in this way—in being treated by a physician—or in not being sick at all?

Polus: It is clear that in not being sick.

Socrates: You see, this—a release from evil—was *not* happiness, as seems likely, but [happiness was] not the acquisition [of evil] at all.

---

70   An ancient physician's most common treatments—cautery, purgatives, and other disagreeable procedures—were all going to hurt.

Polus: These things are [so].

Socrates: And what? Of two men having evil either in body 478d or in soul, which is more wretched, the one treated by a physician and freed from the evil or the one not treated by a physician and [still] having the evil?

Polus: The one not treated by a physician appears [more wretched] to me.

Socrates: And paying the penalty was a release from a very great evil, wickedness?

Polus: Well, it was.

Socrates: You see, it restrains [people] and makes [them] more just, I suppose, and justice becomes the medical [technical skill] for wickedness.

good summary

Polus: Yes.

Socrates: Happiest then is the one who doesn't have evil in his soul, since this appeared as the greatest of evils. 478e

Polus: It is indeed clear.

Socrates: Second [happiest], I suppose, is the one being released [from evil].

Polus: It is likely.

Socrates: And this was the one put [back] into his mind and reproved and who paid the penalty.

Polus: Yes.

Socrates: Then the one having injustice and not released [from it] lives most badly.

Polus: It appears [so].

Socrates: And doesn't he happen to be the one who, acting unjustly in the biggest things and using the greatest injustice, accomplishes his deeds so as not to be put [back] into his mind nor to be disciplined nor to pay a penalty, as 479a *you* say Archelaus and the other tyrants and rhetors and members of a junta[71] have done.

---

71 This is our translation for what is, in essence, as Dodds calls it, a "group-tyrant." Dodds cites Aristotle's observation that "group-tyranny" stands to oligarchy as tyranny stands to monarchy (*Politics* 1292b10 and 1293a31).

Polus: It seems likely.

Socrates: You see, I suppose, my best man, these have accomplished nearly the same thing as someone who, when afflicted with the greatest illnesses, accomplishes for himself that he not pay a penalty concerning the errors of his body and that he not be cured by physicians, fearing like a child to be cauterized and operated on surgically
479b   because it would be painful.[72] Or doesn't it seem like this to you too?

Polus: It [does] to me, of course.

Socrates: Being ignorant, of course, as is likely, of the sort of thing that constitutes the health and excellence[73] of a body. You see, from what we have now agreed, those who escape justice run the risk of doing something like this, Polus—of looking on [the body's] pain and being blind to its benefit and not knowing how much more wretched living without a healthy body is than [living without] a healthy soul (but instead living with [a soul] unsound and
479c   unjust and unholy)—and so they do everything in order not to pay a penalty and be freed from the greatest evil, procuring money and friends for themselves and seeing to it that they be as persuasive as possible at speaking. And if we have agreed on true things, Polus, do you perceive what follows from the argument? Or do you want us to collect these points?

Polus: [Yes], unless it seems best to you to do something else.

Socrates: Doesn't it follow, then, that injustice and acting
479d   unjustly are the greatest evil?

Polus: It appears so, of course.

Socrates: And of course, paying the penalty [appears to be] a release from this evil?

Polus: It is possibly so.

Socrates: And not paying [the penalty appears to be] a continuation of the evil?

---

72   In this section Socrates is surely recalling the reluctant patient whom Gorgias persuaded to submit to the physician's treatment (456b).

73   See "excellence" in the Glossary.

Polus: Yes.

Socrates: Then, second of evils in size is [for one] to act unjustly, but for one to act unjustly and not pay a penalty is naturally the greatest and first of all evils.

Polus: It seems likely.

Socrates: And so, my friend, concerning this [matter] we have *not* gone our separate ways[74]—*you* judging Archelaus happy while he is acting unjustly in the greatest matters and not paying any penalty at all, and *I* thinking the 479e opposite, [that] whether [it is] Archelaus or any other person who acts unjustly and does not pay a penalty, it is appropriate for this person to be wretched in a way different from other people and that the one acting unjustly is always more wretched than the one treated unjustly, and that the one not paying the penalty is always more wretched than the one paying the penalty. Weren't these the things said by me?

Polus: Yes.

Socrates: And hasn't it been shown that these things were said truly?

Polus: It appears [so].

Socrates: Okay. And so if these things are indeed true, Polus, 480a what is the great use of rhetoric? You see, from the things that have now been agreed, it is necessary that one especially keep a watch over himself and see to it that he not act unjustly, since he'll have evil enough [if he does so].[75] No?

Polus: Yes, of course.

Socrates: But if, in fact, he does act unjustly—either he himself or someone else whom he cares about—[then it is necessary] for him willingly to go where he will pay a

---

74 This could be translated (and is by other translators) as a question, "And so weren't we going our separate ways about this matter...." We have chosen the present translation because it shows that Socrates has led Polus around to the place where there is no disagreement between them, and thus Socrates has fulfilled one of the purposes of dialectic—to reach agreement. This represents a key moment in the conversation rather than a simple summing up.

75 This is a *meiosis*—the technical rhetorical term for an ironic understatement. Socrates means that the person he is talking about "will have plenty of evil."

480b
penalty as quickly as possible, to the judge in the same way as to the physician, hurrying lest over time the illness of injustice, festering, make his soul also incurable. Or what shall we say, Polus, if indeed our earlier agreements remain for us? Isn't it necessary for these [statements] to harmonize with those and not otherwise?

Polus: What are we to say, Socrates?

Socrates: For delivering a speech in defense of one's own injustice or [the injustice of] one's parents or companions or children or homeland when [he or they] have acted unjustly, rhetoric is not at all useful to us, Polus, unless
480c
someone were to understand the opposite—that it is necessary to prosecute oneself especially, and then the members of his household and others and whoever of his friends over and over again happens to be acting unjustly, and not to hide but to drag the injustice into the open, in order that he might pay a penalty and become healthy, and to compel him and others not to play the coward but to shut his eyes tight and offer [himself] well and bravely as though to a physician for surgery and cautery, pursuing the good and beautiful, not taking into account the pain, [and] if in fact he has performed unjust actions that
480d
deserve blows, to provide [himself for] a beating, and, if [he is deserving] of chains, to be bound, and if of a fine, to pay [it], and if of exile, to undergo exile, and if of death, to undergo death, being himself the first prosecutor both of himself and of the members of his household—and to use rhetoric for this: to see to it that the injustice [of all of them] become conspicuous and that they be released from the biggest evil—injustice. Are we to say this or are we not, Polus?

480e
Polus: To me, in fact, Socrates, these things do seem out-of-place, though perhaps for you they agree with [what we've said] before.

Socrates: Then, won't those things either have to be let go of, or is it necessary that these [things we've agreed upon now] go together?

Polus: Yes, of course, this is so.

Socrates: And, of course, turning to the opposite situation, if
it is necessary [for a person] to do someone ill, whether
an enemy or anyone [else], if only he himself has not
been treated unjustly by the enemy—you see, one must
be discreet about this—but if the enemy treat another
person unjustly, in every way it must be arranged, both
in acting and speaking, that he *not* pay a penalty and *not*   481a
go before a jury, and if he *does* go, it must be contrived
that he—the enemy—escape and *not* pay a penalty, but
if he has stolen gold, a lot of it, he *not* give it back, but
holding on to it squander it on himself and his family,
[and squander it] unjustly and in an ungodly way, and if
in turn he has performed unjust actions deserving death,
[it must be contrived] that he *not* die, absolutely *never,* but
[become] an immortal [always] being wicked, but if he
does not [become an immortal], that he live the greatest   481b
time being such [an evil person]. For such things rhetoric
will be useful, it seems to me, in fact, Polus, since for the
person who does not intend to be unjust there does not
seem to me to be a big use for it, if indeed there is even
some use, since in the [conversation] earlier there didn't
appear to be any at all.

Callicles: Tell me, Chaerephon, is Socrates serious about these
things or is he having fun?[76]

Chaerephon: To me, Callicles, he seems preternaturally
serious. Still, there's nothing like asking him.

Callicles: By the gods, but I desire to. Tell me, Socrates, are   481c
we to take you now as a serious person or as one who's
having fun? You see, if you are serious and these things

---

76 Callicles' question here uses the word for the serious people in tragedy, but the word is
not conjoined with the word for the low figures of comedy. Instead, Callicles asks whether
Socrates is playing or, as we have translated the word, "having fun." It is not easy, perhaps,
always to tell where the borderline between fun and seriousness lies, and the ancients were
themselves aware of this difficulty. Are the logical conundra and paradoxes raised by such
Presocratics as Parmenides and his student Zeno playfully presented to show the limitations
of language, or are they serious insights into the basic nature of being—or are they both?
And the Platonic dialogues themselves—are they so much play or are they deadly serious—
or are they both? On the term "[to be] serious" see above, note 54 and the Glossary.

that you are saying happen to be true, wouldn't the life of us human beings be turned upside down, and aren't we doing all things the opposite, as is likely, of the way they must be [done]?

Socrates: Callicles, if human beings didn't have some [common awareness of] experience, [there being] one [experience] to some, another different from that to others, but one of us experienced an individually private experience [altogether different from what] the others [experienced], it would not be an easy thing [for one person] to display his own experience.[77] I speak having considered that *you* and *I* now happen to have experienced the same thing, each of the two of us being in love with two things, *I* with Alcibiades, son of Cleinias and with philosophy,[78] and *you* with [your] two, with the Athenian demos and with [Demos] the son of Pyrilampus.[79] And so I perceive— although you are clever—that every time your boy-

repetition

481d

---

77   This sentence is very difficult, and requires much interpolation to make sense. Perhaps Socrates is deliberately obfuscating his meaning. He is certainly not answering Callicles' question directly.

78   This is the first appearance of the word "philosophy" in the dialogue. It is also the first mention of Alcibiades, the son of Cleinias. Alcibiades was perhaps the most controversial Athenian of the last two decades of the fifth century B.C.E. A strong proponent of the Athenian attack on Syracuse, he was suspected in the profanation of the Herms on the eve of the Sicilian Expedition, a suspicion given credibility because he had already been reputed to have mocked the mysteries at private parties (Thucydides 6.27-29). Alcibiades fled to Sparta rather than stand trial in Athens. There he gave the Spartans the advice that enabled them to defeat the Athenians in Sicily and, by the advice to fortify Decelea, to harass them in their homeland, a maneuver that—as Thucydides says (7.27)—was the ruin of Athens. Later, when after some scandalous behavior involving the seduction of a royal wife, he was compelled to flee from Sparta, he succeeded in securing Persian help for Athens, which welcomed him back. Defeated at the Battle of Notium, he fled to the Propontis and was later executed by the Persians. Aristophanes' *Frogs*, produced in 404, probably reflects Athens' feelings about Alcibiades (1425): "the polis longs for him, it hates him, and it wants him back." Near the end of the *Gorgias* (519A), just after the argument that the true statesman makes his fellow citizens better, Socrates will again bring up Alcibiades, and readers will recall that Socrates was unable to make even his beloved Alcibiades virtuous. On Plato's possible purpose in evoking the memory of Alcibiades, see Introduction p. 2, note 2.

79   Pyrilampes' son Demos is described as "good-looking" or "excellent" in Aristophanes' *Wasps* (82) and, according to Lysias (19.25), he equipped a trireme. We suspect he is being mentioned here because his name would yield a pun on *demos* (see Glossary). According to John Burnet, Pyrilampes was the stepfather of Plato, whose father Ariston must have died when Plato was quite young. This would make Demos Plato's stepbrother (John Burnet, *Greek Philosophy: Part I, Thales to Plato* [London: Macmillan and Co., 1928],

favorite[80] speaks and says that things are like this, you are
unable to speak against [him] and you change yourself up
and down;[81] and in the assembly, if while you are saying   481e
something, the demos of the Athenians says that it is not
so, you change and say what it wishes, and towards this
beautiful young man of Pyrilampus you have experienced
other things like these. You see, you are not able to
contradict the wishes and words of your boy-favorite, *who is he referring to*
so that if each time you are speaking someone wonders
at what you are saying on account of these [loves]—how
out-of-place [your statements] are[82]—perhaps you would
say to him, if you wished to tell the truth, that unless
someone keeps your boy-favorite from these words, *you*   482a
won't ever stop saying these things. Consider then that it
is necessary [for you] to hear other such things from me
and do not wonder that *I* am saying these things, but stop
Philosophy, *my* boy-favorite, [who is] the one saying these
things. You see, my friendly companion, he[83] is always
saying what you hear me [saying] now, and he, as far as I
am concerned, is much less impulsive than my other boy-
favorite; you see, this son of Cleinias at different times
[says] different words, but Philosophy always [says] the
same ones, and *he* says the things you are now wondering   482b

---

206). Burnet does not cite his source for this information, and the only place we can find
Pyrilampes mentioned as the stepfather of Plato, after searching the *Thesaurus Linguae
Graecae* (a complete database of all Greek literature through the sixth century C.E.), is
Proclus' commentary on Plato's *Parmenides*. But Proclus lived nearly a millennium later
than Plato, and it is possible that the name Pryilampes, meaning "bright with fire," was
enough to inspire this allegorizing Neo-plationist to invent the relationship. If, however,
Plato is choosing the name because of the pun it yields, Proclus would be acting in the
same spirit by producing his allegorical familial relationship.

80   The term that we have translated "boy-favorite" is *paidika* and contains the same root
      (*pais*) as the word we have translated above in Callicles' question as "having fun." Perhaps
      this is Socrates' way—to be sure, an oblique way—of answering Callicles' question.

81   These words recall Callicles' observation (481c) that Socrates' claims about bringing
      one's friends to justice and letting one's enemies commit crimes scot-free would turn the
      world upside down.

82   Socrates picks up Polus' recent use of this word (475a). See note 53.

83   We have used "he" in English even though Philosophy is a feminine noun in Greek
      (which is why other translators use a feminine pronoun here) because Socrates is calling
      him a "boy-favorite" and so he would be male. Using a feminine pronoun in English
      would preserve the gender of the original but would lose the sense.

at—and you were yourself present at what was said. And so either refute *him* about what I've just been saying [and show how] it is not the utmost of all evils to act unjustly and [though] acting unjustly not to pay a penalty; or, if you will let this go unrefuted, by the dog-god of the Egyptians, Callicles will not agree with you, Callicles, but will be discordant in all his life. Let me tell you, *I* of course think, best [of men], that it is better for me that [my] lyre be out of tune and discordant and that the dance which I

482c   lead [also be discordant] and that most people not agree with me but say things opposite, than that I, being one [person], should be out of tune with myself and say things opposite [to what I say].

    pretensions

Callicles: You seem to me, Socrates, to be sophomoric in your speeches, truly like a demagogue.[84] And now you are speaking like a demagogue, and Polus is experiencing the same experience as that which he accused Gorgias of experiencing at your hands.[85] You see, I suppose, he said that when Gorgias was asked by you, should there arrive by his side a man who didn't know the just things but

482d   wished to learn rhetoric, whether Gorgias would teach him, and [Gorgias] became ashamed and—on account of the character of human beings, because they would be vexed if someone refused [such a request]—said that he would teach him—[and] indeed, on account of this agreement [Gorgias was] compelled to say things opposite to himself—and you are glad at this very thing[86]—and [Polus] was laughing at you rightly then, in fact, as it seems to me. But again now he himself has experienced

essay

---

84   Perhaps the mixing of metaphors here is a mark of Callicles' excitement. Or Callicles may be sarcastically following up Socrates' parody of Polus' use of the word "experience" and be mocking Socrates.

85   Perhaps Callicles' repetition of the word "experience" is a sign of his agitation. But the word also means "suffer," and so perhaps Callicles is emphasizing Polus' passivity in the face of Socrates' argument.

86   This attribution of a bad motive to Socrates—namely, that he delights in leading people down a philosophical primrose path—was made by Polus in 461c. We should note that Callicles asserts that saying things opposite to oneself is shameful and that it is possible to be compelled to say such opposite things. We shall have to see whether he undergoes this same kind of compulsion.

this very thing. And for this very [reason], in fact, *I* don't admire Polus, because he admitted to you that to act unjustly is uglier than to be treated unjustly; from this agreement, you see, he in turn was tripped up by you in words [and] was bridled,[87] being ashamed to say what he was thinking. You see, Socrates, *you*—saying that you pursue the truth—in reality are leading [people] into coarse and demagogic things that are not fine by nature, but by convention.[88] These things are [in] many ways opposite to each other—nature and convention. And so if someone is ashamed and does not dare to say what he thinks, he is compelled to say opposite things. And indeed, having observed this smart [effect], *you* work evil in words, [for] if on the one hand someone speaks according to convention, [you] reply by asking according to nature, and if on the other hand he [speaks about the things] of nature, [you reply by asking] about the things of convention. And so in these matters—acting unjustly and being treated unjustly—while Polus was speaking of the thing uglier according to convention, *you* straightaway were pursuing the argument according to nature. By nature, on the one hand, you see, everything is uglier that is also worse—and this is to be treated unjustly; by convention, on the other hand, to act unjustly [is uglier and worse]. You see, this is not even the experience of a *man*, to be treated unjustly, but of some man-slave,[89] for whom it is better to die than to live—[one] who, being treated unjustly and treated like dirt is not himself able to help himself or another for whom he cares.

But I think that those who establish the conventions[90] are the weak people and the many. And

482e

483a

483b

---

87 This is a joke on Polus' name, which means *colt*. See note 46.

88 This interpretive translation of the sentence has Callicles maintaining that Socrates is actually leading those who converse with him into mistaken notions rather than just offering mistaken arguments. The word we have translated as "custom" (*nomos*) is also the word for "law." See Glossary.

89 The particular word for "slave" here has the same root as the word for "man," and we are trying to capture the repetition.

90 Here Callicles seems to be shifting away from a sense of *nomos* as custom and more to a sense of law.

[it is] for themselves, and for what is advantageous to themselves, that they establish conventions and praise

483c   the praiseworthy and blame the blameworthy. Fearing the more vigorous of human beings and the ones who have the power to have more, [they establish conventions and distribute praise and blame] in order that [the more vigorous] not have more than they, [and] they say that it is a shameful and unjust thing to have more and "this is to act unjustly—to seek to have more than others." You see, I think that [since they are] rather trivial people[91] they are *glad* to have an equal [share]. Indeed, on account of these things, this—seeking to have more than the many—is said by convention to be unjust and shameful, and they call it "acting unjustly." But nature itself, in fact,

483d   I think, reveals this—that it is just that the better have more than the worse and the more powerful [have more than] the more powerless. And that these [statements] are so is clear in many ways, both in other living things and in all the poleis and races of human beings, because in this way the just has been judged, that the stronger should rule over and have more than the lesser. Come on, what sort of justice was Xerxes using when he marched

483e   on Greece or his father on Scythia? Or someone might have a myriad other such things to say. But I think these men are performing these actions according to the nature of the just, and, yes, by Zeus, of course, according to the convention of nature,[92]—not, however, perhaps according to this [convention] that we are laying down. Fashioning the best and most vigorous of us, taking [them] from youth, as though [they were] lions, subduing [them] by

---

91   On "trivial," see note 54.

92   Since the word we have translated as "convention" is often translated as "law," Callicles' phrase could read "law of nature." Dodds, so reading it, writes, "Callicles' coinage is not to be confused with 'natural law' in the Stoic sense . . . or with the modern scientist's 'laws of Nature', which are simply observed uniformities. Callicles' 'laws of Nature' is not a generalization about Nature but a rule of conduct on the analogy of 'natural' behavior." A modern example of Dodds' point would be the extrapolation by social Darwinists of the competitive struggles of natural selection in the animal and plant kingdoms to human capitalist enterprises. Our translation more strikingly perhaps reflects the highly charged and equivocal force of Callicles' expression.

charms and bewitching [them], we enslave them in our   484a
own interests, saying how it is necessary to have an equal
[share] and [saying,] "this is the fine and the just."[93] But
I think, of course, [that] if a man has a sufficient nature,
having shaken all these things off his back[94] and having
broken [free of them] and having escaped [them], having
trampled our learning and deceptions and spells and all
the conventions contrary to nature, [and] then having
risen up [against all of these things in his rebellion] the
slave appears [as] our despot—*there* shines forth nature's   484b
justice. And it seems to me that even Pindar, in his ode,
reveals what I am saying when he says that

> Convention is king of all,
> Of mortals and of immortals;

Indeed, this [convention], he says,

> Acting justly, directs the utmost violence
> With a supreme hand; I call as a witness [to this]
> The deeds of Heracles, since without paying. . .

[Pindar] speaks somehow thus—you see, I don't know
the ode[95]—and he says that Heracles drove off the cattle
without buying them (though Geryon did not give them
[to him]), as though this [behavior] were just by nature   484c
and as though both the cows and all the other possessions
of worse and lesser people were [the possessions] of the
better and the stronger person.

And so the truth is like this, and you will know
it, should you come to the bigger [picture], letting go
already of philosophy. You see, Socrates, philosophy is

---

93   The reader may wish to compare the views of Callicles here with those of the Athenian
      ambassadors to Melos in the Melian Dialogue (Thucydides 5.105), found later in this
      volume.

94   Perhaps, since the verb is used of a horse shaking off his rider, this is another horse
      metaphor, to go along with the puns on Polus' name.

95   As has been observed, Plato is having Callicles distort the meaning of Pindar's ode into
      a view supportive of his own remarks. Plato comically portrays in the *Protagoras* how
      easily the statements of poets could be distorted into wholly contradictory meanings. For
      a fine discussion of the use of this ode in the *Gorgias*, see Dale Grote, "Callicles' Use of
      Pindar's NOMOS BASILEUS: *Gorgias* 484B" (*The Classical World* 90 [1994] 21–31).

a pleasant thing, should someone taste it moderately[96] in the right time of life. But if he waste his time beyond what's necessary, it is the wreck of people. You see, if he should be an entirely good-natured [person] and he should engage in philosophy beyond the right time of life, he—a man intending both to become noble and good and to have a good reputation—must necessarily become

484d   inexperienced in all the things in which it is necessary to be experienced. And, in fact, [such people] become inexperienced in the conventions concerning the polis and of the words it is necessary to use in contracts with people in private and public,[97] and of human pleasures and desires, and, in short, they become inexperienced in every way in [human] habits. And so, when they should come into some action, either private or pertaining to the

484e   polis, they become laughably ridiculous, as, of course, I think, would men engaged in the affairs of the polis also become laughably ridiculous, when in turn they come into your pastimes and arguments. This is consistent with the comment of Euripides:

Brilliant is each in this, and to this he hastens
Spending the biggest part of his day on this,
There, where he himself happens to be better than
        himself.[98]

485a   But where he is lousy, he flees from there and badmouths it, but he praises the other thing [—the set of practices in which he is adept—] from good will for himself, thinking that in this way he is praising himself.

But I think it is most right to have a share of both. On the one hand, it is a fine thing, so long as it is for the sake of education, to have a share of philosophy, and it is not a shameful thing for a young man to engage in philosophy. But when, being already older, a man still engages in

---

96   "Moderately" is the adverb from "moderation," for which see the Glossary.

97   There is a question of whether rhetoric is for public or private use. In Plato's *Phaedrus* (261a–b), though the title character seems to think rhetoric is what is used in public assemblies, Socrates says that rhetoric may be used in public or private.

98   The quotation is from Euripides' lost play *Antiope*.

philosophy, it becomes a most laughably ridiculous thing, Socrates, and *I* of course experience exactly the same thing about those people engaging in philosophy that I do towards those stammering and having fun. You see, when I see a child, for whom it is still fitting to converse[99] like this—stammering and having fun— I am glad, and it appears to me pleasant and free and fitting the age of the child, but when I hear a little boy conversing clearly, it seems to me something bitter and it bothers my ears and it seems to me to be something fit for a slave. And when someone hears a man stammering or sees him having fun, this seems laughable and unmanly and a thing worthy of a licking. And *I* experience the same thing, of course, towards those engaging in philosophy. Seeing philosophy in the company of a young fellow, I delight and it seems to me to be fitting and I think that this person is someone free, and the one not engaging in philosophy [I think] unfree and a person who will never make himself worthy of any business that is fine and noble. But when indeed I see an older [person] still engaging in philosophy and not letting it go, this man, Socrates, seems to me to have need of a licking. You see—what I was now saying—it falls to this man, even if he should have a very good nature, to become unmanly, and to flee the central [affairs] of the polis and the marketplaces, in which the poet says that men become distinguished,[100] and to slink away in retirement to live the rest of his life whispering in a corner with three or four young fellows, and never to utter a free and great and adequate [remark].[101] *accusation of Apology.*

485b

485c

485d

485e

---

99 The verb that we have here translated as "conversing" is the same word that Socrates has used with the sense of "engaging in dialectic." Callicles perhaps is directing a verbal jab at Socrates by saying that this activity is "something fit for a boy or a slave." Callicles does not apply the verb "converse" to a man.

100 Homer, *Iliad* 9.441, where the term we have translated into its usual fifth century sense of "marketplaces" probably meant "assemblies." On casual, learned references to poets, see note 7.

101 Though "adequate" is the manuscript reading, it appears to some editors as anti-climactic, and they have emended the text to read "noble" or "new." But we think that the anti-climax serves Plato's purpose of showing Callicles as flustered and therefore not in control of his rhetoric.

But *I* am more or less friendly towards you. And so I am likely to have experienced now what Zethos [experienced] at the hands of Euripides' [character] Amphion, [in the play] that I mentioned.[102] You see, it comes also to me to say such things to you as he says to his brother—that "you are being careless, Socrates, of the things you must care for, and [with respect to] the noble nature of [your] soul you are [making yourself] conspicuous in the shape of a young fellow, and neither would you rightly put forth an argument in councils of justice nor would you cry aloud a plausible or persuasive [statement], nor would you counsel

486a   a new plan on behalf of another." And, my friend Socrates, don't be vexed with me; you see, I am speaking with good will for you. Does it not seem a shameful thing to you to be such as *I* think you are and [as I think] the others are [who are] always driving further into philosophy? You see, if someone, upon taking hold of you or someone else like you, should drag you away to prison, saying that you are unjust, [even though] you are doing nothing at all that

486b   is unjust, you know that you would not be able to be of use to yourself, but you would become dizzy and stare blankly from not having anything to say, and upon going up to the courtroom and being confronted by a low-life and rascally accuser, you would die, if he wished to punish you with death. "And how is this a wise thing, Socrates— any technical skill that takes a man of good nature and makes him worse,"[103] as one having the power neither of helping himself nor of saving either himself or any

486c   other person from the greatest dangers, but [leaves] him stripped by his enemies of all his substance and merely living without rights in his polis? Such a man—to put it in a rather redneck way—it's okay to punch in the nose and not pay a penalty for it.[104] But, good [friend], be persuaded by me, and stop [this practice of] refuting, and [instead]

---

102   In 484e.

103   These and the subsequent quotations are also adapted from Euripides' *Antiope*. Dodds quotes the Greek, which was reconstructed by A. Nauck in the latter part of the nineteenth century.

104   In Greek, literally, "to box on the ears"; but in our culture, we punch others in the nose.

practice the music of "winning friends and influencing people,"[105] and practice [a subject] from where you will seem to be thoughtful, leaving this wit to others, whether we must call it triviality or nonsense, "from which you'll inhabit empty houses."[106] Don't emulate men engaged in refutation over these petty points but those who make a living and have a [good] reputation and many other good things.

486d

Socrates: If I happened to have a golden soul, Callicles, don't you think that I would be delighted to find one of the stones by which they test gold—the best [such test-stone]—and to bring it to whatever [soul] I thought [to bring it to, in order to see whether] the test-stone agreed with me that the soul was well cared for, [since, when I tested my soul] I would know well that [it] has been sufficiently [well taken care of] and [that] I have no need at all for another test.[107]

Callicles: For what [reason] are you asking this, Socrates?

486e

Socrates: I'll tell you. I now think that having met you I have happened upon such a godsend.

Callicles: What indeed?

Socrates: I know well that, should *you* agree with me about the things on which my soul holds an opinion, these things are at once themselves true. You see, I think that one who intends to test a soul adequately about living rightly and not [rightly] must have three things all of which *you* have—knowledge, good will, and frankness. You see, *I* run into many people who are unable to test [my soul] because they are not wise, as *you* are. And while others are wise, they are not willing to tell me the truth

487a

---

105 More literally, the "poetry of business."

106 The implication is that unless Socrates changes his ways, no one will wish to spend any time with him, and he will be the poorer for it; he will empty out the houses he visits.

107 This a curious metaphor. Metals cannot change into other metals. Yet Socrates seems to suggest here that if he had a leaden soul he might be able to change it into gold and then need another test stone to ascertain that he had successfully changed it. Socrates seems to be expressing delight for his soul, since it is already golden. The problem with the image lies in Socrates' suggestion that metals, like souls, can change.

because they don't care for me, as *you* do. As for these
two foreigners, Gorgias and Polus, these two are wise and

487b   my two friends, but they are more wanting in frankness
and they are more subject to shame than they need to be.
Well, how aren't [they]? The two of them, in fact, have
come to such a degree of shamefulness that, though being
ashamed, each of them was himself daring to say things
in opposition to himself [while standing right] in front of
many people, and [to say] these [opposite] things about
the greatest [matters]. But *you* have all these qualities that
the others don't: [you] have been adequately educated,
as many of the Athenians would say, and you have good

487c   will towards me. What proof do I use? *I* shall tell you. *I*
know that four of you, Callicles, have become sharers of
a wisdom, you and Teisander of Aphidnae, and Andron
the son of Androtion, and Nausikides from Cholargus.[108]
And *I* once heard you deliberating [the question of] how
far one should pursue wisdom, and I know that some
such opinion prevailed among you—not to pour one's
heart into philosophizing to exactness—but you bade

487d   one another to beware lest it escape you that you're being
ruined by becoming wiser than what's necessary. And so,
since I hear you advising me these same things that you
[advised] your own friends, it is a sufficient proof that you
truly have good will towards me. And, of course, that you
are frank and not held back by shame, you yourself say
[it], and the speech you spoke a little before agrees with
you. Indeed, it is clear that this [same situation] holds

487e   about the things [we are] now [talking about]: if in the
arguments *you* agree with me about something, this thing
will at once have been tested adequately by me and you,
and it won't be necessary to carry it to another test. You
see, *you* would never have acquiesced in [an argument]
from a lack of wisdom or from the presence of shame,

---

108   Little is known of Callicles' three friends, and what is known of two of them hints at
selfishness and greed. Plato's audience, which was probably familiar with the history of
these individuals, would catch the dramatic irony. About Teisander nothing is known.
Andron, one of the oligarchy of the Four Hundred, saved himself by denouncing a
colleague; and Nausikides extorted outrageous prices from the poor for his grain.

nor in turn would you deceive me and acquiesce; you see, you are my friend, as you yourself say. And so in reality my and your agreement will already have the finality of truth. And, Callicles, the examination about the [issues] for which *you* censured me is the most excellent of all— what sort of man it's necessary for someone to be and what he [ought to] practice and up to what point, both   488a as an older man and a younger man. You see, if *I* am doing something not rightly in my life, know well that I am making a mistake not willingly but in my ignorance; and so just as *you've* begun to put me in the right mind, do not stop, but reveal to me adequately what this is that I must practice, and in what way I might possess it, and if you catch me agreeing with you now but in later time not doing those things that I have agreed to, think me a complete dolt and and don't [bother] setting me right in   488b my mind later, as I'll be a person worthy of nothing.

But take [this] up for me from the beginning: what do you say the just thing [actually] is according to nature—both *you* and Pindar? [Is it that] the stronger person should, by his strength, carry off the things of the lesser people and the better person carry off [the things of] the worse people and the superior [person] have more than the more trivial one? Or are you saying that the just is something else, or do I recall rightly?

Callicles: But I was saying these things then and I say them now.

Socrates: Which person do you call the better and the stronger?   488c You see, I was not able to learn from you then what you were saying, whether you call the stronger [the ones who are] the physically more powerful, and is it necessary for the physically weaker ones to obey the physically more powerful one—the sort of thing you seem to me then to have revealed too, since the big poleis attack the small ones according to the just-by-nature—because they are stronger and more physically powerful, as the stronger and the physically more powerful and the better are the same; or is it that [the stronger is] better on the one hand,

488d but lesser and physically weaker on the other hand, and stronger on the one hand, but more wretched on the other hand; or is the definition of the better and the stronger the same? Define this very thing for me clearly—are the stronger and the better and the physically more powerful the same or different?

Callicles: But *I* am telling you clearly that they are the same.

Socrates: Aren't the many stronger than the one—according to nature? Indeed, they make even the conventions for the one, as *you* also were just saying.

Callicles: Well, how not?

Socrates: Then the rules[109] of the many are the [rules] of the stronger.

Callicles: Yes, of course.

488e **Socrates:** And so aren't they [the rules] of the better? You see, the stronger are the better, I suppose, according to your argument.

Callicles: Yes.

Socrates: And so aren't the rules of these men excellent according to nature, since, of course, they are stronger?

Callicles: I say so.

Socrates: And so do the many think like this, as you in turn were now saying, that it is just to have an equal [share] and that it is uglier to act unjustly than to be treated unjustly? Are these things so or not? And don't *you* then be caught talking from shame! Do the many think, or do they not, that it is just to have an equal [share] and not a bigger [share], and that it is uglier to act unjustly than to be treated unjustly? Don't grudge answering me this, Callicles, so that, if you should agree with me, I may be strengthened [in this idea] by you, inasmuch as it will have been agreed to by a man adequate at deciding.

489a

---

109   We are using "rules" for the Greek *nomima*, a word related to the word for "convention." It refers to the result of an established convention. This could be a rule, which, has somewhat less gravity than a "law," or it could even be a "law," depending on the context. The various distinctions among these words are not always observed, and it is very difficult to know exactly where one sense ends and another begins.

Callicles: But, of course, the many do think this way.

Socrates: Then, not by custom alone is it uglier to act unjustly   489b
than to be treated unjustly and [not by custom alone]
is it just to have an equal share, but also by nature; and
so it is likely that you were not saying the truth in [the
things you said] before and [that you were] not rightly
accusing me when [you were] saying that custom and
nature are opposite, [and that] though *I* knew [this fact,
that custom and nature are opposite] I was working evil
in my arguments, [so that] if someone spoke according to
nature I drove him to custom; but if [he spoke] according
to custom, [I drove him] towards nature.

Callicles: This man won't stop playing the fool. Tell me,
Socrates, aren't you ashamed, being a man of your age,
to be hunting after names, and if someone makes a   489c
mistake in a phrase, to be making this a godsend? Well,
do you think that I am saying something other than the
fact that the stronger people are the better people? Have
I not been saying to you for a long time that the better
and the stronger are the same? Or do you think that I am
saying that if some trashy mob of slaves and of completely
ordinary people who are good for nothing except for
some physical strength in their body, and *these* should say
things, that what [they say] would be the rules?

Socrates: Well, Callicles most wise, are you saying this [—that
the stronger are the better]?

Callicles: Absolutely, since this follows.

Socrates: But, daimonic one, for a long time *I* too have been   489d
guessing that you were saying something of this sort about
the stronger and I am asking further, since I'm eager to
know clearly what you are saying. You see, I don't suppose
that *you* think two are better than one or that your slaves
are better than you because they are physically stronger
than *you*. But again, tell me from the beginning what you
say the better are, since [you don't say that they are] the
physically stronger. And, wondrous one, teach me more
gently, so that I won't run off from you.

489e   **Callicles:** You are being ironic, Socrates.[110]

Socrates: By Zethos, Callicles—[to swear by the character whom] *you* were using when you were being ironic in many ways towards me! But come, tell me, who do you say these better ones are?

Callicles: Those who are superior, of course.

Socrates: Don't you see, then, that *you* yourself are saying names but are showing nothing? Won't you say, concerning the better and the stronger, whether you are maintaining that they are the more thoughtful ones or some others?

Callicles: But, yes, by Zeus, I am maintaining [that they are] these—in fact, exceedingly so.

490a   **Socrates:** Then, often one thinking person is stronger than ten thousand non-thinking people, according to your argument, and it is necessary for him to rule, and for the others to be ruled, and for the one ruling to have more than those who are ruled. This, you see, is what you seem to me to wish to say—and I'm not hunting for a [mistaken phrase of yours to catch you in a trap][111]—if the one is stronger than the ten thousand.

Callicles: But this *is* what I'm saying. You see, *I* think this is what is just by nature—that the one who is better and

---

110   Callicles' charge here that Socrates is being ironic and Socrates' counationcharge in his reply are the only uses of the word "irony" in the dialogue. One of the difficulties in translating the word is that modern English makes distinctions that are not made in Greek. For us, both sarcasm and irony fall under the genus of saying the opposite of what is meant with an intention of being understood by somebody: in sarcasm, we wish the person addressed to understand the truth; in irony, we wish some third person—either an observer or ourselves—to appreciate the truth. We also distinguish dramatic irony, which consists of words expressing a truth opposite to that stated which are understood not by the speaker but by someone else, either a character in the play or the audience or both. Socratic irony is the pretense, almost painfully elaborate, of stupidity or of being inferior to the interlocutor. Even in the painful elaborateness, which may be seen as a sign of irony, there is deceit, as the interlocutor will probably take the excessively full explanation as indicating stupidity. But when the interlocutor suspects that the deceit is being practiced (and that the comment is what *we* would call "sarcastic"), as Callicles does here, he charges Socrates with irony. Aristotle in the *Rhetoric* (1419b) distinguishes *irony* from *bomolochia*, "buffoonery," but *irony*, says Aristotle, is proper for a civilized person, while "buffoonery" is not.

111   This is our guess of what the Greek text, which seems to be corrupt here, means.

more thoughtful both rules and has more than those who
are more trivial.

Socrates: Hold on here! Whatever else are you saying now? If   490b
we should be in this [place], as we are now, many crowded
together, and if we should have many foods and drinks in
common, and we are men of every kind, some physically
strong, some weak, but one of us, who is a physician, is
more thoughtful about these things, and [if] he be, as is
likely, physically stronger than some, weaker than others,
won't it be that since he is more thoughtful than we, he
will be better and stronger in these matters?

Callicles: Yes, of course.

Socrates: Is he to have more of these foods than we because   490c
he is better, or is it necessary that in ruling he manage all
things but in squandering and using up these things for his
own body he is not to grasp for more, if he doesn't intend
to be punished[112]—but is he to have more than some,
less than others? But if he happens to be the physically
weakest of all, won't [it be] the least of all [shares] [that]
goes to the best [person], Callicles? Won't it be this way,
[my] good man?

Callicles: You are talking about foods and drinks and
physicians and nonsense. *I* am not speaking about these   490d
things.

Socrates: Are you saying the better person is the more
thoughtful? Say yes or no.

Callicles: *I* do, of course.

Socrates: But [you're not saying] that it is necessary for the
better person to have more.

Callicles: Not of foods and drinks, of course.

Socrates: I understand. But perhaps of cloaks, and it is
necessary for the best weaver to have the biggest cloak
and the most and the prettiest [clothes]?

Callicles: What's this stuff about clothes?

---

112 Socrates is speaking of a metaphorical "punishment" for the one who is better and
stronger, from the over-engorgement of his stomach by food.

Socrates: But as for shoes, it's clear that the wisest and best in
490e   these matters should have more. Perhaps it's necessary for
the shoemaker to put on and walk around in the biggest
and the most shoes.[113]

Callicles: What's this stuff about shoes? You're full of
nonsense.

Socrates: Well, if you're not saying that, perhaps you're saying
this: that for a farmer who is thoughtful about land and
[is also] a fine and good man, perhaps it's necessary that
this [farmer] have more seeds and use as much seed as
possible for his land.

Callicles: You're saying the same things over and over again,
Socrates.

Socrates: And, in fact, not only [that], Callicles, but also about
the same things.

491a   **Callicles:** By the gods, won't you stop always simply talking
about hides and launderers and butchers and physicians,
as though our argument were really about them?

Socrates: Won't *you* say what things the stronger and more
thoughtful person has more of and justly grasps for [still]
more of? Will you neither put up with my interjecting [an
answer to this question] nor you yourself say?

Callicles: But *I* have, of course, been saying [it] for a long
time. First, with respect to the stronger—who they
are—I am not speaking of shoemakers or butchers, but
491b   [of those] who are thoughtful in the matters of the polis,
how it should be well inhabited, and [they are] not only
thoughtful but manly, being adequate for the things
they plan to accomplish, and they don't get weary from
softness of soul.

Socrates: Best of Callicleses, do you see that *you* are not
accusing me of the same things that *I* am accusing you

---

113 Since the shoemaker has only two feet Socrates is obviously pulling Callicles' chain.
Callicles does not seem to be responding in good humor. Why doesn't Callicles walk away
in disgust? Perhaps it is the presence of the others that keeps him in the conversation.
Another possibility is that he is trapped because the conversation is occurring in his
home.

of? *You* say that I am always saying the same things, and
you blame me. But *I* accuse you of the opposite—that you
are never saying the same things about these matters,
but at one time you were defining the "better" and the
"stronger" as the "physically stronger," and later as the
"more thoughtful," and now in turn you come having
something else: some more manly men are said by you
[to be] the stronger and the better. But, [my] good man,
be released [from this confusion once and for all], saying
who you say are the better and stronger, and at what.

491c

*said
summary*

Callicles: But *I* have said of course that they are the ones who
are thoughtful and manly in the matters of the polis. You
see, it is fitting for these men to rule over the poleis, and
this is the just thing too—for them to have more than
others, for the rulers [to have more than] the ruled.

491d

Socrates: What? [To have more] than themselves, friend?

Callicles: What's that?

Socrates: The ones ruling [to have more than] the ones being
ruled?

Callicles: What's that you're saying?

Socrates: I am saying that each one is the ruler of himself.
Or is this not at all necessary, for a person to rule over
himself, but [only] over others?

Callicles: What do you mean by "ruling over himself"?

Socrates: Nothing complicated, but, as the many [say], being
self-restrained and in charge of oneself, ruling over the
pleasures and desires in oneself.

491e

Callicles: How sweet you are: you are saying that the stupid
ones are the self-restrained.

Socrates: Look, how [am I saying that]? There is no one who
wouldn't know that I am *not* saying that.

Callicles: Yes, you absolutely are, in fact, Socrates! Since how
happy would a man become serving as a slave to anyone?
But *this* is what I, speaking frankly, am saying to you is
by nature fine and just: that it is necessary for the one
who's to live rightly to allow his desires to be as big as

492a   possible and not to curtail them, but to be adequate to serve them through manliness and prudence when the desires are as big as possible and always to have his fill of them whenever [any] desire should arise. But this, I think, is impossible for the many. For this reason they blame such men [as can fulfill their desires] because of a sense of shame, hiding their powerlessness, and, indeed, they say that wantonness is a shameful thing—which [is what] *I* was saying before—enslaving the people [who are] better in [their] nature; and they themselves, being without the power to provide fulfillment to their

492b   pleasures, praise self-restraint[114] and justice because of their unmanliness. Since for as many as it was their lot [in life] from their beginning to be the sons of kings, or for those [who are] sufficient by nature to provide for themselves some rule—either a tyranny or a junta—what in truth would be uglier and worse than self-restraint and justice for such people—for whom, when it was possible [for them] to have enjoyment of the good things (there being nothing to stop [them])—[than that] *they* should lay on themselves as their master the conventions and speech and blame of the many [mere] human beings? Or how would these men, the ones "ruling" even these [good] things in their polis, not have become wretched

492c   by this fine thing—justice and self-restraint—when they can provide nothing more to their own friends than to their enemies? But in truth, Socrates, [the truth] *you* say you are pursuing is this: luxury and wantonness and freedom, if [each] has a mercenary force [behind it][115]— this is excellence and happiness—and these other things are pretty words, [social] contracts contrary to the nature of human beings—nonsense and worth nothing.

---

114   Self-restraint is our transliteration for the Greek word *sophrosyne*. It refers to the active self-control involved in refraining from seeking sensual pleasures. It emphasizes a little more than "self-control" and considerably more than "moderation" the active effort of the will in resisting pleasure. See also the Glossary under "self-restraint."

115   Callicles is thinking in terms of power with this bold metaphor of freedom having a mercenary force to support its desires.

Socrates: Not <u>ignobly</u>, of course, Callicles, are you making an   492d
attack on the argument, since you are a frank man. You
see, *you* are now clearly saying what the others think but
are unwilling to say. And so *I* have need of you to slacken
in no way, in order that it should become entirely clear
how one must in reality live. And tell me, with respect to
the desires, are you saying that they must not be checked
if someone intends to be such as it is necessary [for him
to be], allowing the biggest possible desires to obtain
fulfillment for themselves from any source whatsoever—
and this is excellence?   492e

Callicles: *I* do say these things.

Socrates: Then those needing nothing are not rightly said to
be happy?

Callicles: Well, in that way, stones and corpses would be most
happy.

Socrates: But, indeed, the life of those you are talking about
is, in fact, also terrible. You see, I wouldn't wonder that
Euripides is saying the truth in these [verses], when he
says:

> Who knows whether to live is to die,
> And to die is to live?[116]

and *we* in reality perhaps are dead.[117] You see, *I've* heard   493a
already from one of the wise men how *we* are dead now
and the body is our tomb and this [part] of the soul
where the desires are happens to be [the kind] of thing
that is persuaded and changes suddenly up and down;
and again, with respect to this [part of the soul], some
subtle man, speaking mythically—perhaps a Sicilian
or an Italian—leading [us] astray by means of a name,

---

116 It is not known from which lost play these lines come.

117 The idea that what we call life is really death and what we call death is really life has a
long tradition in both pagan and Christian literature (for example, Plato, *Phaedo* 64bff.,
and Augustine, *Confessions* 1.6). It takes on a clever reversal in Lucretius' *On the Nature
of Things,* where the poet shows that what we call the punishments of death are really the
sufferings of our lives (3.978–1023).

493b

because [this part of the soul] is a thing involved with persuasion[118] and [a thing] inclined toward belief, called [the mind] a jar[119] and the mindless [he called] leaky[120] and this [part] of the soul of the mindless people, where the desires are, is the wanton and not covered [part] of it,[121] so that the jar would be perforated—likening [the desiring part of their soul to a leaky jar] on account of its inability to be filled. This man is showing you the opposite, indeed, [of what you said], Callicles, how of [all of the people] in Hades—indeed he is speaking of the hidden[122]—these would be the most wretched—the [leaky ones][123]—and they would carry water to the perforated jar by another such perforated thing, a sieve. And then he

493c

says that the sieve, as the one speaking told me, is the soul; and he likened the soul of the mindless ones to a sieve (as a perforated thing), inasmuch as it is unable to stay watertight on account of disbelief[124] and forgetfulness.[125]

---

118   The usual meaning of the word we have translated as "involved with persuasion" (*pithanon*) is "persuasive." But the word appears, though rarely, to have also a more passive meaning, "persuadable," which would perhaps reinforce the meaning of the word that we have translated as "inclined toward belief" (*peistikon*.) Our translation preserves the ambiguity in the term since one can be "involved with persuasion" either as the one who is persuaded or the one who is doing the persuading.

119   The word for "jar" in Greek is *pithon*, a word quite similar to the word *pithanon*, which we have translated as "involved with persuasion"—enabling Socrates to construct an elaborate pun. Unfortunately, the pun is not possible in English, and we acknowledge the truth that Cervantes puts in the mouth of his Don Quixote that reading a translation is like looking at the back of a tapestry.

120   Another untranslatable pun: the word for "leaky" also means "uninitiated."

121   In other words, this part of the soul is not covered and thus its contents are not preserved.

122   The text says "unseen" but we have used "hidden" to catch the Hades-hidden pun (*haidou-aides*) that is in the Greek text.

123   Or [uninitiated]; see note 120.

124   The term that we have translated as "disbelief" seems to refer to a lack of belief in the doctrine of Pythagoras—a belief that would have been required by Pythagorean initiates. A "leaky" or "uninitiated" individual would have made a poor member of the Pythagorean brotherhood. Socrates' words at the beginning of this analogy, that this subtle Italian (probably a Pythagorean) has led us astray, are certainly still valid: the meaning of this analogy is quite perplexing.

125   A good memory was a requirement for Pythagoreans, as it was for Plato. The Pythagoreans invented all kinds of memory exercises, and Plato has Socrates require a good memory for those who would be philosophers (*Republic* 486c-d).

And though these [images] are very likely somewhat out-of-place, yet they show what *I* wish to have shown you, if somehow I might be able to persuade you to change your move [in this conversational game of draughts and], instead of a life that is greedy and wanton, to choose a life [that is] orderly and adequate and content with the things it happens to have. Am I persuading you to change [to the   493d belief that] the ordered are happier than the wanton, or [is it that] even if I should speak mythically[126] of many other such things you would not change your mind at all?

Callicles: This [latter statement] you have said more truly, Socrates.

Socrates: Come, indeed, as I now tell you of another image from the same school. You see, examine whether you are saying something like this about each life, the self-restrained and the wanton—that to each of two men there are many jars, and to one of them the jars are sound and   493e full—one [jar] with wine, another with honey, another with milk, and many others with many things—but the flowing sources of each of these things is scarce and difficult [to tap], [for they are] accompanied by many difficult toils. And so the one [man], having gotten his fill, would not pipe in [more good things] nor think about anything, but he would be calm because of the [good] things [that he has obtained]. And for the other one, the flowing sources [of good things are the same as] for the first—possible to find out, but difficult [to obtain]—but his vessels are perforated and cracked, and he is compelled to fill these day and night or suffer extreme pains. Then,   494a if each life is such [as I have described it], do you say that [the life] of the wanton person is happier than the life of the orderly person? As I say these things, am I at all persuading you to concede that the orderly life is superior to the wanton one, or am I not persuading [you]?

---

126 This unexpected phrase anticipates the striking use of "myth" in 523a. On the latter use of *myth* see Appendix C.

Callicles: You are not persuading [me], Socrates. You see, to that man who has been filled there is no pleasure at all, but this is, as *I* was just saying, to live like a stone, after he is filled, neither still feeling joy nor feeling pain. But the sweet life is in this—in pouring in as much as possible.

494b

Socrates: Won't it be necessary, should there be much pouring in, that there be much going out, and that there be some great perforations for the outflows?

Callicles: Yes, this follows.

Socrates: *You're* talking of the life of some ravenous bird, not of a corpse or a stone. Tell me also: are you speaking of the sort [of life in which] a hungry [person] is hungry and eats?

Callicles: *I* am, of course.

494c   **Socrates:** And [of the sort of life in which] a thirsty [person] is thirsty and drinks?

Callicles: I am saying that, and [of the sort of life in which] the one who has all other desires has the power, while feeling joy, to live happily filling them.

Socrates: Excellent, best of men. Well, finish as you've begun, and [see to it that] you don't hold back because of shame. And, as it seems, I too must not hold back because of shame. And first, say whether a man who's scratching at his itchy scabs and is able to scratch [them] bounteously and goes though his whole life scratching [them] is living happily.

494d   **Callicles:** How out-of-place you are, and simply[127] a demagogue.

Socrates: According to you, Callicles, I dumbfounded Polus and Gorgias and made them feel shame, but *you* are not dumbfounded and you do not feel shame; you see, you are manly. But just answer.

Callicles: I say then that the one scratching his scabs would live pleasantly.

127   The word we have translated as "simply" (*atechnos*) is used in Aristotle's *Rhetoric* (1355b35) for the kinds of persuasion without craft (like torture, extortion, etc.).

Socrates: And so, if pleasantly, happily?

Callicles: Yes, of course.

Socrates: If he scratches only his head—or still, what shall   494e
I ask you? Look, Callicles, what would you answer,
if someone should ask you about all the [parts of the
body] that are connected[128] to these in order. If these
[conclusions] are so, the crown of the matter is the life
of a lewd masturbator—isn't it terrible and shameful and
wretched? Or will you dare to say that these people are
happy if they have a bounty of what they want?

Callicles: Aren't you ashamed, Socrates, to drive the
arguments to such things?

Socrates: Well, am *I* driving [the arguments] there, noble
one, or that man who says that [those] who feel joy in this
way without limitation, however they feel joy, are happy,   495a
and who does not define what sorts of pleasures are good
and bad? But still, even now, state whether you say that a
pleasant thing and a good thing are the same or whether
there is anything of [the things that are] pleasant that is
not good?

Callicles: In order that the argument not be made contradictory
by me—if I should say that [they] are different—I say that
[they] are the same.

Socrates: Callicles, you are destroying [our] first words
[together], and you won't still be examining reality with
me adequately, if you continue to say what is contrary to
what you believe.[129]

Callicles: Well, *you* also, Socrates, [are doing the same].   495b

---

128 Here we follow the ms. reading, where the text suggests that Socrates is about to annoy
Callicles again by asking about scratching the parts of the body proceeding downwards
from the head to the genitals. Callicles would be at least as annoyed as he was earlier
when Socrates made his *ad absurdum* argument of the shoemaker having a right to wear
the most shoes.

129 In 491e, Callicles said that he was speaking frankly. In 487e, Socrates had used almost
the same language as he uses here to say that if he and Callicles agreed on something,
this agreement would be an assurance of its validity. On saying, in dialectical arguments,
what one truly believes, see Appendix B, rule 11.

Socrates: Then let me tell you, neither am *I* doing the right thing—if indeed I'm doing this—nor are *you*. But, divinely blessed one, consider whether this is not the good, to experience enjoyment in every way; you see, if this is so, both these things that have now been hinted at and many shameful things appear to follow, and many other things too.

Callicles: So *you*, of course, think, Socrates.

Socrates: And *you*, Callicles, are really firm in these [conclusions]?

Callicles: *I* am, of course.

495c   **Socrates:** And are we to take the argument in hand, since you are serious?[130]

Callicles: Absolutely, of course.

Socrates: Indeed, come now, since it seems so, go through this for me: you call knowledge something, I suppose?

Callicles: *I* do, of course.

Socrates: Weren't you also now saying that courage is something [combined] with knowledge?

Callicles: Well, I was saying [that].

Socrates: And so weren't you saying, with respect to these two things, that courage is different from knowledge?

Callicles: Absolutely, of course.

Socrates: And what? [Were you saying that] pleasure and knowledge are the same or different?

495d   **Callicles:** Different, I do suppose, most wise [Socrates].

Socrates: And [that] courage is different from pleasure?

Callicles: Look, how not?

Socrates: Come, indeed, so that we shall remember these things—that Callicles of Acharnae has said that a pleasant thing and a good thing are the same, but that knowledge

---

130 These words recall the very question Callicles asked about Socrates when he took over the conversation from Polus (481b).

and courage are different from each other and from the good.[131]

Callicles: And Socrates of Alopece, of course, does not agree with us concerning these things. Or does he agree?

Socrates: He does not agree; and, in fact, I think that neither 495e will Callicles, when he will look at himself rightly. You see, tell me, do you think that those who doing well are experiencing the opposite experience of those who are doing badly?[132]

Callicles: *I* do, of course.

Socrates: And so, if they are opposite one another, aren't they necessarily like health and disease? You see, I do suppose, a person is not healthy and sick at the same time, and he is not at the same time freed from both health and sickness.

Callicles: What are you saying?

Socrates: Taking separately any [part] of the body you wish, examine [it like this]. A person has a sickness in his eyes, 496a I suppose, which is named *ophthalmia*?

Callicles: Look, how not?

Socrates: And, I do suppose, he's not also healthy in them at the same time?

Callicles: No, not in any way.

Socrates: And what [about] when he is freed from the ophthalmia? Is he then freed from the health of his eyes, and in the end is he released from both [health and illness] at the same time?

---

131 The district of Acharnae was in the western part of Attica, nearest to the border across which invaders would come from Sparta and its allies during the Peloponnesian War. As a result, the Acharnians suffered most of the people of Attica and were most intent on revenge against Athens' enemies. In Aristophanes' play *Acharnians*, the people of Acharnae are presented as hyper-militarists and extreme nationalists.

132 Perhaps Plato here is equivocating between the idiomatic and literal usages of the phrases "doing well" and "doing badly." For Socrates here, as for Cicero and the Stoic tradition, there would be no difference between prospering and acting well morally. Like Thoreau, who plays upon the etymologies of words, teasing us with the etymological and developed sense of words, so Plato. Here Plato is asking us to question whether what we usually call prospering really is, philosophically speaking, "doing well."

Callicles: Least of all, of course.

Socrates: You see, it would be a wonder, I think, and an illogical thing, no?

Callicles: Absolutely, in fact.

Socrates: But in turn, I think, [a person] takes and loses each of the two things?

Callicles: I say [so].

Socrates: And it's the same with strength and weakness?

Callicles: Yes.

Socrates: And speed and slowness?

Callicles: Yes, of course.

Socrates: And with respect to good things and happiness and the things that are the opposite of these, the bad and the very wretched, [a person] takes hold of each and in turn is released from each?

Callicles: Entirely, I do suppose.

496c **Socrates:** If, then, we should find some things that a person both is freed from and at the same has, it is clear that these things would not be the good and the bad. Shall we agree on this? And after examining [the matter] very well, answer.

Callicles: But I agree in a way that's beyond what is natural!

Socrates: Come, indeed [let's return] to what's been agreed before. As for being hungry, were you saying before that being hungry is pleasant or painful? I mean the [condition] itself of being hungry.

Callicles: *I*, of course, [say that it is] painful. I say, however,
496d that for the person who is hungry eating is pleasant.

Socrates: And *I* [do too]. I understand. But then being hungry, of course, is itself painful. Isn't it?

Callicles: I say [it is].

Socrates: And isn't it [the same] about being thirsty?

Callicles: Absolutely, of course.

Socrates: And so shall I ask still more [questions], or do you agree that every need and desire is painful?

Callicles: I agree, but do not ask.

Socrates: Well, do you say that, for a person who is thirsty, drinking is indeed nothing else than pleasant?

Callicles: *I* do, of course.

Socrates: And concerning what you are speaking about, "being thirsty" is, I do suppose, a "feeling pain"?

Callicles: Yes.

Socrates: But to drink is both a fulfilling of a need and a pleasure? 496e

Callicles: Yes.

Socrates: And don't you say that in drinking there is feeling joy?

Callicles: Very much so.

Socrates: For the one who is thirsty, of course.

Callicles: I say [so].

Socrates: [When he's] feeling pain?

Callicles: Yes.

Socrates: And so do you perceive the logical consequence, that whenever you say that a person who is thirsty drinks, you are saying that he feels pain at the same time that he feels joy? Or is this not happening at the same place and time, whether in soul or body, as you please? You see, I think it makes no difference at all. Are these things so or not?

Callicles: They are.

Socrates: Yet truly you are saying that it is impossible, in fact, for one doing well to be doing badly at the same time.[133]

Callicles: Well, I do say so.

Socrates: But, of course, you have agreed that it *is* possible for 497a a man who is distressed to feel joy.

Callicles: It appears [so].

---

133 For the ambiguity, see note 132 above. For "doing well" it is possible to read "prospering"; for "doing badly" it is possible to read "to be badly off.".

Socrates: Then feeling joy is not to do well nor [is] being distressed [to do] badly, so that the pleasant is a thing different from the good.

Callicles: I don't know what you are quibbling about, Socrates.

Socrates: You *do* know, but you are kidding,[134] Callicles. Go on still to what's ahead.

Callicles: Why are you talking nonsense?

497b   **Socrates:** So that you may see how you, as one who is wise, are setting me straight. Hasn't each of us ceased both being thirsty and feeling pleasure at the same time by drinking?

Callicles: I don't know what you are saying.

Gorgias: Don't [be this way], Callicles, but answer for our sake, too, in order that the arguments might be completed.[135]

Callicles: But Socrates is always this way, Gorgias; you see, he keeps on asking about small things that are worth little and he keeps on refuting.

Gorgias: Why does it make a difference to you? This is not your prerogative at all,[136] Callicles. But submit to being refuted by Socrates as he might wish.

497c   **Callicles:** [Go ahead]—*you*—ask these small, narrow things, *if* it seems best to Gorgias.

Socrates: You are a happy man, Callicles, because you have been initiated in the Big before the Small;[137] and *I* didn't

---

134   The Greek term "are kidding" derives from the name of a woman who pretends stupidity. "Kidding" is used to duplicate the alliteration in English of the *k* sound that Plato seems to be after (kidding, Kallicles).

135   Perhaps Gorgias is retaliating for Callicles' intervention in 458d, when Gorgias, himself severely discomforted, was eager to extricate himself from *his* dialectical exchange with Socrates.

136   This is an attempt at a neutral translation for a phrase that might also mean, "this is not your judgment to make" or "there's no penalty for you to pay" or "it's not for you to calculate the value of the discussion."

137   Socrates is punning on Callicles' use of "small." Here the reference is to the Big and Small grades of the Eleusinian Mysteries. To be eligible to participate in the Big rites, one must already have participated in the Small. But perhaps there is also a reference to the kind of rhetorical argument that Aristotle discusses in the *Rhetoric* (1397b12), the greater and lesser, the *argumentum a fortiori*.

think that was permitted. And so answer from where you left off, about whether, when each of us ceases being thirsty, he also [ceases] feeling pleasure.

Callicles: I say [he does].

Socrates: And doesn't a man who [ceases being] hungry also cease feeling pleasure at the same time, and [isn't this the case with] the other desires and pleasures?

[handwritten note: how so, I can drink when not thirsty, and have pleasure]

Callicles: These things are [so].

Socrates: Doesn't he cease having both pains and pleasures at the same time?   497d

Callicles: Yes.

Socrates: Yet truly, as *you* agreed, he does not, in fact, cease from having goods and evils at the same time. But are you not agreeing now?

Callicles: *I* am, of course. And so, indeed, what [of it]?

Socrates: [It is that] these things are not the same, friend—the good things as the pleasures and the bad things as the distressing things. One makes a cessation of some of these at the same time, you see, but not of others, [since] they are different. And so how could the pleasures be the same as the good things or the distressing things the same as the bad things?

And if you wish, examine it also like this—I think, you see, that not even in this way will it be agreed by you.   497e
But consider: do you not call those [people] good who [are good] by the presence [in them] of good things, just as [you call] beautiful [those] in whom beauty is present?

Callicles: *I* do, of course.

Socrates: And what? Do you call thoughtless [men] and cowards *good men*? In fact, you were just now not [calling them such], in fact, but you were saying that courageous and thoughtful men [were good]; or *don't* you call [the courageous and thoughtful men] good?

Callicles: Yes, it follows.

Socrates: And what? Have you ever seen a mindless child feeling joy?

Callicles: *I* have, of course.

Socrates: And haven't you ever seen a mindless man feeling joy?

Callicles: *I* think so, of course. But what is this [you are asking]?

498a   **Socrates:** Nothing, but answer.

Callicles: I have seen [this].

Socrates: And what? [Have you ever seen] a man who has a [good] mind feeling pain and feeling joy?

Callicles: I say [so].

Socrates: And which ones feel joy and feel pain more, the thoughtful or the thoughtless?

Callicles: *I*, of course, think there's not much difference at all.

Socrates: But even this is sufficient. In war, have you ever seen a cowardly man?

Callicles: Well, how not?

Socrates: What, then? When the enemy were withdrawing, which ones seemed to you to feel joy more, the cowards or the courageous?

498b   **Callicles:** Both [seemed] to me, of course, [to feel joy], [but perhaps the cowards more].[138] Unless, of course, [they felt joy] about the same.

Socrates: It makes no difference. But, then, the cowards also feel joy?

Callicles: Absolutely, of course.

Socrates: And the thoughtless [also feel joy], as it seems.

Callicles: Yes.

Socrates: And when the [enemy] are attacking, do only the cowards feel pain or also the courageous?

Callicles: Both.

Socrates: Similarly, then?

---

138   The words we have bracketed—"but perhaps the cowards more"—reflect Dodd's emendation.

Callicles: Perhaps the cowards [feel pain] more.

Socrates: And while the [enemy] are withdrawing, they feel joy more?

Callicles: Perhaps.

Socrates: And so don't both the thoughtless and the thoughtful and both the cowards and the courageous feel pain and feel joy about the same, as *you* say, but the cowards more than the courageous?   498c

Callicles: I say so.

Socrates: Yet truly the thoughtful and the courageous are good, of course, but the cowards and the thoughtless, bad?

Callicles: Yes.

Socrates: Then the good and the bad feel joy and feel pain in about the same way?

Callicles: I say so.

Socrates: And so are both the good and the bad good and bad in about the same way? Or are the bad even more good and more bad?[139]

Callicles: But, by Zeus, I don't know what you are saying.   498d

Socrates: Don't you know that you are saying that the good are good by the presence of good things, and the bad [are bad by the presence] of bad things? And [don't you know that you are saying] that the good things are pleasures, and bad are the afflictions?

Callicles: *I* [do], of course.

---

139 Presumably because as cowards they feel more joy at the departure of the enemy [and so they are more good because joy = good] and because they feel more pain at the attack of the enemy and so are more bad (because pain = bad). But the conclusion as phrased certainly does sound odd: the bad are more good than the good! This is similar to the character Virgil's argument in Canto 6 of Dante's *Inferno* (6.106–108), that on the Day of Judgment, as the joy of those in Heaven will be greater, so the pain of those in Hell will be greater too. Dante explicitly tells us that Virgil is adapting an argument from Aristotle. The argument is from *De Anima* (412a–413a), and probably reflects, as does the argument here in the *Gorgias*, discussions that took place in Plato's Academy about a human being as a composite of body and soul. In Dante, Aristotle's thought would, of course, have been filtered through Thomas Aquinas.

Socrates: And for those who are feeling joy, aren't good things present—the pleasures—if they are feeling joy?

Callicles: Well, how not?

Socrates: And when good things are present, the ones who are feeling joy are good?

Callicles: Yes.

Socrates: And what? To those who are distressed, aren't evils—the pains—present?

Callicles: They are present.

498e   **Socrates:** And do *you* say that by the presence of bad things, in fact, the bad are bad? Or do you no longer say [so]?

Callicles: *I* [do], of course.

Socrates: Then the good are those who would feel joy, but the bad are those who would feel distressed?

Callicles: Yes, of course.

Socrates: And the ones who are more [good and bad feel joy and feel pain] more, and the ones who are less [good and bad feel joy and feel pain] less, and [those who are good and bad] in about the same way [feel joy and feel pain] in about the same way?

Callicles: Yes.

Socrates: And do you say that the thoughtful and thoughtless feel joy and feel pain in about the same way, and the cowards and the courageous too, or do the cowards [feel joy and feel pain] still more?

Callicles: *I* do [say so], of course.[140]

Socrates: Indeed, calculate in common with me what follows from what [we've] agreed; you see, they say that it is twice
499a   and thrice a fine thing both to say and examine fine things. We say that the thoughtful and brave person is good. No?

Callicles: Yes.

---

140   Callicles answers—illogically—an either/or question with "I do [say so]." Perhaps Plato is portraying how Callicles has been lulled into unthinking affirmations; or perhaps he is showing Callicles' underlying intellectual laziness.

Socrates: And that the thoughtless and cowardly person is bad?

Callicles: Yes, of course.

Socrates: And again the one who feels joy is good?

Callicles: Yes.

Socrates: And the one who feels distress is bad?

Callicles: Necessarily.

Socrates: [And you say that] the good person and the bad person feel distress and feel joy similarly but [that] perhaps the bad [person feels distress and feels joy] even more?

Callicles: Yes.

Socrates: And so won't the bad person become bad and good similarly to the good person or won't the bad person become even more good [than the good person]? Don't these conclusions also follow those earlier ones, if someone says that pleasures and good things are the same? Aren't these [conclusions] necessary, Callicles?[141]   499b

Callicles: I've been listening to you for a long time, Socrates, agreeing completely with you, knowing in my heart that should someone, playing with you, give you anything whatsoever, you gladly take hold of it, as young men do. As though, indeed, *you* think that I or anyone else whatsoever of human beings doesn't think that some pleasures are better, others worse!

Socrates: Ho, ho, Callicles, how rascally you are towards me,   499c and you use me just as you would a child, at one time saying that these things are so, but at another time [that things are] different, deceiving me. And I did not think in the beginning [of our exchange] that I would be deceived by you intentionally, since you are my friend. And now I was told a falsehood, and, as it seems, it is necessary for me, according to the old saying, to make the best of what I've got and to accept this—what you've given. Is it indeed

---

141   The conclusions are "necessary" in the sense of following logically from the previous statements, but they are just as hard to swallow as the conclusions reached earlier with Polus about letting one's enemies go free if they did wrong but punishing one's friends.

[the truth], as it seems, what you are now saying—that some pleasures are good, but others bad? Eh?

499d   **Callicles:** Yes.

Socrates: And the beneficial pleasures are good, but the harmful ones, bad?

Callicles: Yes, of course.

Socrates: And beneficial, of course, are the [pleasures] doing some good thing, and bad are the [pleasures doing] some bad thing?

Callicles: I do say so.

Socrates: And so, do you mean [pleasures] like these, the sort that we were just speaking of [that are] for the body— pleasures in eating and drinking, if these are the pleasures that produce health in the body or strength or some other bodily excellence—that some of these are good, but others

499e   are bad, [producing] the opposites of these [results]?

Callicles: Yes, of course.

Socrates: And it's the same for pains—some are useful, some, grievous?

Callicles: Well, how not?

Socrates: And so mustn't one both choose and engage in the useful pleasures and pains?

Callicles: Yes, of course.

Socrates: And not the grievous ones?

Callicles: Indeed, [this] is clear.

Socrates: You see, I suppose, it seemed to us—to me and Polus—if you remember, that for the sake of good things all things must be done. And [along with us], does it seem this way to you, too—[that] the end of all actions is the good[142] and for the sake of the [good] all things must

500a   be done but not [the good] for the sake of other things? Shall we include *you* too as one of the three voting for this view?

---

142   This statement, that the end of all actions is the good, anticipates the opening line of Aristotle's *Nicomachaean Ethics*.

Callicles: *I*, of course, [shall vote with you].

Socrates: For the sake of the good things, then, it is necessary to do the other things and the things that are pleasant [as well], but not the good things for the sake of the pleasant things?

Callicles: Yes, of course.

Socrates: Is it for every man to choose from the pleasures the sort of things that are good and the sort that are bad, or is there need of a person who has the technical skill [to choose] each?

Callicles: [There is need of] a man who has the technical skill.

Socrates: Let us recall what *I* happened to say to Polus and Gorgias. I was saying, you see, if you recall,[143] that some practices were just for pleasure, providing for it alone, being ignorant of the better and worse,[144] but that others were knowing what is good and what is bad; and of the [practices concerned with] the pleasures I posited cookery as an experience and not as a technical skill, but [of the practices concerned with] the good [I posited] medicine as a technical skill. And, by [the god of] friendship, Callicles—you yourself!—think it necessary *not* to play with me, and *don't* answer whatever pops into your head contrary to what you [really] think, and do not in turn take what [I say] as though I were playing [with you]. You observe that the arguments we are having are about this: about what a person—even one who has a small intellect— should be serious about more than [anything else]—or [perhaps, better] this—how one ought to live, whether [aiming] at [those actions towards] which *you* are urging me, indeed, [maintaining that] these are the actions of a man—to speak among the people and practice rhetoric and engage in the affairs of the polis in the way in which

500b

500c

---

143   This is the second time in a few lines (the previous time was at 499e) that Socrates has brought up Callicles' ability to remember. In view of the earlier comments on memory (see note 125), perhaps Socrates is casting aspersions on Callicles' memory. Socrates would be suggesting, not very nicely, that Callicles is a leaky jar.

144   Socrates is personifying the practices, which he calls "ignorant."

you, today's [politicians], engage in them—or [aiming at] this—[my] life in philosophy—and the ways in which this [life] is different from that [other life]? And so perhaps it is best, as *I* have just undertaken [to do], to distinguish [these lives], and for us after we have distinguished [them] and have agreed with each other—if these *are* two lives—to examine in what they differ from each other and [to determine] which of the two [lives] one ought to live. And so perhaps you do not know what I mean.

Callicles: No, indeed, [I don't].

Socrates: But *I* shall speak more clearly to you. Since we have agreed, *you* and *I,* that there is something good on the one hand, and something pleasant on the other, and that the pleasant is different from the good, and that each of the two has its own concern and method of possessing [it]— the hunt for the pleasant and the hunt for the good—first agree with me or [don't agree] that this very thing is so. Do you agree?

Callicles: I say [that it is] like this.

Socrates: Come, indeed, and concerning what *I* was saying to these men, agree completely with me [about what I was saying], if I then seemed to you to be saying true things. I was saying, I suppose, that cooking does not seem to me to be a technical skill but an experience, but [that] medicine [is a technical skill], [when I was] saying that it examines both the nature of what it cares for and the cause of the things it does and [that] it is able to give an argument for each of these things—[this is] medicine.[145] But the other [—cooking—] goes quite simply to the [producing] of pleasure, towards which it has all of its care, examining neither the nature nor the cause of pleasure— completely without an account, so to speak—not adding up anything thoroughly, [and] saving a memory of what has usually occurred only by a routine and experience,

500d

500e

501a

---

145 Socrates begins and ends this long "that" clause with the word "medicine." We have tried to capture this trope as best we could, but for clarity we have added "this is."

by means of which indeed it provides pleasures.[146] And so   501b
examine first whether these things seem to you to have
been said sufficiently and whether there are some other
such matters concerning the soul, some having to do with
technical skill that have some forethought for what is best
for the soul but others that make small account of [what is
best]; and consider in turn, just as [in the case of cooking],
only the *pleasure* of the soul, how pleasure might come
into being for it, and neither look nor care for which of
the pleasures is better or worse—but care only that the
pleasures be gratified, whether [they be of the] better or   501c
worse [kind]. You see, Callicles, to me [these activities
that aim only at pleasure] seem to be [this way], and *I* of
course say that such is a pandering both of the body and
of the soul and of anything else of which someone cares
for the pleasure without examining the superior and the
worse. And do *you* put together the same opinion as we
about these things or do you say something else?

Callicles: *I* do not, of course, but I'll yield in order that the
argument advance for you and that I be pleasing to
Gorgias.

Socrates: Is this [true] about one soul but it is not [true] about   501d
two and many?

Callicles: No, but [it is true] about two and about many.

Socrates: Isn't it [possible] to be pleasing to multitudes at the
same time, not at all looking for what is the best thing?

Callicles: *I*, of course, think so.

Socrates: Are you able to say what the practices are that do this?
But rather, if you wish, while I am asking [about them],
say what seems to you to be one of these [practices], and
say what doesn't. And first let us examine flute-playing.   501e

---

146   Socrates' complaint about cooking here seems to be that it aims only at producing but not
also at understanding pleasure. Perhaps he would say "the unexamined pleasure is not
worth enjoying."

Doesn't it seem to you, Callicles, the sort of thing that pursues only our pleasure and considers nothing else?[147]

Callicles: It seems [so] to me, of course.

Socrates: And don't all such things—for example, cithara-playing in contests?

Callicles: Yes.

Socrates: And what of the rehearsals of the choruses and the process of composing dithyrambs[148]? Doesn't it also quite appear as some such [thing] to you? Do you think that Kinesias,[149] Meles' son, considers a bit how he will say something such that those who hear it might become better, or [do you think] that he intends to be pleasing to a crowd of spectators?

502a

Callicles: This [latter] is clear, of course, Socrates, about Kinesias, of course.[150]

---

147   We have followed the tradition of translating the playing of this instrument as "flute-playing," though, since the instrument had a reed, it more nearly resembled an oboe or clarinet. Despite the authority of Socrates here, the statement that flute-playing (or playing a reeded wind instrument) aims only at pleasure does not ring true. The Spartans, for example, marched into battle to the sound of such playing. In the Republic, Socrates discusses extensively the role of music in educating the guardians. Music, according to Socrates, has the power to act directly on the passions, without and even against reason. The use of music, along with gymnastics, is to "tune" the soul properly—to make the soul harder or softer as necessary—to prepare the guardians for the fulfillment of their political responsibility—leading their society in peace and war—and even more for the fulfillment of their intellectual responsibility—searching for the truth of being. See, e.g., *Republic* 410a-412a.

148   Exactly what the dithyramb was and how the name was derived are mysteries whose solutions are lost in the mists of time. It appears to have been a kind of wild song for Dionysus, irregular in its structure, sung in choruses and accompanied by a reeded wind instrument at the festivals for the god; it is believed to have been the forerunner of tragedy. Aristotle's discussion of the dithyramb in the *Poetics* (49a19–31) is itself vexed and hence does not offer conclusive evidence.

149   Though Kinesias was a popular poet of dithyrambs (see previous note) in the last part of the fifth century, he is subjected to a good deal of criticism by the comic poets (e.g., Aristophanes, *Clouds* 333), as well as by Plato in the current passage. Kinesias' corruption of the genre, according to his critics, seems to have consisted of pomposity, immorality, and an inept use of figures of speech. But, we should recall, the same public that loved him also loved the great tragedians (whom Plato's Socrates would banish from his republic). In the absence of a text, perhaps it would be prudent for *us* to withhold censure.

150   Perhaps the double use of "of course" is meant to leave no doubt that Kinesias aims at only pleasure. No redeeming social value in his work!

Socrates: And what of his father Meles? Did he seem to you to play the cithara looking at what is best?[151] Or is it that *he* did not look even on what was most pleasant? While singing, you see, he used to cause distress to the spectators. But indeed, examine [this]: don't both cithara-playing as a whole and the composing of dithyrambs seem to you to have been discovered for the sake of pleasure?

Callicles: To me [they do], of course.

Socrates: What about that venerated and wondrous process of   502b
composing tragedy, for which there has been enthusiasm? Is its concern and enthusiasm, as it seems to you, only to please the spectators, or [is its concern] also to fight hard—if something be pleasant and pleasing to them, but also grievous [to them]—to see to it that it does not tell this thing; but if something happens to be unpleasant and beneficial, this it will say and sing, whether the [spectators] should feel joy in it or not? In which of these two ways does the composing of tragedies seem to you to be arranged?

Callicles: This, indeed, is clear, of course, Socrates, that it   502c
is rather directed towards pleasure and to pleasing the spectators.

Socrates: And weren't we just now saying, Callicles, that this sort of thing is pandering?

Callicles: Yes, of course.

Socrates: Come, indeed, if someone were to strip off from all poetry melody, rhythm, and meter, would anything be left besides words?[152]

---

151 This later perhaps became the *summum bonum* of Roman Stoicism.

152 Perhaps John Milton had this passage in mind when he wrote of the beautiful figures of tragedy (*Paradise Regained* 4.343–50):

> Remove their swelling epithets, thick laid
> As varnish on a harlot's cheek, the rest,
> Thin sown with aught of profit or delight,
> Will far be found unworthy to compare
> With Sion's songs, to all true tastes excelling,
> Where God is praised aright, and godlike men,
> The Holiest of Holies, and his saints;
> Such are from God inspired, not such from thee.

Callicles: Necessarily.

Socrates: And so aren't these words spoken to a big crowd and to the people?

Callicles: I say [so].

Socrates: Then the poetic [skill] is a kind of public speaking?

502d **Callicles:** It appears [so].

Socrates: And so wouldn't rhetoric be a public speaking? Or don't the poets seem to you to be making rhetoric in the theaters?

Callicles: [They seem so] to me, of course.

Socrates: Now, then, *we* have discovered a rhetorical [activity] for such a populace of children and women and men alike and slaves and free people, [an activity] that we don't esteem; you see, we say that it is a pandering.

Callicles: Yes, of course.

Socrates: Well: and what is the rhetoric for the populace of
502e Athens and the other peoples in the poleis of free men—whatever is this [rhetoric] for us? Do rhetors seem to you always to be speaking for what is best, aiming at this—how because of their words the citizens will become as good as possible; or [do the rhetors] also,[153] stirring themselves to be pleasing to the citizens for the sake of their own private [benefit while] making light of the common [good], talk to the peoples [in the different poleis] as though [they were talking] to children, trying only to please them, but, of course, without caring at all whether they will be better
503a or worse on account of these things [that they say]?

Callicles: This is no longer a single matter that you are asking. You see, there are some who, caring for the citizens, say what they say, but there are also others such as *you* describe.

Socrates: This will be enough. You see, if this is two-fold, the one [kind] of this [speech-making] would be, I suppose, a pandering and shameful public speaking, but the other

---

153 Perhaps by "also" Socrates means, "like the tragic poets" he has just been speaking about.

would be a fine thing—to provide for how the souls of the citizens will be as good as possible and to fight hard [to achieve this result], saying the best things, whether they be more pleasant or more unpleasant for the hearers. But 503b *you* have not ever seen this rhetoric; or, if you are able to say who of [all the] rhetors *was* such, why haven't you pointed out to me who he is?

Callicles: But, by Zeus, *I* am not, of course, able to say [that] any of current rhetors [is such].

Socrates: What? Of the rhetors of the old days, are you able to say one who was responsible for the Athenians' having become better after he began to speak publicly [to them], having been worse in earlier time? You see, *I* don't know who this man is.

Callicles: What about Themistocles—don't you hear what a 503c good man he was? And [what about] Cimon and Miltiades and this Pericles[154], who has lately died, whom *you*, also, heard?

---

154   These individuals are a Mt. Rushmore of fifth century Athenians, despite all having sometimes grave imperfections. Themistocles (524–459), a political man of extraordinary resourcefulness and genius, led Athens, in the war against Persia, spectacularly to victory at the Battle of Salamis, but in the years after the war was ostracized by the Athenians, and later, when he was implicated in some shady dealings with Persia, was condemned by Athens to death *in absentia*; accounts vary on whether he died by suicide or natural causes. Cimon's greatest achievement was victory over the Persians at the Battle of Eurymedon in 466 and a peace agreement with Persia; but when, a few years later, he and his various pro-Spartan policies fell into disfavor, he was ostracized and his peace with Persia abandoned. Miltiades was the leader of the Athenians at the Battle of Marathon in 490, the astonishing victory over Persia that delayed for a decade the Persian advance on Greece; but after the battle he used the Athenian fleet to settle a personal grievance against the island of Paros, and, upon his defeat, he was tried and fined by Athens but died of gangrene before he could pay. Pericles, the democratic (but, as Thucydides says, virtually monarchical) ruler of Athens during its period of greatest power in the Aegean, led his polis at the beginning of the Peloponnesian War; but he generated a good deal of hostility towards himself and was fined by the Athenians at some time near the commencement of the war. (Thucydides is remarkably silent on the circumstances of Pericles' troubles with the law, and other sources are inconsistent. A. W. Gomme, A *Historical Commentary on Thucydides* [Oxford: Clarendon Press, 1956] vol. ii., pp. 184–189, marshals and evaluates the inconclusive evidence on the case.) The common thread for all four, as Socrates will observe later in the dialogue (514b ff.), is that Athenian disfavor towards these men proves that they had not actually improved the citizenry.

Socrates: [These men made citizens better only] if it is in fact true, Callicles, what *you* were saying before [about] excellence, that it is filling completely the desires both of oneself and of others; but if this isn't [true], but instead that which in the later argument *we* were compelled to agree [is true]—[namely,] that of the desires, some, being filled, make the person better, [and] these one should accomplish, but others, [being filled, make the person] worse, [and these one should] not [accomplish], and [that] there is some technical skill [of distinguishing the two kinds of desires, then are you able to say[155]] that such a man from those [you have named] has existed?[156] *I* don't [see], of course, how I can name one.[157]

503d

the just element of rhetoric.

Callicles: But if you seek well, you'll find [one].

Socrates: Indeed, let us see, examining in this way without trembling [in fear], whether any of these men turned out such. Come, the good man—the one who speaks for what is best—concerning the things he would say, won't speak without purpose, but won't he [speak while] keeping his eye on something? [He is] just like all the other craftsmen who look at their own work, [when] each brings [what he brings] to his work, not choosing [it] without a purpose, but [choosing what he brings] to it to make sure that what he works on has a form.[158] For example, if you wish, look at the painters, the house builders, the ship makers, all other craftsmen—any of them you wish—at how each places in some ordered arrangement what he places and forces one [part] to be fitting with another and to be harmonious [with it] until the whole [structure] should be sustained as an ordered and beautified thing; and indeed, the other

503e

504a

---

155 We accept the second half of Dodds' proposal for the lacuna here in the text.

156 As Dodds says, "This long sentence is loosely and elliptically constructed, and in its last two clauses is defective or corrupt." We have tried to fill in the missing parts and to make as good a sense of the text as possible.

157 Dodds gives this last line to Callicles and begins Socrates' speech with the line we have assigned to Callicles. We have followed the distribution of parts assigned by John Burnet in his edition (Oxford: Clarendon Press, 1903), as it seems to us to make better sense than Dodds' distribution.

158 The word in Greek is *eidos,* for which see note 23.

craftsmen, even those whom we have now been speaking of—the ones [who are concerned] with the body, both the trainers and the physicians—they, I suppose, beautify the body and put it in order. Shall we agree that this is so or not?

Callicles: Let this be so.

Socrates: Then a house that happened [to have] order and beauty would be useful, but [a house that happened to have] disorder [would be] worthless?

Callicles: I say [so].

Socrates: And isn't this the same for a ship, too?

Callicles: Yes.   504b

Socrates: And do we say truly [that this is so] also for our bodies?

Callicles: Yes, of course.

Socrates: And what is the soul?[159] Will it be useful when it happens [to have] disorder, or [when it happens to have] some order and beauty?

Callicles: It is necessary from what [was said] before to agree with this too.

Socrates: And so, what is the name of that which has developed in the body from order and beauty?

Callicles: Perhaps you are speaking of health and [physical] strength.

Socrates: *I* [am], of course. And what in turn is the name   504c
of that which has developed in the soul from order and beauty? Try to find and to say the name as [you did] in the case of the [body].

Callicles: Why don't you yourself say [it], Socrates?

Socrates: But if it is to you more pleasant, *I* shall say it. And *you*, if *I* seem to you to speak well, affirm [it], but if not, refute [me] and do not nod [in agreement]. You see, it seems to me that the name for the ordered arrangements

---

159 Socrates shifts his syntax. We might expect, "What about the soul?" but he does not speak to satisfy our expectations.

of the body is *healthy;* [and] from this, health comes into being in [the body] and the rest of the body's excellence. Are these things [so] or not?

Callicles: They are.

504d   **Socrates:** And for the orderly and beautiful things of the soul [the names] are *conforming-to-custom*[160] and *custom,* from [which qualities] people become conforming-to-custom and beautiful. And these [things] are justice and self-restraint. Do you say [so] or not?

Callicles: Let it be.

Socrates: And so, looking at these things, won't that rhetor— the one who both has the technical skill and is good— bring the words he says and all his actions to souls, and if he should give a gift, give [it], and if he should take something away, take it away, always keeping his mind 504e   on this: how by his work justice might come into being in the citizens there in their souls and injustice might be taken away, and self-control come into being in them and wantonness be taken away, and the rest of excellence come into being in them and evil go away. Do you go along [with this] or not?

Callicles: I go along.

Socrates: You see, Callicles, what benefit [would there be], in fact, to give to a body [that is] sick and wretchedly lying [in bed] many foods and the most pleasant ones, or drinks or anything else—anything whatsoever that will not benefit [the body] because it is too much, or, according to the just argument, the opposite—too little? Are these things so?[161]

---

160   The words "custom" and "conforming-to-custom" are the noun and adjectives from *nomos,* the word-cluster that is often distinguished from the nature-natural cluster from *physis.* The English word "customary" can sometimes be used to translate the adjective. Though in Greek the adjective can refer both to activities and people, in English we do not ordinarily refer to people practicing a custom as "customary." Thus, for example, we might say that eating turkey on Thanksgiving is "customary," but we would not refer to the people eating it as customary. On the controversy concerning custom and nature see Introduction pp. 8 ff.

161   This is, of course, a statement of the "doctrine of the mean," attributed to Aristotle but writ large in Greek culture.

Callicles: Let them be [so].   505a

Socrates: You see, I don't think that it is profitable for a person to live with a wretched body; you see, it's necessary to live wretchedly like that. Or is it not so?

Callicles: Yes, [it is].

Socrates: And concerning the complete fulfillment of desires, such as when a hungry person eats as much as he wishes or a thirsty person drinks [as much as he wishes], won't the physicians allow the healthy person as many things [as he wishes] but the sick person (to put it in a word) they never allow to have a fill of what he desires? *You,* too, agree with this, of course?

Callicles: *I* do, of course.

Socrates: And concerning the soul, best of men, is it not the   505b
same way? As long as the soul is wicked, being mindless and wanton and unjust and unholy, it is necessary to hold it back from its desires and not to enable it to do things other than those by which it will be better; do you say [so] or not?

Callicles: I say [so].

Socrates: You see, it's superior thus, I suppose, for the soul itself?

Callicles: Yes, of course.

Socrates: Isn't to restrain [the soul] from the things it desires to chasten [it]?

Callicles: Yes.   *self-restrain*

Socrates: Then for the soul to be chastened is superior to wantonness, as *you* were now indeed thinking.

Callicles: I don't know what you're saying Socrates, but ask   505c
someone else.

Socrates: This man won't stay to be benefited even while he himself is experiencing this very thing that the argument is about—being chastened.

Callicles: Nor, of course, do I care at all about any of the things *you* are saying, and I answered you about these things for the sake of Gorgias.

Socrates: Well? And so what indeed shall we do? Shall we break up in the middle of the argument?

Callicles: You yourself will decide.

505d
Socrates: But they say that it's not right to leave tales in the middle, but that [it is right] to put a head [on a tale], in order that it not go around headless.[162] And so answer the remaining things, in order that our argument might take on a head.

Callicles: How violent you are! But if you are persuaded by me, you will bid farewell to this argument, or you will converse with someone else.

Socrates: And so who else is willing? You see, let's not leave the argument unfinished, of course.

Callicles: Won't you yourself be able to finish the argument, either speaking according to your own [mind] or answering yourself?[163]

505e
Socrates: In order that the saying of Epicharmus[164] come to pass

What two men were saying before this, I, being one, have become adequate [to say].

But it looks as though it will most necessarily have to be this way. If we shall do [this], *I*, in fact, think that we must all be competitive [with each other] towards knowing what is true and what is false in what we are arguing about; you see, it is clear that this is a good common for all. And so *I*
506a
shall go through the argument as it seems to me to be; but

---

162   Socrates is here punning on the word for "head," which can also mean "completion." Perhaps the meaning "completion" derives from the fact that one builds a column from the bottom up, and the "head" of the column, i.e., the *capital*, is put on last. Perhaps the ancients drew pictures of human beings also in this way, starting with the feet and drawing the head last.

163   Perhaps Callicles feels that he has been manipulated and that in essence Socrates is both asking and answering.

164   Epicharmus (540–450) was an early writer of comedies on mythological themes, not themes that were political. His career was spent in Syracuse, a polis that, living under a series of tyrants, did not enjoy the comedic freedom of Athens. Olympiodorus, an ancient commentator on the *Gorgias,* says that Epicharmus in one of his plays has a character take both parts of a conversation and that Socrates is making reference to this passage, but, as Dodds observes, Olympiodorus may very well have been guessing.

if to any of you I don't seem to be saying things that agree with myself, it is necessary [that you] take hold [of them] and refute me. You see, *I*, in fact, am not at all saying what I am saying as one who knows, but I am seeking [knowledge] in common with you, so that, should the one who speaks, going off in a different direction from me, show something, *I* shall be the first one to agree [with him]. I am saying these things, however, if it seems to be necessary to continue with the argument. But if you [who are standing around watching our argument][165] don't wish to, let's say goodbye already and go away.

Gorgias: But to me it seems necessary not to go away yet, but   506b
to go through the whole argument. And it appears to me to seem [so] to the others, too. *I* myself, of course, you see, wish to hear you going through the rest [of the argument] yourself.

Socrates: But indeed, Gorgias, I myself would gladly still converse with this Callicles, until I had given him back Amphion's phrase for that of Zethus; but since *you*, Callicles, are not willing to carry through the argument with me to the end, then, as you hear me, take me on if I seem to you to say something not well. And if you refute   506c
me, I shall not become angry with you as *you* have with me, but you will be written up as my greatest benefactor.

Callicles: Argue with yourself, good man, and go on.

Socrates: Indeed, hear me taking up the argument from the beginning. Then, are the pleasant and the good the same?

—They are not the same, as Callicles and *I* agreed.

—And must the pleasant be done for the sake of the good, or the good for the sake of the pleasant?

—The pleasant for the sake of the good.

---

165 The shift to the second person plural indicates that Socrates is addressing more people than just Callicles. We have indicated the shift (which in Greek is evident from the form of the verb) by adding the words in brackets.

506d

—And is the pleasant that thing which, [when] it is present, we enjoy and [is that thing] good, [because of] which, [when it] is present, we are good?

—Yes, of course.

—For truly *we* are good, in fact, and all other things, too—as many as are good—[when] some excellence is present?

—It seems to me, of course, to be necessary, Callicles.

—But, indeed, the excellence of each thing—of an implement and of a body and in turn of a soul and of every living thing—does not of course come most beautifully by chance, but by its ordered arrangement and correctness and technical skill, whatever [technical skill] is rendered to each of these things. Are these [statements so]?

—Well, *I* say [so].

506e

—Then it is by an ordered arrangement that the excellence of each thing has been ordered and made beautiful?

—*I*, of course, would say [so].

—Is it, then, that some appropriate ordered beauty of each object, having come about in each object, provides each good of the objects?[166]

—It seems so to me, of course.

—And a soul also that has its own ordered beauty is then superior to one lacking ordered beauty?

—Necessarily.

—Yet truly the soul having ordered beauty is, of course, beautiful in an ordered way?

---

166 Socrates is here using the rhetorical figure "polyptoton," the use of the same word in different cases in proximity. At the end of the Gettysburg Address, where Lincoln speaks of a government *of* the people, *by* the people, and *for* the people, he is employing a polyptoton. Our translation, by the heavy use of prepositions here (*of* each object, *in* each object, *of* the objects), has tried to keep something of the flavor of the polyptoton, a goal made rather difficult by the nature of English, which, unlike Greek, does not make much use of cases.

—Well, how will this not be the case?

—And, of course, the [soul] beautiful in an ordered way is 507a
self-restrained?

—Very necessarily.

—Then, the self-restrained [soul] is a good soul. *I* am
not able to say other things, [things that are] contrary to
these, dear Callicles. But if *you* are, teach me.

Callicles: Argue [on], good man.

Socrates: Indeed, I say that if the self-restrained [soul] is
good, the soul that has experienced what is opposite to
self-restraint is bad; and this was the thoughtless and
wanton soul.

—Yes, of course.

—And, truly, the self-restrained person would do fitting
things concerning gods and people; you see, a person not
doing what is fitting would not be self-restrained.

—It is necessary that these things are so. 507b

—And truly, a person who did fitting things concerning
people would be doing just things; and concerning gods,
[he would be doing] holy things; and the one doing just
and holy things is necessarily a just and holy person.[167]

—These things are [so].

—And, indeed, he is, of course, necessarily courageous.
You see, it is not characteristic of the self-restrained person
to chase after and to flee from what is not fitting but [it *is*
characteristic of the self-restrained person] to chase after
and pursue matters and people and pleasures and pains
that he should, and, remaining at his post, to be strong
where he should; so that it is quite necessary, Callicles, 507c
that the self-restrained man, as we have described him in
detail, being just and courageous and holy, is completely
good, and that the good man does well and nobly what he
does, and that he who does well is divinely blessed and
happy, but the wicked man and the one acting badly is

---

167 These "baby steps" in the argument must be quite annoying to Callicles.

wretched. And this would be the one who is opposite to the self-restrained man—the wanton one—whom *you* praise.

And so *I* put these things thus and I say that these things are true: and if [they] are true, the one wishing, as it seems, to be happy must pursue and practice self-restraint, and must flee wantonness [as fast as our] feet can take us,[168] and he must provide for himself most of all not to have *any* need of being chastened, and if he or someone else of his household, either a private citizen or his polis, should have need [of being chastened], he must apply a punishment and chasten—if he intends to be happy. To me, of course, this seems to be [what we must set our eyes on in order to live properly], and it is necessary to live looking on this object and, constraining together all [our] own things and those of the polis for this [object], to see to it that justice be present and that the person who will be blessedly happy have self-restraint so as not to act allowing his desires to be wanton and [so as not to act] undertaking to fulfill these [desires]—[since fulfilling them would be] to lead the unendingly evil life of a pirate. You see, such a person would be friendly with neither another human being nor a god; he would not have the power of acting in common, and without acting in common there would not be friendship. And wise people say, Callicles, that acting in common and friendship and self-restraint and orderliness and justice hold heaven and earth and gods and human beings together, and on account of these [things that are held together] they call this whole an ordered beauty—[a *cosmos*]—my companion, and not a disorder and wantonness. But *you* do not seem to me to apply your mind to these things, even [though you are] wise concerning them, but it has escaped you that a geometric equality has great power both among gods and among humans, but *you* think that

507d

507e

508a

---

168 Socrates is shifting from the third person singular to the first person plural. Such shifts in person are often consciously deliberate in ancient literature and show that the speaker, "telling a tale about a person, is suddenly carried away and assumes the point of view of the person himself" (Longinus, *On the Sublime* 27.1).

it is necessary to practice graspingness.[169] You see, you are careless of geometry.[170] Let it be.

Indeed, either we must refute this argument—how [it is] not by the possession of justice and self-restraint that the happy are happy and by [the possession of evil] that the wretched are [wretched]—or, if this [argument] is true, we must examine the matters that go along with it. All those matters, Callicles, go along with what *you* asked me before, whether I was being serious when I was speaking and said that one must prosecute oneself and his son and his friend, if he acted unjustly, and that for *this* purpose rhetoric must be used. And the [points] about which you thought Polus was going along with me out of shame—[they] were true: namely, that to act unjustly is worse than to be treated unjustly, in the same degree by which [it] is uglier; and that it is necessary for one who will correctly be a rhetorician to be a just person who has knowledge of just things—what Polus in turn said that Gorgias had agreed to through shame.

Since these matters are so, let's examine what *you* are reproaching me with, whether it is said well or not, that indeed *I* am not able to help either myself or anyone of my friends or household, nor to save [myself or a friend or a member of my household] from the greatest dangers, but that I am [available] to anyone who has a wish—in the same way as those who have lost their civil rights [are available] to anyone who wishes—to be punched in the nose—to use your youthful expression—or deprived [of my] money, or thrown out of the polis, or, ultimately, killed. And to be in this position, according to your argument, is indeed the ugliest thing of all. And, indeed, while my [argument] has

508b

508c

508d

---

169 The term that we have translated as "graspingness" comes from the Greek for "to have more" (*pleonexia*). It is a key word in political and moral discourse. See Glossary.

170 There was a tradition dating back to at least the Middle Ages that over the entrance to Plato's Academy was a sign reading: "Let no one enter who is incapable of understanding geometry." In the *Republic*, Plato has Socrates tell his interlocutor Glaucon that geometry is about knowing and that its subject matter is being (*Republic* 527a-b). If these encomia to geometry be true to Plato's and Socrates' spirit, Socrates' criticism of Callicles here would be a deep insult.

Switching argument to discussion of which one is worse: to treat unjustly or to be treated unjustly.

508e

509a

509b

509c

already been often stated, it doesn't hurt [for it] to be said again. I deny, Callicles, that being punched in the nose unjustly is a very ugly thing, nor, of course, is being cut either in my body or my purse, but [I do say that the act of] striking me and of cutting me and my things unjustly is both uglier and worse, and [the act of] stealing my things and of kidnapping me and of robbing me and, in a word, of acting unjustly towards me and my things is worse and uglier for the one acting unjustly than for me, [the one] being treated unjustly. And these things that we've said before in our earlier arguments, as *I* say, are, to put it in a rather red-neck way, held down and tied [down] by iron and adamantine arguments—as of course they would seem—[arguments] that if *you* or someone more youthful than you does not break, it will not be possible for someone who says something different from what *I* am now saying to be speaking well, since I, of course, always have this same argument—that *I* do not know how these matters are—and that, let me tell you, of the people whom *I* have met, as indeed now, no one who says anything different fails to be laughable.[171] And so *I* again establish that these matters are this way: and if they are this way and [if] injustice is the greatest of evils for the one acting unjustly and [if] still greater than this greatest [evil]—if it is possible—[is] for the one acting unjustly not to pay a penalty, then what would in truth be the [sort of] help that would make a person an object of laughter if he didn't have the power [of providing that sort of help] to himself? Indeed, [won't it be] the help that turns away from us the greatest harm? But it's extremely necessary for this to be the ugliest [kind of] help—not to have the power to help either oneself or one's friends and householders; and second [ugliest] [will be the lack of power] to turn away from us the second greatest harm; and third [will be the

---

171   The logic of this sentence seems to dissolve: the beginning, with "since," is not followed up, as far as we can tell, by a logical consequent. Being an object of ridicule—what Callicles has said of Socrates (482d, 484e, 485a, 485c)—is the worst thing for a Greek. For his part, Socrates is suggesting that he has made Gorgias, Polus, and Callicles all laughing stocks. It is, perhaps, not a very tactful thing to say.

inability to turn away] the third greatest harm and the rest in the same way; and as is the greatness of each evil by nature, so nobility is the power of someone to provide help for each evil, and shame is not [having the power of providing help]. Is it otherwise or is it so, Callicles?

Callicles: It's not otherwise.[172]

Socrates: Of these two, then, acting unjustly and being treated unjustly, we say that the greater evil is to act unjustly, the lesser to be treated unjustly. And so what would a person provide himself to help himself, in order to have both these benefits—that of not acting unjustly and that of not being treated unjustly? [Is it a matter of] power or will? This is what I am saying: if he [simply] doesn't *wish* to be treated unjustly, will he not be treated unjustly? Or if he obtains the *power* of not being treated unjustly, will he not be treated unjustly?   509d

Callicles: This indeed is clear, of course: that [he will not be treated unjustly] if he [provides such] power [for himself].

Socrates: And indeed, what about acting unjustly? If he does not wish to act unjustly, is [the wish] sufficient—you see, he *will* not act unjustly—or even for this is it necessary to provide himself some power and technical skill, so that unless he learn and practice them, he will act unjustly?[173] Why don't you answer me this very [question], Callicles, whether we—Polus and *I*—seem to you to have been rightly forced to agree in the earlier arguments or not, when we agreed that no one wishes to act unjustly but that all those who act unjustly [do so] unwillingly?   509e

Callicles: Let this be so for you, Socrates, in order that you may go through the argument.[174]   510a

---

172 A very grudging acceptance, noted by the litotes.

173 This anticipates the argument in Boethius' *Consolation of Philosophy* about will and power (4.2).

174 A clear violation of the "rules of dialectic" (see Appendix B), which requires that the participants say what they believe. Callicles just wants to eat lunch. He is no longer interested in persuading those who are present of the truth of his position. His remarks indicate fatigue, certainly not the persistence that would be required of intellectual courage. He is an example of what Socrates in the *Phaedo* calls a "misologic" person, one who from failure in argument or from frustration comes to hate argument (*Phaedo* 89d).

{**Socrates:** And for this, as is likely, some power and [some] technical skill must be provided so that we not act unjustly.

Callicles: Yes, of course.}[175]

Socrates: And so, what technical skill is there of providing that one not be treated unjustly or [be treated unjustly] as little as possible? Consider whether you think as I do. You see, to me it seems like this: either one must rule in his polis or even be a tyrant or one must be a partner to the prevailing civil society.[176]

510b   **Callicles:** Do you see, Socrates, how ready *I* am to praise you, should you say something well? You seem to me to have said this very well.

Socrates: Consider, indeed, whether I seem to you to say this well also: every person seems to me to be a friend to every [other] person as much as possible and especially—as the ancient wise men say—[in the case of] like to like.[177] Does it seem so also to you?

---

175 We have agreed with some editors, though not with Dodds, in excising these two lines, which appear to be interpolations by copyists, because they are inconsistent with the preceding and following lines.

176 "Civil society" is our translation of the Greek *politeia*, an important word, and the Greek title of the dialogue that is traditionally called Plato's *Republic*. Modern usage makes "republic" refer to a form of government, though the Latin means, etymologically, "public matter" or "public thing." The narrow sense in English of "republic" as a governmental regime does not capture the rich meaning of the entire polis' life (see the Glossary). Plato's *Republic* itself deals with a great deal more than a form of government. Leo Strauss argues that *politeia* means something like the "way of life of a community" and that therefore typical translation of *politeia* as "constitution" is too narrow, at least in its contemporary usage as a "form of government" or even as "a document establishing a form of government." Classical political philosophers such as Plato, he adds, understood that the way of life of a community was crucially dependent on the form of its government, and so "constitution" does capture an important element of the meaning of *politeia*. Strauss uses "regime" as his translation of *politeia*. The problem with "regime" in contemporary usage is that it carries the connotation of illegitimate government. See Leo Strauss, *Natural Right and History* (University of Chicago Press, 1953), 135-137.

177 Whether friendships are composed of individuals who are alike or complementarily different was a matter of debate in the fifth and fourth centuries (and the debate is reflected in our contrasting expressions—"birds of a feather flock together" and "opposites attract"). In general, the ancient theorists of friendship concluded that in the best friendships there exists an identity of virtue.

Callicles: [It seems so] to me, of course.

Socrates: And so where a wild and uneducated tyrant is ruling, if there should be someone much better than he in the polis, would the tyrant indeed fear him and would [the tyrant] be incapable of being a friend with his whole mind to this person?[178]

510c

Callicles: This is so.

Socrates: Nor, if someone were much more trivial, would this man [be a friend to the tyrant]. You see, the tyrant would disdain him and would not ever be eager for his [company] as he would be for a friend's.

Callicles: This is also true.

Socrates: Indeed, there remains only this man as a worthy friend to such [a tyrant]—[the one] who, being of a similar character—blaming and praising the same things—is willing to be ruled and to be under the one ruling. This person will have the power to be great in the polis,[179] and no one will act unjustly towards him and go away happy. Isn't it so?

510d

Callicles: Yes.

Socrates: Look, if someone of the young men in this polis was thinking, "In what way might *I* have the power to be great and [bring it about that] no one act unjustly towards me?" this, as is likely, would be his path: straightaway from youth on he would make a habit[180] of feeling joy in and

---

178 Socrates is saying that because a tyrant would fear anybody superior to himself—perhaps thinking that such a man might be planning to take his place—he would surround himself with inferiors, who will be sycophants rather than friends. A similar argument is made in the *Hiero* by Xenophon, a contemporary of Plato, who was also a follower of Socrates. In Xenophon's dialogue, the tyrant Hiero explains to the poet Simonides (who is clearly superior to Hiero) his inability to have friends (*Hiero* 3-6). That true friendship requires equality is stressed by Aristotle in his discussion of friendship (*Nicomachaean Ethics* 1157b25–1158b11).

179 For consistency, we could have translated this, "This person will have great power in the polis." But the current translation, which is equally accurate, is more obviously oozing with Socratic irony in this context.

180 For Aristotle, the essence of ethics—from the same word that we have translated "make a habit of"—is the formation of good habits. If, as is likely, these same views were current in Plato's Academy and well known to those in the Academy, the present passage would be redolent with irony.

disliking the same things as his master and to see to it that he be as much like him as possible. Isn't it so?

Callicles: Yes.

Socrates: And so it will have been accomplished by this person, as your argument [goes],[181] that he won't be treated 510e unjustly and that he will have great power in his polis.

Callicles: Yes, of course.

Socrates: And so, then, [what about] also not acting unjustly? Or is it very necessary [that he will act unjustly], if he will be like the unjust person who is ruling and [if] by [standing at the tyrant's] side he will have great power? But *I*, of course, think [the situation will be the] complete opposite: he'll have the wherewithal to act unjustly as much as possible and, while acting unjustly, not to pay a penalty. Isn't this the case?

Callicles: It appears so.

511a **Socrates:** And so, he'll possess the greatest evil, being wretched and deformed in his soul through the imitation of his master and his power.[182]

Callicles: I don't know how every time you turn[183] the arguments up and down, Socrates. Or don't you know that this man [who] imitates [the tyrant] kills that man [who does] not imitate [the tyrant], if he wants, and deprives him of his possessions?

---

181   The word "your" is plural. Socrates might be reminding the others present that this is the now discredited argument of all his interlocutors, perhaps including the new politically active young men of the polis whom he has just mentioned. Socrates' comments show that the implications of Gorgias' remarks, though brief, are being explored throughout the dialogue.

182   It is not clear—and our translation preserves the lack of clarity—whose power is doing the corrupting: is the individual being corrupted though imitation of the master's power or through his own power?

183   Here Callicles is making one of the usual charges against the practitioner of dialectic— that he is somehow playing fast and loose with the arguments, manipulating and twisting them like a sophist, i.e., making the better argument the worse and the worse the better. Some of Plato's dialogues (e.g., *Euthydemus*, *Protagoras*, *Cratylus*) show how easy it is to manipulate arguments, and perhaps the line between honest dialectic and sophistic eristic (wrangling for the sake of victory) is not so clear. If dialectic is the best mode of philosophy, its corrupt form would be the worst.

Socrates: I know it, good Callicles, if I'm not deaf, hearing [this] often from you and just now from Polus and also from almost everyone else of the people in the polis. But *you* listen to me, too: he kills as he wishes, but [it is the act of] a wicked person [killing] one who is good and noble.   511b

Callicles: And, indeed, isn't this also irritating?

Socrates: Not, of course, for the one who has a mind, as the argument shows. Or do you think that it is necessary for a human being to provide for this—how he might live as long as possible, and to care for those technical skills that might always save us from dangers, just as *you* are   511c now bidding me to care for the rhetorical [skill that] saves [people] in the law courts.

Callicles: Yes, by Zeus, and [in so doing I] am, of course, counseling you rightly.

Socrates: What, best of men? Does the knowledge of swimming also seem to you to be a solemn thing?

Callicles: Not to me, of course, by Zeus.

Socrates: Yet truly it, too, of course, saves human beings from death when they fall into some such thing where there is need for this knowledge. But if this seems a small matter to you, *I* shall mention a greater matter to you, the   511d pilot's [skill], which saves not only souls but also bodies and property[184] from the ultimate dangers, just as rhetoric does. And this [skill of the pilot] is unassuming and beautiful in an ordered way and does not solemnify itself in posturing as though it were regularly accomplishing some high-falutin' feat, but, having accomplished the same things as skillful lawyering, if it brings you safely here from Aegina—I think this is done for two obols— and if it brings you from Egypt or from the Black Sea, for this great good deed—saving (I was now saying)   511e you yourself and your children and [your] property and women, and going back to the harbor—[it charges] at

---

184 Dodds says this is a stock phrase for "lives and property" and that no play on souls and bodies is intended. But literary people often play on the literal meaning of stock phrases, and we see no reason to assume that such a play on words is not occurring here.

very most two drachmas, and [when] that man who has the [pilot's] technical skill has accomplished these things, he disembarks alongside the sea and rambles around his ship with a modest gait. I think, you see, he is calculating that he knows it is unclear whether he has benefited any of those who sailed with him [in] not allowing them to be drowned and [whether] he has harmed any of them,

512a   since he knows that he has not unloaded them [onto the shore] better than he had loaded [them onto the ship],[185] in either their bodies or souls. And so he calculates, on the one hand, that if someone held in the grip of great and incurable diseases in his body has not choked, this man is wretched because he has *not* died and has not at all been benefited by him; and, on the other hand, [he wonders] if someone has many illnesses, even incurable ones, in what is more honorable than the body—the soul— and he must live, [whether] he will have benefited him also, by saving [him] from the sea or from a courtroom, or from

512b   some other place—but he knows that it is not superior for a corrupt human being to live; it is necessary, you see, for him to live badly.

On account of these things it is not the custom for the pilot to solemnify himself, even though he saves us, nor of course, my wondrous fellow, does the machine-maker, who sometimes has no less power of saving us than a general, a pilot, or anyone else.[186] You see, sometimes he saves whole poleis. Doesn't [this] seem to you to be very like skillful lawyering? And if he wished, Callicles, to say what *you*

512c   [people are saying], making his business a solemn thing, he would bury you with his arguments, arguing and urging that it is necessary [for us all] to become machine-

---

185   Readers might wonder how much people in the transportation industry actually worry about the moral effect of their services. Does a bus driver taking people across town think, "Will this passenger be better morally when he gets off the bus on Third Avenue than he was when he boarded on Amsterdam Avenue?" Do even school bus drivers worry about the moral effect of driving children to school?

186   The word we have translated as "machine-maker," *mechanopoion*, sometimes means "maker of war engines," but the word might also refer to those who make the mechanical parts of ships. Socrates' point seems to be that the machine-maker doesn't put on airs even though his work also has the power to save many lives.

makers, as there are no other things [that matter]. You see, he would have an adequate argument. But nonetheless *you* do disdain him and his technical skill, and, as though in reproach, you refer to him as a *machine-maker*, and you would not be willing to give your daughter to his son nor would you be willing to take his daughter. Yet, from what [you say when] you praise your own things, by what just argument do you disdain the machine-maker and the other people whom I was now talking about? I know that you would say that you are better and [that you are descended] from better people. But with respect to *better*, if it is not what *I* say [it is], but this itself is excellence— [simply] to save oneself and one's things (whatever sort [of person] one happens to be)—then your blame of the machine-maker and the physician and the others whose technical skills have been created for the sake of saving [lives] is downright laughable. But, divinely blessed man, see whether the noble and the good aren't something different from saving and being saved. You see, this— how much time one lives—must not be the concern of [one who is] truly a man, and he must not be infatuated with his life, but, relying on the god in these matters and believing the women [when they say] that one may not escape the appointed day, he must examine this—how he might live as best as possible the time that he is about to live: is he to make himself like the civil society in which he lives—and now it is also necessary for you, then, to become most like the demos of Athens, if you intend to be considered a friend to it and have great power in this polis; and concerning this, see whether it does profit you and me, so that, daimonic one, we shall not experience what they say [happened to] the Thessalian women when they were pulling down the moon:[187] [namely,] have the

512d

512e

513a

---

187 In the *Clouds* of Aristophanes, one of the characters, Strepsiades, talks about hiring a Thessalian witch to draw down the moon (749), that is, to cause an eclipse. Thessaly is the area on the northeastern Aegean to which Crito tries to induce Socrates to escape (*Crito* 45c, 53d). Its reputation for witchcraft among Athenians probably resulted from its cultural distance from Athens and the prejudice that attends strange foreign places. The metaphor here, suggesting that the kind of power that Callicles advocates is as phony as the manipulation of the heavens by witches, is perhaps intended to antagonize Callicles.

to be a phony, but at the cost of doing the unjust.

513b

choice of this power in the polis [but] at the cost of the things dearest [to us]. If you think that any human being will give you such a technical skill, which will make you, though being unlike the civil society, have great power in the polis, whether for the better or for the worse, you are not, as it seems to me, Callicles, deliberating rightly; you see, it is necessary to be not an imitator but [one who is] naturally similar to these [people], if you intend to work out something legitimate concerning friendship with the demos of Athens and, yes, of course, by Zeus, with [Demos] the son of Pyrilampos. And so, whoever brings it about [that you are] most similar to these, that person will make you what you desire, a person who deals with the matters of the polis—a political and a rhetorical man.

513c

You see, each [person] takes delight in the character of those making the same arguments [as he makes] and is annoyed by another [argument], unless *you* say something else, dear. What do we say to these things, Callicles?

Callicles: I don't know how [it is that] you seem to me to speak well, Socrates, but I have experienced the experience of the many:[188] I am not wholly persuaded by you.

513d

Socrates: You see, Callicles, an erotic desire in your soul for the demos resists me; but if perhaps we should thoroughly examine these very same things often and better, you would be persuaded. And so recall that we said how there are two methods of caring for each—body and soul—one attending to pleasure, the other to [what is] best, [this latter] not giving gratification [to pleasure] but fighting hard against [it]. Weren't these the definitions we reached then?

in tension

Callicles: Yes, of course.

Socrates: And so, doesn't the one, the method [that aims] at pleasure, happen to be ignoble and nothing but a pandering? Eh?

---

188 "The many" (*hoi polloi*) are usually not afforded any respect by the participants in a Platonic dialogue, nor are they by Callicles himself (e.g., 483b), so it is perhaps remarkable that he identifies with the "many" here.

Callicles: Let it be so for you, if you wish.   513e

Socrates: But, of course, the other [method aims at] how what we are caring for—whether it happens to be a body or a soul—might be as good as possible?

Callicles: Yes, of course.

Socrates: And so, mustn't we undertake to care for the polis and the citizens in this way—to make these citizens as good as possible? You see, indeed, without this, as we discovered in our earlier [arguments], [there is] no benefit in bringing forward any other good work at all, unless the intention of those who are about to take either a lot of money or rulership over some [other people] or any other power be noble and good. Are we to establish [this] as so?   514a

Callicles: Yes, of course, if it is pleasing to you.

Socrates: And so, Callicles, if, intending to act for the demos in matters relating to the affairs of the polis, we are going to call each other to building [projects], either walls or dockyards or holy places—[calling each other] to the greatest building projects—would it be necessary for us to examine ourselves and test first whether we know the technical skill or whether we don't know it—[the technical skill of] construction—and [ask] from whom we learned [it]? Would this be necessary or not?   514b

Callicles: Yes, of course, [it would be].

Socrates: And so in turn [should we examine] this next, whether we have ever built a building in private either for one of our friends or for ourselves and whether this building is noble or shameful. And if when looking at our teachers, we found that they had been good and esteemed and that we had built many noble buildings [in company] with our teachers and also [had built] many private buildings of our own after we had departed from our teachers, then, with the circumstances so disposed, it would be [the job of those of us] who had mind to go on to public works. But if we are unable to show either a teacher   514c of ours or any buildings at all[189]—or [if we showed] many that were worth nothing at all—it would thus be mindless indeed, I do suppose, to undertake public works and to urge each other to them. Are we to affirm that these

514d   things are said rightly or not?

Callicles: Yes, of course.

Socrates: And so aren't all other things like this, and if, while undertaking to act publicly, we were urging one another on—as [though] we were adequate physicians—we'd examine [each other], I do suppose, *I* you and *you* me. [You'd say,] "Come, by [the] gods, how fares the body of Socrates himself in the matter of health? Has someone else, either a slave or a free person, yet been freed from an illness because of Socrates?" And, I think, *I* would look into other such things about you. And if we found

514e   that because of us no one had become better in his body, no one of the foreigners or the town folk, neither a man nor a woman, by Zeus, Callicles, wouldn't it in truth be laughable for people[190] to come to such [a degree] of mindlessness, that—before showing privately how we happened to act in many matters, and [how we happened to] set many things right, and [how we happened to] expose adequately the naked truth about our technical skill—we would, as the saying goes, undertake to learn pottery at the jar and ourselves undertake to act publicly and to urge other such [individuals to do so too]? Would it not seem to you mindless to act in this way?

---

189   We find noteworthy this respect afforded to those who have esteemed teachers; perhaps it reflects a human bias in favor of pedigrees, whether biological or intellectual. The same phenomenon may be observed in concert program notes, where a musician's teachers are listed, the assumption being that a musician who studied with such and such a teacher must be good. Perhaps this judgment assumes excellence because of difficult entrance requirements: a famous teacher would not take on a mediocre student. The same prejudice applies generally. We naturally (but often erroneously) suppose someone who has studied at Stanford or Harvard to know something. Socrates is preparing the ground for the discussion about whether there are true teachers of politics.

190   While some editors have eliminated "people" because it marks a shift from the first person plural to the third person, we follow Dodds in accepting the ms. reading and the interpretation "that what is shocking is not that Socrates and Callicles should behave in this way but that anybody should," (Dodds, p. 354) and that after this statement the argument shifts back to the case of Socrates and Callicles.

Callicles: To me, of course, [it would].

Socrates: And now, best of men, since *you* yourself are just   515a
beginning to do the business of the polis[191] and you are
urging me [to do the same] and you are rebuking [me]
because I am not doing [so], shall we not examine each
other? Come, has Callicles yet made anyone of the citizens
better? Is there anyone who, having been wicked and unjust
and wanton and mindless earlier, has, because of Callicles,
become a noble and good person, either a foreigner or a
townsman, or a slave or a free man? Tell me, if someone   515b
should examine you about these things, Callicles, what
will you say? Whom will you say you have made a better
human being by your company? Are you shrinking to
answer whether there is any work of yours [when you
were] still acting in private, before you undertook to act
publicly?

Callicles: You are a lover of winning, Socrates.[192]

Socrates: But, of course, [it's not] from love of winning that
I ask, but as one truly wishing to know in what way you
think it is necessary to engage among us in the affairs of
the polis. Coming into the business of the polis, will you   515c
care for anything other than that we the citizens be as
good as possible? Or haven't we often already agreed that
it is necessary for the political man to do this? Have we
agreed or not? Answer. We *have* agreed. *I* shall answer on
your behalf. And so if it is necessary for the good man to
provide this for his own polis, tell me, recalling those men
about whom you were speaking a little earlier, whether
they still seem to you to have been good citizens—Pericles   515d
and Cimon and Miltiades and Themistocles.

Callicles: To me, of course, [they do].

---

191 Here we have a stronger suggestion than the rather oblique hints in 508d and 509a that
Callicles is a rather young man.
192 Perhaps Callicles is punning. Instead of being a lover of wisdom, *sophia*, Socrates is a
lover of *nike*, victory. Instead of the reading "lover of winning" (*philonikos*), there is the
variant "lover of strife" (*philoneikos*). Either way, the pun would apply. With Dodds, we
keep "lover of winning."

Socrates: And so, if they were good, it is clear that each of them was making the citizens better instead of worse. Was each doing so or not?

Callicles: Yes.

Socrates: And so, when Pericles was beginning to speak in the demos, the Athenians were worse than when he spoke his last?

Callicles: Perhaps.

Socrates: Indeed, not "perhaps," best one, but "necessarily" from the things we've agreed to—if, of course, that man was a good citizen.

515e   **Callicles:** And so, indeed, what [follows]?

Socrates: Nothing. But tell me the following about this [point]—do the Athenians say about themselves that on account of Pericles they have become better, or [do they say] the exact opposite—that they were ruined by him? You see, I, in fact, hear this—that Pericles, having first set up the system of payment for public services, made the Athenians lazy and cowardly and talkative and money-loving.[193]

Callicles: You hear these things from the people with cauliflower ears.[194]

Socrates: But I no longer hear these things, but I know clearly, and you do, too, that at first Pericles had a good reputation and [the people] charged him with no shameful crime—when they were worse; but when because of him they had

516a   become noble and good—at the end of Pericles' life—they charged him with theft and nearly punished him with death, [and] it is clear that [they thought of him as] being a wicked man.

---

193 Socrates is referring to the payment for serving on juries, on active military duty, and in councils. These payments enabled more men to serve, especially in the navy, and made them a potent political force.

194 This expression refers to young men of Spartan sympathy. Since the Spartans engaged in boxing for fun, they would have had beaten ears, and this is a derogatory term to refer to Spartan sympathizers, who, presumably, would have imitated this fashion.

Callicles: And what follows? Because of this was Pericles a bad man?

Socrates: Well, of course, if he were a caretaker of asses and horses and cows, he would have seemed a bad one if, after he had taken them by his side [in a condition of] not kicking him or butting [him] or biting [him], he [then] exhibited [these animals] doing all these things on account of wildness. Or doesn't [a person] seem to you a 516b bad caretaker of any living being at all, who, taking [the animals] by his side [in a condition of being] rather tame, exhibits them [later] as wilder than he received them? Does it seem so or not?

Callicles: Yes, of course—so that I might be pleasing to you.

Socrates: And please me [by] answering this, too: is the human [animal] also one of the living things, or isn't he?

Callicles: Well, how not?

Socrates: Wasn't Pericles taking care of human beings?

Callicles: Yes.

Socrates: And so, what [follows]? Wasn't it necessary for [the human beings for whom Pericles was caring], as we have just agreed, to have become more just instead of more unjust by his [activities], if indeed that man took care of 516c them as a [man] good in the affairs of the polis?

Callicles: Yes, of course.

Socrates: And so, the just are, of course, gentle, as Homer said.[195] What do you say? Isn't it so?

Callicles: Yes.

Socrates: But [Pericles] let [them] go wilder than the way [they were when] he took them by his side, and [they were wilder] towards himself, the [very] one towards whom he least of all wanted [them to be wild].

Callicles: Do you want me to agree with you?

Socrates: If, of course, I seem to you to be saying the truth.

---

195 Homer seems actually to have put it a bit differently: "the wild are unjust" (*Odyssey* 6.120).

Callicles: Indeed, let these things be so.

Socrates: And so, if they were wilder, [they were] more unjust and worse?

516d **Callicles:** Let it be [so].

Socrates: Then, from this argument, Pericles was *not* good in the affairs of the polis.

Callicles: Not, as *you*, of course, are saying.

Socrates: No, by Zeus, nor as *you* [are], in fact, from what you have agreed to. And again, tell me about Cimon.[196] Didn't they whom he had cared for ostracize him so that they wouldn't hear his voice for ten years? And they did these same things to Themistocles and punished him with exile.[197] And Miltiades, the one [who had been victorious] at Marathon,[198] they voted to throw in the pit,[199] and if [it had not been] on account of the prytanis,[200] wouldn't he have fallen into [it]? Yet these, if they were good men, as *you* say, would not ever have suffered these things. Those, of course, who [end up being] good charioteers don't fall out of their chariots in the beginning [of their careers], but [it's] *after* they have taken care of their horses and have become better charioteers—[*that's* when] they fall out. These things are not [so] either in charioteering nor in any other work. Or does it seem so to you?

516e

---

196   In 461, when there was an earthquake in Sparta, the Spartans feared that their resident-slaves, the helots, would rise up. Against much political opposition Cimon carried a measure authorizing Athens to send troops to help Sparta. In the last moments, Sparta turned the Athenians away, perhaps from fear of having a "foreign" army on her land. The Athenians, whose motives, at least in their own minds, were pure, were outraged and resented Cimon, whom they ostracized. Ostracism was a response to political disfavor, and was not the same thing as exile, which was a punishment for serious crimes.

197   Themistocles was ostracized in 471, when he fell out of political favor. Two years later he was suspected of having collaborated with the Spartan traitor Pausanias and was punished by exile. He spent the remainder of his life under the protection of the Persians, whom he had so brilliantly defeated in the Persian Wars.

198   Socrates is mentioning the victory of Miltiades at Marathon to distinguish this Miltiades from his Uncle Miltiades, the tyrant of the Chersonese.

199   The pit was a cleft in the rock behind the acropolis into which criminals of the polis were thrown as a form of execution.

200   The Prytanis was the man chosen by a daily lot to serve as chair of the Council. He would have been chosen by lot from the one of the ten tribes that was holding its turn as the executive committee of the Council.

Callicles: Not to me, of course.

Socrates: Then, as it seems, our earlier arguments were true—
that *we* don't know any man at all who has been good at   517a
political affairs in this polis. And *you* have agreed that
there is no one of those who are around now [who is good
at political affairs]. But of those [who lived] before—and
you preferred them—have appeared as equal to those who
are living now [in not being good at political affairs], so
that [it follows that], if they were rhetors, neither did they
use true rhetoric—you see, [if they had], they would not
have fallen—nor [did they use true] pandering.

Callicles: But let me tell you, Socrates, there is a big gulf
between what anyone today has ever done and the deeds
of those whom we have spoken of.   517b

Socrates: Daimonic man, *I* don't fault them, of course, in their
capacity as servants of the polis, but they seem to me to
have been more successfully servile than the men [who are
around] now and [and they were] abler at finding out for
the polis the things it desired. But, you see, with respect
to changing the desires of the citizens and not bowing to
them, persuading and compelling them to change [so that]
they might become superior—in a word, the [politicians
of the past] were no different from those [who are around   517c
now]—and this [making others superior] is the only
work of a good citizen. *I,* too, agree with you that [earlier
politicians] were cleverer at providing ships and walls and
dockyards and many other such things. And so we, *you*
and *I,* are doing a laughable thing in our arguments: you
see, in all the time we've been engaging in dialectic we
haven't stopped at all, [but we are] always being carried
round [in a circle] to the same [place], being ignorant of
what the other of us is saying. And so *I,* of course, have
often been thinking that *you* agreed and knew how this
same business is double both about the body and about   517d
the soul and [how] one of the two is a servile [business],
by which it is possible to find foods, if our bodies are
hungry, and drinks, if they are thirsty, and, if they are
cold, cloaks, beds, shoes, and other things that our bodies

come to desire. And I am speaking to you through these images with the specific purpose that you might easily learn. You see, [I think that you have agreed that] the provider of these things is a peddler, or an importer, or a

517e   craftsman of these things—a bread-maker, or a cook, or a weaver, or a leather-cutter, or a currier, and [I think you have agreed that] it is not at all wondrous that one who has [one of these occupations] will seem to himself and to others [to be] a carer of the body—to everyone who does not know that alongside all these [types of activities] there *is* a gymnastic and medical technical skill that in reality *does* care for the body, [a technical skill] that is fitting to rule over all these [other] technical skills and to use their works because it knows what is useful and grievous about

518a   foods and drinks for the [true] excellence of the body, and all these other [providers] are in reality ignorant; [and I think you have agreed that,] indeed, therefore, these [—the bread-maker, cook, weaver, leather-cutter, and currier—] are properly slaves and servants and not free about the body's business, but [that] the other technical skills[201]—the gymnastic and the medical [technical skills] are— according to the just [argument], the masters of these. And so, with respect to these same things that are about the soul, you seem to me at one time to understand what I am saying and you agree as one knowing what *I* am saying; but a little later you came saying that there have

518b   been noble and good people as citizens in the polis, and when *I* ask who, you seem to me to have brought forward people who are very similar about the affairs of the polis, as if, were I asking about the gymnastic affairs who have been good or who are the ones who take care of bodies, and you, being very serious, would tell me, "Thearion, the bread-maker, and Mithaikos, the one who has written on Sicilian cooking, and Sarambos the retailer—these have been wondrous carers of bodies, one because he provides

---

201 Part of what makes this sentence difficult is the shifting between singular and plural. A few lines earlier, Socrates had referred to the gymnastic and medical technical skill in the singular, that is, as *one* technical skill; now he is referring to them in the plural, as *separate* technical skills.

wondrous breads, another [because he provides wondrous] food, the third [because he provides wondrous] wine."

only pleasure, not good or bad.

And so perhaps you would be annoyed if *I* said to you, "Sir, you understand nothing at all about [the] gymnastic [technical skill]. You are speaking to me about servants and about people who are providers of desires, people who don't understand at all [what is] noble and good about these things, [people] who, should they thus happen to overindulge and fatten people's bodies and be praised by those people [whom they have fattened], would [actually] be destroying their original flesh; and they [who have lost their flesh] in turn through inexperience will not blame those who gave [them] feasts as the ones responsible for [their] illnesses and for the throwing out of their original flesh; but [they will blame] those who just happen to be present with them and are sharing some advice, when the overindulgence of that time catches up with them, the [overindulgence] that brings disease a long time later since [it has] come without health—[those who are now suffering from their overindulgence] will blame and find fault with *these* [people] and will do something bad [to them], if they can, but they will praise those earlier [individuals who actually were] responsible for the evils.

really insulting to Callicles

So the politicians are most to blame

You also, Callicles, are now doing something very much like this: you are praising people who have given feasts and regaled the people with what they've desired. And they say that these have made the polis great; but they do not perceive that it is swelling and ulcerous on account of those men of old.[202] You see, without self-restraint and justice they have filled the polis with harbors and dockyards and walls and tribute and such nonsense. And so when there should come the same crisis of weakness [as that which afflicts a body through the bloated overindulgence of its desires], they will blame those counselors [who are] *then* present, but the ones responsible for the evils—Themistocles, and Cimon, and Pericles—they will praise; and perhaps they'll take hold

---

202 I.e., the so-called statesmen like Pericles and Themistocles mentioned earlier.

519b

of you,[203]—if you're not cautious—and of my partner Alcibiades, when they destroy their original possessions in addition to what they have acquired, though [you and Alcibiades] are not [wholly] responsible for the evils but perhaps [only] sharers in the responsibility.

And *I*, in fact, now see and I hear a mindless thing happening about the men of old. You see, I perceive, when the polis lays its hands on one of those who have engaged in its affairs as a man who has acted unjustly, [those men are] annoyed and complain that they are suffering terrible things, since, as their argument goes, having done many good things for the polis, they are [now being] unjustly destroyed by it. But the whole thing is a lie. You see, no

519c

man who stands before his polis, not one at all, would be unjustly destroyed by that very polis before which he stands. You see, the situation is likely the same [for] those engaging in the affairs of the polis as [for] sophists. You see, the sophists, too, though wise in other respects, do engage in this out-of-place[204] [behavior]: you see, while saying that they are teachers of excellence, they often accuse their students of acting unjustly towards them, depriving them of their wages and of not returning [any]

519d

other thanks after they have experienced good [treatment] from them.[205] And what would be more lacking in reason than this argument, that those who have become good and just people—having had [their] injustice taken away by their teacher, on the one hand, and having gotten justice, on the other—would act unjustly by this [injustice] that they do not possess? Does this not seem to you out-of-place, friend? How you have truly compelled me to give a public address, Callicles, [since] you are not willing to answer!

---

203 As Callicles had threatened Socrates earlier, describing how inept he would be in court, so Socrates seems to be threatening Callicles here for his failure to understand the true goods.

204 This is the key word *atopos* (see note 53).

205 The sophist Protagoras in Plato's caricature of him in the *Protagoras* (328b-c) claims to have let his students decide whether to pay him and how much.

Callicles: And weren't *you* [the one who was] unable to speak, unless someone answered you?

Socrates: It seems likely, of course, [that I was wrong]; [for] now I am stretching out many of my speeches since you are not willing to answer. But, good man, speak, by [the god] of friendship. Doesn't it seem to you lacking in reason that someone who says he has made another into a good person should [then] blame him because through him [this other], having become good and being [so], is then wicked?   519e

Callicles: To me it does, in fact, seem [lacking in reason].

Socrates: Don't you hear [the sophists] who say such things, affirming that they educate human beings to excellence?

Callicles: *I* do, of course. But what would you say about people [who are] worth nothing?   520a

Socrates: What would you say about those who, affirming that they are in charge of the polis and take care that it be as good as possible, in turn accuse it—whenever they happen to [do so]—of very great wickedness? Do you think that these people are different from those [sophists]? Blessedly happy one, the sophist and the rhetor are the same thing, or nearly the same and virtually the same,[206] as *I* was saying to Polus. But *you*, on account of ignorance, think the one thing—rhetoric—all lovely, and you disdain the other. But in truth, sophistic is finer than rhetoric by as much as law-making [is finer than] jurisprudence, and gymnastics [is finer] than medicine:[207] and *I*, of course, was thinking that [it was] only to public speakers and sophists that I   520b

---

206   This sort of redundant expression has the technical name *pleonasm*. Perhaps pleonasm was a characteristic of the style of Gorgias and his students, a characteristic that Socrates is parodying here. Quintilian, a first century C.E. writer on rhetoric and education, describing pleonasm as "a superfluity of words" (*Institutes* 8.53), censures the expression "I saw it with my eyes," since "I saw it" would have been enough. But when a luminary like Virgil writes, "I heard his voice with my own ears"(*Aeneid* 3.359), Quintilian praises the redundancy as showing a justified heightened emotion. In other words, context (or famous authorship) determines whether something is to a beholder the laudatory or blameworthy kind of pleonasm.

207   Because, perhaps, of the principle that a gram of prevention is worth a kilogram of cure (to put it metrically).

didn't concede [the right] to blame that "thing" they teach [—the people—] as wicked to themselves; or, by the same argument, [I was thinking that] at the same time they [must] accuse themselves because they have not benefited those whom they claim they benefit. Isn't it so?

520c   **Callicles:** Yes, of course.

Socrates: And, of course, I do suppose, as is likely, the right is conceded to them alone to lavish their good work [on their customers] without a wage, *if* indeed they were saying the truth. You see, concerning some other good result that a person receiving a good result receives[208]—for example, becoming swift on account of a trainer, perhaps he would withhold his gratitude from [the trainer], if the trainer had lavished [his services freely] on him and had not agreed on a wage—[trusting] that he would get money at precisely the same time that he gave a share of speed [to

520d   his customer]. You see, it is not from slowness, I think, that people act unjustly, but from injustice. Eh?

Callicles: Yes.

Socrates: And so if someone removes this very thing, injustice, he will not fear that he will ever be treated unjustly, but for him alone [it will] be safe to lavish a good service—if in reality someone had the power to make [people] good. Is it not so?

Callicles: I say [so].

Socrates: On account of these things, it is not at all shameful, as it seems, to take money counseling other counsels,[209] as, for example, about house-building or other technical skills.

520e   **Callicles:** It is likely, of course.

---

208   Yet another pleonastic Gorgias-like jingle. Socrates' parodying of Gorgias' style with these silly jingles would annoy his hearers in the dramatic context and delight Plato's readers. Most translators ignore these jingles both because these verbal pyrotechnics are cumbersome to produce and not so very jingly (as our translation shows) and because, at least in modern English, they are bizarre. Gorgias' audience, however, seemed to like them.

209   Another jingle.

Socrates: But, in fact, about this action—[teaching] how someone might be as good as possible and manage his own house or polis as excellently as possible—it has been thought shameful to say that he would not give counsel unless someone gave him money. Eh?

Callicles: Yes.

Socrates: You see, it is clear that this is responsible [for the situation that they don't have to ask for their wages ahead of time]—that this alone of good services makes the one having the good experience desire to do good in return, so that it seems to be a noble sign, if, after having done this good service, [a person] will experience a good [service] in return. But if not, [it is] not [a noble sign]. Are these things so?

Callicles: They are.   521a

Socrates: Distinguish for me which care of the polis you are urging me towards—fighting hard for the Athenians that they be as good as possible, as a physician [would fight for his patients], or caring for them like a servant and courting their gratitude? Tell me the truth, Callicles: you're just, you see; as you began speaking frankly to me, finish saying what you think. Even now speak well and nobly.

Callicles: I say then that [I am urging you to care for them like] one who is a servant. *still Callicles doesn't agree.*

Socrates: Then, most noble one, you are urging me to pander?   521b

Callicles: If it's more pleasing for you to call [yourself] a [lowly] Mysian, Socrates, since unless you do these things of course. . . .[210]

---

210 The point seems to be that what Callicles calls "acting like a servant" Socrates calls "pandering." So to call someone a Mysian is to use an uglier for a less offensive term. In the same way, one person's "friendliness" is another's "fawning obsequiousness"; one person's "innocent flirtation," another's "leering harassment." In political terms, one person's "serving the people" is another's "looking to see which way the wind blows." The Mysians were a tribe from Thrace in the northern Aegean (*Iliad* 13.7)—hence the word *Mysian* refers to a people, but the word *mysos* also means "uncleanness" or "defilement," and hence the word can refer to a detested thing. Thus to use a *Mysian* word is to use the opposite of a euphemism—using an uglier word for a nicer one. Perhaps— if mere translators might be allowed to add to the rhetorical lexicon—this would be a "kakophemism."

Socrates: Don't say what you've often said—that a person who wishes will kill me—so that *I* in turn won't say, "A man who is wicked of course [will be killing] a man who is good." [And don't say] that he will rob me if I've got anything, so that *I* won't say in turn, "He's robbed me, but he won't know how to make use of [my] things,[211] but, as he has robbed me unjustly, so when he takes the things, he will use them unjustly, and if unjustly, shamefully, and if shamefully, badly."

521c

Callicles: How you seem to me to trust that you would not experience any of these things, that living out of the way you wouldn't be dragged to a courtroom by some perhaps entirely wretched and insignificant person!

Socrates: Then, Callicles, I am mindless, truly [I am], if I don't think that in *this* polis anyone might experience anything that might happen. I, however, know this well: that if I shall go into a courtroom risking any of the things that *you* are talking about, [it will be] someone wicked who is dragging me in—you see, no one good would drag a person not acting unjustly [into court]—and [it would be] not at all out-of-place,[212] of course, if I should die. Do you want me to tell you why I expect these things?

521d

Callicles: Yes, of course.

Socrates: I think that with *few* [other] Athenians [who ever lived]—in order not to say [that I am] the only one—I truly take in hand the technical skill of politics, and [I am] the *only* one of those [alive now] to practice political affairs. And so, inasmuch as [I am] arguing the arguments that I argue[213] aiming not at thanks, but at [what is] best, not at what is most pleasant, and not wishing to do what you advise, I won't know what pretty things I am to say in the courtroom. And the same argument has come to me that I was saying to Polus. I shall be judged as a physician is judged among children, when a cook is doing

521e

---

211   Perhaps Socrates' meaning here is that no proper use will be made of the items stolen, and if the use is not proper, then it is no real use at all.

212   Another use of *atopos*.

213   Another jingle.

the accusing. Consider, you see, what such a person would say in defense of himself when he is being arrested on such [charges], if someone should accuse him, saying, "Children, this man here has done many bad things to you yourselves, and he is destroying the youngest of you [by his] cutting and cauterizing; and drying you up and throttling [you], he is putting you in perplexity;[214] giving [you] most bitter potions, he is compelling [you] to be hungry and thirsty—not [doing] as *I* am, feasting [you] on many sweet things of all kinds." What do you think a physician caught in this evil would say? Or, if he said the truth—"I *did* do all these things, children, in the interests of [your] health"—how great a shout do you think such jurymen would cry out? [Would it] not be loud?   522a

Callicles: Perhaps.

Socrates: It *is*, of course, necessary to think [so].[215] And so don't you think that he would be in complete perplexity about what he must say?   522b

Callicles: Yes, of course.

Socrates: Let me tell you, even *I* know that I would experience such an experience[216] coming into a courtroom. You see, I won't be able to speak of the pleasures that I've furnished to them—which *they* think of as good services and benefits—and *I* don't envy those providing [them] nor [those] to whom they are provided. And if someone says that I, putting them into perplexity, am destroying the younger people or that I, saying bitter words either in private or in public, am making accusations against the older people, I shall be able to say neither the truth—[that]   522c "*I* do say all these [accusations and bitter words] justly,

---

214   The term we have translated as "perplexity" is, in Greek, *aporia*, a word that means a place where there is no way out. Socratic dialectic often plunges its participants into a dead end where they admit to perplexity. Acknowledging that one does not know what he thought he knew is the essential first step in pursuing truth.

215   The mss. give this sentence to Callicles, but we are persuaded by Dodds and the parallels he cites in showing that "perhaps" does not go along with "it is necessary." We think that Callicles here is answering perfunctorily, for he has lost any real interest in continuing; for Socrates, however, the argument is important, and so he is affirming this point.

216   Another jingle.

[handwritten margin note: talking about Socr's death]

and, indeed, I am acting for your [benefit], gentlemen of the jury"—nor anything else. So that perhaps I *shall* suffer this, whatever happens.[217]

Callicles: Does a person in the polis, in such a condition and being unable to help himself, seem to you, Socrates, to be excellent?

Socrates: If, of course that one thing were there for him, Callicles, which *you* have often agreed to: if he had helped himself [by] having neither said nor done anything 522d unjust either to human beings or to gods. You see, this has often been agreed by us to be the strongest help for oneself. And so, if someone were to refute[218] me [by saying that I] had lacked the power to help myself or another [by not speaking or acting justly], I would be ashamed, having been refuted both among the many and the few, even if I, being alone, [were refuted by] one person; and if on account of this lack of power [to show that I had not spoken or acted unjustly] I should die, I would be vexed. But if from want of pandering rhetoric I, in fact, should come to my end, I know well that you would see me 522e bearing my death easily. No one—whoever's not wholly without reason and courage—fears death—but he fears acting unjustly. You see, for the soul to arrive in Hades

217 In Dodds' interpretation, these two sentences would read:
> And if someone says that I, putting them into perplexity, am destroying the younger people or that I—saying bitter words either in private or in public—am making accusations against the older people, shall be able neither to say the truth—[that] [522c] "I do say all these [accusations and bitter words] justly, and, indeed, I am acting for your benefit, gentlemen of the jury (to use *your* word for these people)"—nor [to say] anything else. So that perhaps I *shall* suffer this, whatever happens.

The meaning would be that Socrates does not accept such individuals as true jurors since they do not really understand what justice is. Plato would have Socrates use the term in the same way as he does in the *Apology* (40a and 41a), where he says that the term "gentlemen of the jury" truly refers only to those who voted for acquittal. Despite Dodds' argument that this use of "gentlemen of the jury" is an allusion to the *Apology*, it seems unlikely that a reader would be expected to remember this particular quotation (if in fact the writing and publication of the *Apology* even preceded that of the *Gorgias*). Nevertheless, as stated earlier (Introduction pp. 13-14), Socrates' trial and execution hover in the background of the entire dialogue, and no word can be read without this memory.

218 The word we have translated as "refute" is also the word for "convict." Socrates seems to be playing with the two meanings. Perhaps for Socrates to be refuted *is* to be convicted.

full of many unjust deeds is the utmost of all evils. And if you wish, *I'm* willing to tell you an account of how this is so.

Callicles: But since you've finished everything else, finish this too.

Socrates: Hear a very fine account indeed, as the saying goes,[219]   523a
one you'll consider a tale, as *I* think, but *I* an *account*.[220]
The things that I shall say, you see, are [things] I intend
to say as truth.[221] *Beginning of the myth.*

Well, as Homer says, Zeus and Poseidon and Pluto divided the rule for themselves when they took it from their father.[222] And so there was this law about men in the [time] of Kronus—always and even now it still exists among the gods—that whoever of men had gone through his life justly and piously, when he should die, would go to   523b
the islands of the divinely blessed[223] and live in complete happiness apart from evils, but the one [who had gone through life] unjustly and godlessly, went to the prison house of punishment and justice, which indeed they call Tartarus. The judges of these [men] in the time of Kronus

---

219   The saying seems to be not much more meaningful than our "Once upon a time."

220   The words "tale" (*mythos*) and "account" *(logos)* are interchangeable, for both words can signify a real or fictive world, and a Greek author could use either word to say that his story is either true or false. See Appendix C.

221   The claim that this manifestly false myth is true (Socrates is making it up for the occasion with many elements pointedly designed to pertain to Callicles) raises the matter of truth in fiction. Such truth is twofold: (1) the consistent and convincing illusion of reality; (2) the meaning, based on that illusion, that is yet relevant and applicable to the abstract and psychic world in which we live. The data of a story are to be accepted as real unless they are self-contradictory. For example, when the stage directions of *Hamlet* say "Enter ghost," then the reader must accept the existence of the ghost, whatever his personal belief about ghosts. Such acceptance is what Coleridge calls "the willing suspension of disbelief"; it is of equal importance to continue the acceptance not only during the experience of the work of art but also during the period of criticism. Only by doing so can we hope to understand the truth of the art. Whether we choose to accept that truth after we understand it is, of course, optional with each reader. Here we may wonder whether Socrates is presenting his story in such a way as to elicit any kind of receptive hearing by Callicles.

222   The reference to Homer is *Iliad* 15.187–93. We learn from Hesiod (*Theogony* 73) that the taking over of the rule was not peaceful but violent.

223   Socrates is using the word for "divinely blessed" (*makarios*) since the happiness is that given by the gods. See note 62 for a discussion of this word.

and when Zeus was still newly holding the rule were living [men and they were judging] living [men], making judgments on that day in which they were about to die.[224] And so the cases were judged badly. And so Pluto and the caretakers who were from the islands of the divinely

523c   blessed went to Zeus and said that people were roaming to each of the two places and not [arriving appropriately where they] deserved. And so Zeus said, "But *I* shall stop this [from] happening. Now, you see, the cases are adjudicated badly. You see, those being judged are judged while clothed. You see, they are judged while living. And so," he said, "many who have wicked souls have been clothed in beautiful bodies and in pedigree and in wealth, and, when the decision comes, many witnesses for them come forward bearing witness that they have lived justly.

523d   And so the judges are discombobulated by these things, and, at the same time, they also, while being clothed, are making judgments—their eyes and ears and whole body having put a veil before their own soul. And all these things are in their way, both their own clothes and those of the ones being judged. And so," he said, "first we must stop their foreknowing of their death; you see, now they do foreknow [the time of their death]. And so this

523e   [order] has indeed been given to Prometheus—[that] he stop them [from knowing]. Next, they must all be judged naked: you see, it is necessary for them to be judged once they have died. And it is necessary for the judge to be naked, [and,] having died, to look immediately with his very soul on the very soul of each one who has died, [on the soul of each] who is bereft of all his relatives and [who] has left behind on the earth all his ordered beauty, so that the decision be just.[225] And so, recognizing these [facts]

---

224 It is unclear *who* are about to die— the ones being judged, the ones judging, or both.

225 We take this comment as referring to both the wealth and physical beauty of the deceased—in short, to all forms of physical splendor—for such splendor has nothing to do with the virtue of the deceased's soul. One might wonder whether some such motive also inspired nudity in the Greek games. At a certain point it became the rule that, in addition to the athletes, the trainers also had to be naked (Pausanias, *Description of Greece* 5.6.8). Plato is outdoing the Olympic rules by requiring the judges also to be naked.

before *you* have [recognized them], *I* have made my own
sons judges, two from Asia, Minos and Rhadamanthos,
and one from Europe, Aiakos.[226] And so, these, when they   524a
have died, will adjudicate on the meadow, at the place
where three roads meet, [towards which a single road
leads and] from which two roads lead away, the one to
the islands of the divinely blessed, the other to Tartarus.
And Rhadamanthos will judge those from Asia, and
Aiakos those from Europe. And to Minos I shall give
the prerogatives to make the final decision,[227] if the two
others should be in perplexity—so that the decision about
the crossing [to Tartarus or to the Islands of the divinely
blessed] may be as just as possible for people."

And these are the things, Callicles, that *I* have heard
and believe to be true. And from these words I reckon   524b
something like this to follow: death, as it seems to me,
happens to be nothing other than the separation of two
things, soul and body, one from the other. And when
they have been separated from each other, each of the two
continues its state not much less than when the person
was living, the body [having] its [same] nature and cares
and experiences—all of them evident. For example,   524c
if someone's body was big by nature or by nurture or
both while he was living, then, even when he has died,
his corpse will be big, and if [he was] fat [in life], fat in
death, and the other [qualities] in the same way. And if
in turn he was accustomed to grow hair, his corpse also
is long-haired. And if someone was a person who always
needed a whipping and had signs of blows to his body

---

226 This seems like nepotism on Zeus' part. Is it possible that Socrates is being ironic, since
he has just asked that the judges be naked and dead so that their pedigree won't interfere
with the justice of their judgments? What could be a finer pedigree than to be the sons
of Zeus? Or can it be that the rules are simply different for the sons of Zeus? And yet,
isn't such a presumption of superiority what all monarchs would declare for themselves?
Zeus' action is unquestionably undemocratic.

227 If Callicles is a stand-in for Critias, and if Rhadamanthos was the hero of Critias' play
Rhadamanthos (see Introduction, p. 14-15), and if to Plato's readers it was transparent
that Callicles was the stand-in—admittedly, a lot of if's—then there might be a dig at
Callicles in the subordinate role given Rhadamanthos. It is much to be lamented that our
actual knowledge of the era in which Plato lived is so sketchy and that remarks like this,
until more evidence is discovered, must remain in the area of speculation.

from whips or other trauma while living, so the body of this person when he has died has these marks to see. Or if his limbs were broken or deformed when he was alive,

524d   these things are the same in the dead man. And in one word, [the qualities with which] his body was equipped while it lived are clearly also those of his body when it has died, either all [the qualities] or many of them for some time. And this seems to me to be [the case] also of the soul, Callicles: when the soul has been made naked of its body, all [its qualities] are evident in the soul—both those of nature and [those that developed from] the experiences that the person had in his soul on account of his practice of each deed. And so when they arrive before the judge,

524e   those from Asia before Rhadamanthus, Rhadamanthus, after setting them near [himself], looks at the soul of each, not knowing whose soul it is, but often taking hold of the Great King [of Persia] or some other king or member of a junta he sees nothing healthy in [the individual's]

525a   soul, but [sees it] full of beatings and scars from false oaths and unjust acts, concerning which each action of [the individual] has marked his soul—all [his actions] twisted from falsehood and swaggering and nothing straight—because [this individual] was nurtured without truth; and from his actions of license and luxuriousness and hubris and lack of self-restraint [Rhadamanthus] sees his soul full of parts that don't fit together[228] and [full of] shamefulness. And upon seeing this [soul] he sends it dishonorably straight to the guardhouse where, once it comes, it will endure its appropriate sufferings.

525b   It is fitting for everyone who is being punished— rightly punished by another—either to become better and [thus] be benefited or to become a paradigm[229] for the others, so that others, seeing what a person who is

---

228   The word translated as "parts that don't fit together" is literally the word from which we derive "asymmetry."

229   The enlightened age that produced rhetoric considered examples that were adduced from reality superior to those from imagination. As a modern student of Gorgias and of rhetoric, Callicles is likely to disdain such invented paradigms as conjured by Socrates here in his myth. See the entries "experience" and "paradigm" in the Glossary.

suffering suffers and being afraid may become better.[230]
Those benefited and paying a penalty [imposed by] gods
and human beings are those who have made curable
mistakes; yet even *they* have a benefit from their pains and
sufferings, both here and in Hades.[231] You see, [it] is not
[possible] to be freed from injustice in another way. Those   525c
who should act unjustly in the most extreme [ways] and,
on account of such [extreme] injustices, would become
incurable—from these [people] come the paradigms, and
they themselves are no longer benefited at all, inasmuch
as they are incurable, but other [people] *are* benefited—
those who see these [individuals] suffering the greatest
and most painful and most fearsome sufferings for all
time on account of their mistakes, simply strung up as
perpetual paradigms there in Hades in the prison house,
visions and warnings of unjust [acts] to those who are
always arriving [there].[232]

Of these [paradigms of incurable criminals] *I* say   525d
that one will be Archelaus,[233] if Polus says the truth, and

---

230 It is of course a question how the dead can serve as an example when they are in the
underworld and those who are alive are still on earth. Dodds suggests that what may save
Plato here is his theory of reincarnation. But this solution has its own major problems:
according to Plato's *Meno* (81b–e) and *Phaedo* (75c–e), souls forget their earlier lives
when they are reborn in new human bodies, and so they could not share the rehabilitative
benefits of their suffering and serve as examples; in addition, the so-called theory of
reincarnation may not be intended as serious by Plato (see, for example, W.S. Cobb,
"Anamnesis: Platonic Doctrine or Sophistic Absurdity?" *Dialogue* 12 (1973)604–28);
and, finally, reincarnation is nowhere mentioned in the myth that Socrates tells here in
the *Gorgias.* Perhaps Plato, though speaking of the underworld, has some sort of view like
that of Lucretius (*On the Nature of Things* 3.978–1023), that the afterlife is experienced
now, that the sufferings attributed to the afterlife are variant versions of the punishments
we suffer in this life. Or, of course—and this seems most likely—Socrates may simply
be pulling Callicles' chain. It is a mistake to twist consistency out of Plato's dialogues:
Plato does not produce an organized, systematic philosophy, as some later thinkers try
to do, but Plato produces a series of separate dialogues, each with its own point and each,
perhaps, intended for a different audience.

231 Plato's underworld thus becomes a type of Purgatory, where sins are cleansed.

232 One might wonder how those who are arriving in Hades, already having committed
irredeemable wrongs, can benefit from the example of these sufferers. Only those who
hear about the sufferers, say, from a person like Er, who comes back from the dead at the
end of the *Republic,* or from Dante, after he has returned from his tour of the afterlife,
could possibly benefit.

233 On Archelaus, see n. 61.

another— whoever might be such a tyrant. And I think that many of these paradigms are from tyrants and kings and members of juntas and those who've managed the [affairs] of the poleis. You see, they err the greatest and most unholy errors on account of the license [they enjoy].²³⁴ Even Homer is a witness to these things; you

525e   see, he has made kings and members of juntas the ones punished forever in Hades—Tantalus and Sisyphus and Tityus. But Thersites²³⁵ and any other wicked person who was a private citizen—no one has made *him* afflicted with great punishments as though [he were] incurable—you see, I think, it wasn't possible for [Thersites to make the greatest mistakes]; and therefore he was happier than those for whom it was possible. But, you see, Callicles,

526a   it's from the powerful that the exceedingly wicked people come; and even among these there is nothing that hinders good men from arising, and, of course, [one] of those [powerful persons] who becomes [good] is exceedingly deserving of admiration. You see, Callicles, it is a difficult thing, and worthy of much praise, for someone who has great license to act unjustly to live his life through with justice. But a few *do* become such—since both here and there they *have* come into being—and I think also that they *will* in the future too—noble and good men with

526b   respect to that excellence of justly taking in hand the things that someone would turn over [to them]. And one who was very esteemed [by the Athenians] and also by the other Greeks was Aristides, the son of Lysimachos. But, best man, many of the members of juntas have become evil.

---

234 We are trying, not very successfully, to capture a jingle. The sense is "they make the greatest mistakes" but the verb "to make a mistake" has as its direct object a substantival form of the verb. "To err an error" strains English idiom. An alternative, "to sin a sin" is better English but introduces a religious element not present in the Greek.

235 Thersites, Homer says, was the ugliest man at Troy, deformed and unpleasant, who tried to make himself amusing to the warriors. He was hated by both Achilles and Odysseus (*Iliad* 2.217–220). And yet, when he scolds Agamemnon (*Iliad* 2.225–42), he is, as Homer points out, voicing what the Greeks are inwardly thinking.

And so, the very thing that I was saying, when that Rhadamanthus takes someone like this, he knows nothing else at all about him, not who he is nor from what [family], than that he is someone wicked. And after sizing up this person he sends him to Tartarus, putting a sign [on him showing] whether he seems curable or incurable. And the person sent to Tartarus, arriving there, suffers   526c
the appropriate [punishments]. And sometimes, looking on another [soul] that has lived in a holy way and with truth, [the soul of] a private man or of someone else— especially, I say, of course, Callicles, of a philosopher [who] in his life [had] done his own things and had not had his hand in everything²³⁶—[the judge] admires [him] and sends him to the islands of the divinely blessed. And Aeacus [does] these same things—each of these [two judges] makes his judgment while holding a staff. But Minos sits as the overseer, alone holding a golden scepter,   526d
as Homer's Odysseus says that he saw him

Holding a golden scepter, making judgments on the dead.²³⁷

And so, Callicles, I have been persuaded by these accounts, and I look for how I shall present my soul to the judge as healthy as possible. And so, bidding farewell to the honors of the many, I, looking for²³⁸ the truth, shall in reality try [to see] how I might have the power to live as good a man as possible, and [so] to die, when I die. And I call on all   526e
other people, and I summon you especially, as far as I have the power, to this life and this contest, which I say is opposed to all the contests here,²³⁹ and I reproach you because you won't be able to help yourself when you have the trial and the decision that I was just speaking about;

236 Socrates seems to approve of minding one's own business—a euphemism for staying out of public affairs—in the Republic (433a). The opposite view—that an interest in all things human justifies snooping into a neighbor's business—is wittily asserted in Terence's comedy, The Self-Tormentor (1.1.25).

237 Odyssey 11.569.

238 An alternative text would read, instead of "looking for truth," "practicing the truth."

239 Perhaps Socrates means that the kind of life he advocates is quite different from the kind usually struggled for.

527a   but upon going to that judge, the son of Aegina,[240] when he takes hold of you and leads [you], *you* will gape and *you* will be dizzy there no less than *I* here, and perhaps someone will punch you in your face dishonorably and treat *you* shabbily in every way.

And so, perhaps these things will seem to you to be spoken as a tale, an old lady's [tale], and you will look down on these things, and, in fact, it would be nothing wondrous to despise these things, if, as we searched, we'd somehow be able to find things better and truer than these. And now you see that you, being three, who are

527b   the wisest of the Greeks of today—you and Polus and Gorgias—are not able to show how it is necessary to live some other life than this one, a life that appears to be beneficial even there [in the world after death]. But among such arguments, while the other ones are refuted, this argument alone holds its ground, that acting unjustly is to be avoided more than being treated unjustly, and altogether a man must take care not to seem but to be good, both in private and public; and if someone in some way becomes bad, he must be punished, and this good [takes] second [place] after being just—to become [just]

527c   and, while being punished, to pay a penalty. And all pandering both for oneself and for others, both for few and for many, must be avoided. And rhetoric, and every other action, must be used always for what is just.

And so, persuaded by me, follow [me] there, where, when you have arrived, you will be happy both living and dying, as the argument shows. And allow someone to look down on you as a mindless person and treat you shabbily, if he wishes, and yes, by Zeus, *you*, confidently

527d   [allow someone] to strike you with this dishonorable blow; you see, you will experience nothing terrible, if you are in reality noble and good, a person practicing

---

240   Why does Plato have Socrates mention Aeacus' mother Aegina, after whom the island is named? Perhaps Socrates wishes to annoy Callicles by the mention of this island, which was a traditional enemy of Athens. The rest of this sentence is also not likely to win over Callicles.

excellence. And then, when we have practiced [excellence] in common in this way—*then*, if it should seem useful, we shall in turn apply ourselves to political matters, or *then* we shall deliberate about the sort of thing that seems good to us, since we'll be better at deliberating than we are now. You see, it is shameful that, being [what] we now appear to be, we would then act like brassy teenagers, as [though] we were something [important]—we who never have the same impressions about the same things—and these are about the greatest matters; to such a degree of ineducation   527e
have we come. And so, let us use the argument as our guiding authority, the one that now discloses itself, which shows to us that this is the best way of life, to live and die practicing both justice and the rest of excellence. And so let us follow this and call on others to do so too, and [let us not follow] that way that you believe and call on me to follow—you see, *it* is worth *nothing*, Callicles.

Appendix A

Speeches from Thucydides' *History of the Peloponnesian Wars* that Reflect Themes of Plato's *Gorgias*

Thucydides (c. 460–400), author of *The History of the Peloponnesian Wars,* writes in a genre that he intends to be factual, not fictional. Thucydides is full of facts, and his "theory"—if he has one—is not easy to discern. Unlike those historians for whom a theory of history is the major preoccupation, Thucydides submits himself to his data and tries to record and observe them. If he has a focus, it is on the mechanisms of power and war as they affect poleis and the individuals who inhabit them.

Thucydides seems also to have no explicit theory of human nature—except to assume that it will not change. Nor has he an explicit formula for human motivation. For Thucydides, human beings are not merely symptoms of historical forces; instead, human beings are themselves "forces." As a result, Thucydides fills his book with characters who make speeches as well as do deeds; indeed, for many their speeches *are* their deeds.

Thucydides is interested in the laws that govern human beings when they act collectively, and for him the job of the historian is to trace this movement, this process, in groups of men. In the story of Athens, its rise and fall, Thucydides had a perfect paradigm of social growth. Other states have been larger, but in their very largeness lurked a complexity that defies analysis—such as the causes of the rise and downfall of Egyptian civilization. But in Athens Thucydides has a specimen like that which a scientist puts under a microscope. Unlike those scientists who, to see a very small object, must use an electron-microscope, which kills the specimen and lets them see it only as dead, Thucydides uses an electron-microscope that enlarges and vivifies. He sees not a dead specimen, but one engaged in dying, a whole culture committing suicide.

The speeches presented here portray that cultural suicide. Its origins lie perhaps in the not quite worthy social values that inform the Athenian Empire as those values are revealed in the first speeches presented, of the Athenian travelers and of Pericles. The next speeches, those of Cleon and Diodotus, show the abandonment of even a pretense of honor as the arguments are framed on expediency alone. The Melian Dialogue shows the Athenians as interested in power alone for its own sake, with even expedience minimized. And the last speech in this collection, that of Alcibiades to the Spartans, shows how handily a clever speaker who is concerned only for his own power can make a plausible case for betraying his own polis to her mortal enemy. All the amoral powers Gorgias and Polus claim for rhetoric are present in Alcibiades' words. Is it any wonder that Athenian disfavor fell on Alcibiades' mentor—Socrates?

The *Gorgias* is the dialogue of Plato most concerned with the real world of politics, a world that includes both the destructive struggle for power in political communities and the even more destructive struggle for power among different political communities. "War," the first word of the dialogue, is one kind of such struggle and metaphorically anticipates the various kinds of struggle that will be portrayed in the dialogue. The practical, political character of the *Gorgias* is reflected in its scrutiny and assessment of the greatest practical leaders of Athens' golden age—Miltiades, Themistocles, Aristides, Pericles, Nicias, and Alcibiades—men whose careers shape Athens from the rise of her empire as a consequence of her supremacy in the Persian Wars to the fall of that empire as a consequence of her losses in the Peloponnesian War.

The Peloponnesian War is the dramatic backdrop to many of the Platonic dialogues, and it is so in the case of the *Gorgias*, a dialogue that, since it deals with the nature and power of rhetoric, naturally keeps coming back to matters relating to the war, in which rhetoric and its ability to shape political power figure critically. The dialogue refers directly or indirectly to many events that occurred during the twenty-seven year conflict, making it impossible to establish a precise dramatic date.[1] This chronological ambiguity has the effect of making the conversation, which could have lasted no more than a few hours, seem to take place over the whole period of the war. The character of Callicles perhaps reflects Athens over the course of the war. At the beginning of the dialogue a charming, civilized individual, by the end he expresses views incompatible with civic life and makes claims nearly identical to those of the unnamed representatives of Athens in the Melian Dialogue, the section of Thucydides' *Peloponnesian Wars* acclaimed for its frank portrayal of *realpolitik*. In Callicles Plato has shown us in microcosm what Athens became as a result of her involvement in the war.

To help understand Plato's *Gorgias*, with its frequent references to Athenian politics before and during the Peloponnesian War, we have thought it desirable to review briefly Thucydides' history of the war, our main extant account of most of the period that the dialogue subsumes. Since many of the speeches of the participants in the Thucydides' history echo and elaborate the arguments in the Platonic dialogue, not as they were found in the relatively civil setting of Callicles' house but in the hurly-burly world of political assembly, we have included translations of several of the key speeches here.

---

1   See Introduction, p. 13-14.

1. Speech of the Athenian Travelers to the Spartan Assembly (1.72–78)

Thucydides distinguishes between the "truest cause" for the war—which he says was also the "most unnoticed in speech"—and the "openly spoken-of causes." The truest cause was that "the Athenians were becoming great, and the fear [they thus] provided the Lacedaemonians" (1.23.6; 1.88). The openly avowed causes were events that took place in remote and insignificant places, events that excited brewing tensions among the Greek poleis. These events involved Athens and Corinth, an important ally of Sparta. Corinth sent an embassy to Sparta calling for a declaration of war against Athens. When the Corinthian ambassadors arrived, there happened to be in Sparta an embassy from Athens that had come on other business. The Athenians requested permission to address the Spartan assembly in reply to the speech of the Corinthians. Thucydides says that the Athenians wished "to show the Spartans that it was necessary to deliberate about all this matter not quickly," and "to show by signs how great their polis was in power" (1.72). To accomplish these purposes, the Athenians recount the development of the Athenian Empire, explaining the motives that led Athens to acquire its empire—a complicated mixture of fear, honor, and interest.

And so, upon coming before the Lacedaemonians, [the Athenians]   1.72.2
said that they also wished to speak to the multitude of them, unless
something should prevent [it]. And the [Lacedaemonians] bid them
come forward, and the Athenians, coming up, spoke the following:

We have not embarked on our embassy to respond to your allies,   1.73.1
but to discuss what our polis has sent us [to discuss]. And [though]
we have perceived no small outcry against us, we have come not
intending to refute the accusations of the [other] poleis—you see,
neither our arguments nor those [which they have spoken] should be
made for you as jurors[2]—but so that you will not easily be persuaded
about great matters by [your] allies] and plan a worse [course];[3]
and, at the same time, [we have come] wishing to show, concerning

---

2   The speaker is saying that he will present a deliberative rather than a forensic speech.
Aristotle divides the separate types of oratory speeches into forensic—those that deal
with the past and take place in the courtroom—and deliberative—those that deal with
the future and take place in assemblies (See *Gorgias*, note 2). The enemies of Athens,
the present speaker is suggesting, have made a speech suitable for the law courts; the
Athenian claims that he will respond with a speech suitable for a legislative assembly.

3   This is a sophist-inspired remark. Gorgias claims that a rhetorician can be more persuasive
about medicine than a trained physician (456b). Socrates, like the sophists, was accused of
making the worse argument the stronger (*Apology* 19b.) Here the Corinthians are accused
of making the worse argument, and the Spartans are warned not to be persuaded by it.

the whole argument that has been made against us, that we do not inappropriately possess what we have acquired and that our polis

1.73.2   is [indeed] worthy of account. And why is it necessary to speak of matters of times long gone by, the witnesses of which [are] more the sounds of stories than [an actual] view of the things that will be heard about?[4] Concerning the Median Affairs[5]—that is, concerning the many things that you yourselves know—even if [these things] will be annoying to those pelted over and over again by them, it is necessary to tell [them again]; you see, when we were acting, there was a danger in [bringing about] the benefit—[a benefit] in which you shared a part of the result— and let us not be deprived [of the benefit] of the whole account, if there is some benefit [to be had].[6]

1.73.3   And the story [of what we did] will be told not more for the sake of laying blame than [for the sake] of a witness and a demonstration of the sort of polis against which you will be beginning a contest, if you don't plan well. You see, we say that at Marathon we alone took a risk before the barbarian and that when he came later—since we were not adequate to ward him off by land—we boarded our ships with [our] whole people and fought a sea-battle together at Salamis—[a battle] that kept him ([as he] was sailing) from destroying the Peloponnese city by city, [and his sailing] would have produced a situation [in which the Peloponnesians] would not have had the power to help each other against [his] many ships. And [the barbarian] himself produced the greatest evidence [of the claim we make on behalf of our polis]: you see, when he was defeated by our ships, as though he no longer had a power that was a match [for us], he quickly withdrew with the major [part] of his army.

---

4   The language of oratory is continuing here. The Athenian suggests that though he will give a speech about what needs to be done in the future—the subject matter of deliberative oratory—it is nevertheless necessary to understand what was done in the past—the appropriate subject matter of forensic.

5   These are the Persian Wars. Though Herodotus explained at length (1.123–130) how the Persians under Cyrus took over the empire of the Medes, to the Greeks the Medes and Persians were indistinguishable. An analogy would be American references during the Cold War to all members of the Soviet Union as Russians, though to the separate peoples of the Soviet Union it was quite important whether they were Georgian or Ukrainian or Chechnyan or Russian.

6   The speaker here may be drawing a contrast of part and whole. In addition, he is cleverly minimizing how much he will talk about his polis, though this minimizing is achieved by the violated logic of the sentence. The contrast he draws between the two parties is not entirely what would be expected. We would expect, "And you shared in the benefit of the war, and we had a share, too." Instead, the logic is: "You had a share, and we should not be deprived of our share."

And certainly, when this occurred, and when it was clearly shown that 1.74.1
the affairs of the Greeks depended on ships, we provided the three
most beneficial things for this [effort]—a very large number of ships,
a very clever man as general, and a most tireless zeal. Concerning the
four hundred ships, in fact, [we provided] a little less than two thirds
of them, and [we provided] Themistocles as archon, [and he was
the person] most responsible for the sea-battle's taking place in the
narrows— a [circumstance] that clearly saved the business, and on
account of this [result] you yourselves honored him—a foreigner —
most of those who visited you. And we also showed the most daring 1.74.2
zeal, we who— when, in fact, no one came to help us by land, the
other [poleis] up to [ours] having already submitted to slavery—left
our city behind and destroyed our domestic [possessions], deeming
it right neither to abandon the common [cause] of the surviving
allies nor to become useless runaways to them; but we boarded the
ships to face the risks and did not become angry because you were
not helping [us] at first.[7] So we say that we conferred benefit on you 1.74.3
no less than we obtained it.[8] *You,* you see, from inhabited cities and
for [the purpose of] dwelling [in them] in the future, when for the
most part you feared for *yourselves* and not for *us,* [only then] did
you come to help; at any rate, when we were still safe, you were *not*
by our side, but *we,* setting out from a [polis] that no longer existed
and taking on risks on behalf of [a polis] existing [only] in slight
hope, we saved the day for you and for ourselves. But if [at first], like 1.74.4
others, being afraid for our land, we had made an approach to the
Median [enemy], or [if] later, as though [we were already] entirely
destroyed, we had not dared to board our ships, it would have been
necessary for you, since you didn't have enough ships, not to fight
a sea battle, but the business would have advanced calmly for [the
Mede] in the way he had planned.

Then, Spartans, because of our zeal and the intelligence of our resolve 1.75.1
at that time, do we deserve to be overly resented by the Greeks because

---

7   Note how crassly the Athenian speaker praises Athens for her goodness in the face of
     the allies' lack of help and how he also praises Athenian steadfastness even while the
     other Greeks were submitting to slavery as subjects of Persia. One might wonder whether
     such self-praise and such candid criticism is likely to win over the audience. It is not
     difficult, as Socrates says, to praise Athenians to Athenians. But it is a rule of rhetoric
     that a speaker not alienate his audience. The Athenian, however, may be speaking in
     this way deliberately, as a display of Athens' power. Thucydides, an any rate, says that it
     was in order to display the power of Athens that the Athenians came before the Spartan
     assembly (1.72).

8   The phrasing is such as to leave vague the benefit Athens received. .

1.75.2   of the empire that we have taken possession of? You see, we did not take it by being violent, but [we took possession of it] when you were unwilling to remain [to fight the] remnants of the barbarian [force],

1.75.3   [and] the allies came to us needing [us] to stand as leader. And out of this work we were compelled first to bring [our empire] forward to this [present situation], mostly because of fear, and then because

1.75.4   of honor, and later also because of benefit [to us]. And then it didn't seem safe [for us] to run the risk of letting [the empire go] when [we were] hated by many and when some [of our allies] rebelled and were suppressed and when you were no longer friendly to us in the same way but were suspicious and at odds [with us]. You see,

1.75.5   those who were revolting would have been on your side. And it is a blameless thing for all, in matters of the greatest dangers, to manage [their affairs] well [so that they come out] advantageously.

1.76.1   At any rate, Lacedaemonians, *you* rule the poleis in the Peloponnese, having set them up as a benefit to you; and if, standing your ground through everything, you then became hateful in your leadership, we know well that you, no less [than we], would have become grievous to [your] allies and have been compelled either to rule strongly or to

1.76.2   run risks for yourselves. Thus, we have done nothing at all wondrous or apart from the human way, if we received an empire that was given [to us] and did not let it go, being conquered by the [three] biggest [motives]—honor, fear, and benefit—nor again were we the first to have acted so, but [we acted in conformity with] the established [practice] that the lesser is kept in check by the more powerful, and at the same time we were thinking that [we] were right [to do so] and [we were] seeming [so] also to you, until you, making a calculation of what is advantageous, began to use the justice-argument—[an argument] that no one ever [paid any attention to] when it lay in his

1.76.3   power to obtain something by strength. And worthy to be praised [are] any who, having exercised human nature to rule others, act more justly than their underlying power [would allow them to act].

1.76.4   And so we think that others, if they were in our situation, would show especially how moderate *we* are. But from [our] goodness a bad reputation, more than praise, has unfairly embraced us.

1.77.1   You see, even [though] we suffer loss in contract trials with our allies, and [even though] we have made the trials [to be conducted] with impartial laws in our own [polis], we have the reputation of

1.77.2   loving to go to court. And no one looks at those who have an empire somewhere else and are less moderate than we towards their subjects [and asks] why [their lesser moderation] is not blamed. You see,

those who have a license to use force don't need to go to trial. But, 1.77.3
accustomed to associate with us on an equal [basis] our allies—if, a
bit contrary [to what] they think necessary, they somehow suffer a
loss either [because of] a judgment or [because of the] power [that
we exercise] on account of the empire—do not feel gratitude [about]
not being deprived of [even] more, but [instead] bear their loss
[with] more difficulty than if from the first we had put aside the law
and were openly making a grab. And [if we had behaved] in that way,
they would not at all have protested, [saying] that it was not necessary
for the lesser to be under the one who is stronger. People [who] are 1.77.4
being treated unjustly, it seems, are angrier than those treated with
violence; you see, one thing seems to be a greedy grab by an equal,
but the other thing seems to be a matter of being compelled by a
stronger. At any rate, those who suffered more terrible things from 1.77.5
the Mede [than they have from us] endured those things, but our
empire seems harsh—in all likelihood. You see, the present situation
always weighs on the subjects. And so, of course, if you destroyed 1.77.6
us and ruled [our empire], you would quickly alter the good will
you received because of the fear of us; [and] if indeed you exhibited
the sort of things you showed then, when you led [the Greeks] for
a short time against the Mede, you also would then know similar
[reactions to those we know]. You see, you have for yourselves legal
arrangements that don't mix with other people and, in addition,
when each [of you] goes out [of your polis] you use neither those
[laws] nor those the rest of the Greek world observes.

And so deliberate slowly as [though you were deliberating] not 1.78.1
about small [matters], and do not be persuaded by others' judgments
and accusations and [thus] assume trouble for yourselves. And
understand ahead of time, before it comes to pass, how great is the
miscalculation of war. You see, as it is expanded,[9] it loves to place 1.78.2
luck around many things, [around things] from which we are equally
distant, and [around things] in which the risk for each of the two of
us is unclear. And people, when they are going to war, do first— 1.78.3
[fight]—what they ought to do later, and [only] when they have
already suffered do they take hold of arguments [—which is what
they ought to do first]. But since as yet [we see] neither ourselves nor 1.78.4
you making this mistake, *we* say to you, while we both still can freely

---

9   What is being expanded is ambiguous. Virtually all translators think it is the war and
     that as war expands, it involves more and more luck. Another possibility is that it is
     miscalculation that, as it is expanded, loves to attribute things to chance. Either way, the
     subject—war or miscalculation—is being personified.

choose goodwill, not to dissolve the treaty nor to transgress oaths, but to resolve our disagreements by adjudication according to our contract. If [you do] not, making the gods witnesses of our oaths, we shall try to ward off those who start a war [in whatever way] you would begin [it]."[10]

2. Pericles' Funeral Oration (2.34–46)

After hearing from both sides, Sparta voted to go to war against Athens, but, in true Spartan fashion, to do so gradually, only after gathering all her own and her allies' forces. She sent envoys to negotiate with Athens, in the hope that Athens would back down in the looming confrontation. Pericles, the principal leader in Athens at this time, counseled his fellow citizens to refuse to give in, claiming that giving in would lead only to more demands. At the same time, he proposed a naval strategy that would enable Athens—the greatest sea power of the Greek world—to defeat Sparta—the greatest land power. Pericles, recognizing the proportional asymmetry in the two poleis' powers and envisioning a long war, warned Athens that to win she would have to refrain from attempting to extend her empire (1.144). When the war finally did begin, the Spartans acted exactly as Pericles had foreseen they would: they invaded and ravaged Attica, trying to lure the Athenians out of the walls of their city to engage them in a land battle. The Athenians, instead, sent out naval expeditions. In Pericles' Funeral Oration, which is presented here, Thucydides puts into the Athenian leader's voice an explanation of why those who died in the first year of the war did not die in vain.

2.34.1   In this winter, Athenians, employing their ancestral custom, publicly made a funeral for those who were first to die in this war, doing so

2.34.2   in the following way. After [the Athenians] made a tent, the bones of those who have died are laid out for three successive days, and each

2.34.3   [mourner] brings to his own [family member] what he wishes. And when the funeral [takes place], wagons carry the cypress coffins— one for each tribe—and the bones of each man are [in the coffin] of his tribe. And for those who are missing—who are not found for

2.34.4   burial—one empty bier that has been prepared is brought. And [any] man of citizens and foreigners [who] wishes joins in the funeral, and

2.34.5   women who are related are present wailing at the tomb. And so they put [these coffins] into the public tomb, which is in the most beautiful suburb of the polis, and they always bury in [this tomb] those [killed]

---

10   This is the speaker's shift from the third to the second person (from *those* to *you*). On such shifts in person see *Gorgias*, note 56.

in the wars, except of course those [whom they buried] at Marathon; judging *their* virtue to be preeminent [the Athenians] made [their] tomb there [at Marathon]). And when [the fallen soldiers] lie hidden   2.34.6 in the earth, a man chosen by the polis, who seems not to be unwise in [his] judgment and [who] is suitable in [his] worthiness, speaks over them a praise [that is] fitting. And after this they go away. Thus   2.34.7 do they bury; and through the whole war, whenever it fell to their lot, [the Athenians] used the custom. And so, for these first ones [who   2.34.8 fell], Pericles son of Xanthippus was chosen to speak. And when the right moment came,[11] going forward from the tomb to a high altar that had been made—that he might be heard as well as possible by the crowd—he spoke the following:

Many of those who have previously spoken here praise the man   2.35.1 who established the custom of this oration, how a fine thing it is that [the oration] be spoken for those buried from the wars. But to me it seemed to be enough that when men have become good by deed, by deed also their honors be shown—the sort of things you see even now around this tomb that has been publicly provided—and that the credibility of the virtues of many not be risked by one man's speaking both well and worse.[12] You see, speaking in a measured way   2.35.2 is difficult[13] on [a matter] in which the appearance of truth is scarcely established. You see, the hearer who both knows [what happened] and is well-minded [towards the dead] would quickly consider something to have been set forth rather deficiently in comparison with what he wishes [to hear] and knows [to have happened], and the one who is inexperienced [would consider what is said] to be made

---

11   Literally, "when the right moment seized [him]." It is hard to tell where personification begins and psychology ends. Perhaps the Greeks had a sense that the moment was what was in control. We use idioms for external psychic causality in modern English too, as in our expressions, "An idea came to me" or "I was struck by a thought."

12   The Greek has the word "and" where we might expect "or." Perhaps Pericles (or Thucydides) means just what the text says: that the credibility depends on the speaker, who sometimes will speak better, sometimes worse. This distinction between "the many" and "the one" is a motif in ancient literature: the one always is superior to the many (see *Gorgias* note 188), except here in Pericles' neatly rhetorical inversion.

13   The speaker here seems to be trying to lower his audience's expectations. A speaker makes this sort of comment in a prepared address only when he knows that he will be able to overcome the presumed difficulty.

too much of, resenting [the praise of the dead],[14] if he should hear something beyond his own nature. You see, praises spoken about others are endurable up to this point: to the extent to which each thinks himself capable of doing something of the things he has heard; but [people] begrudge the one surpassing [achievements of their level] and are unbelieving [concerning another's accomplishments].

2.35.3   But since it seemed to those [who lived] long ago that it is a noble thing for this [oration to take place], it is necessary for me, following the custom, to fulfill the wish and expectation of each of you to the greatest degree possible.

2.36.1   I shall begin with the ancestors first. You see, it is just and at the same time fitting that in the following [remarks] this honor of remembrance be given to them. You see, always inhabiting this land, they passed it free to a succession of descendents up to this [time]

2.36.2   thanks to [their] virtue. They are worthy of praise, and still more are our fathers: you see, in addition to what they received, they acquired as much empire as we have [today]—not without effort—[and then]

2.36.3   they left [it] to us, the present [generation]. And *we* ourselves who are still living now—especially we who are in the established part of our life[15]—have for the most part, expanded [our empire] and have in all ways prepared the polis to be most self-sufficient both for war

2.36.4   and for peace. As for the deeds of these [earlier individuals] in war, by which each [of these things] was acquired, if either we ourselves or our fathers zealously warded off the barbarian or a Greek who was attacking in war, *I* shall let [these things] go, not wishing to draw out a speech among those who know [what happened]. But from what sort of [cultural] practice we have come to these [circumstances] and with what sort of civil society and from what sort of ways it has become great—after showing these [things] first, I shall go on to the praise of these men, thinking [the praise] that is spoken would

---

14   The word translated "resent" [*phthonos*] is often translated as *envy*, but the Greek word indicates something different from envy. *Envy* is wanting what another person has; *resentment* is the pain one feels at another's deserved success and is sometimes accompanied by *begrudging*. I may envy my neighbor his car: I want *that* particular car as my own. I may resent his success in growing roses: I feel pain at the beauty of his roses. I may begrudge him success in growing roses: I can't grow roses, and so I don't want him, or anyone else, to be able to grow them either. In the present instance, Pericles is suggesting that the pain a member of the audience may feel at the praise given to the fallen soldiers may be accompanied by begrudging: if a member of the audience does not have the ability to perform a heroic deed, he begrudges this ability to everyone else too. On "resentment" and related terms, see the Glossary under "Resentment."

15   This would be between ages forty and sixty.

not to be unfitting and that it would be advantageous in the present [situation] for the whole crowd of townsfolk and foreigners to hear.

You see, we employ a civil society that does not seek to emulate the laws of [our] neighbors,[16] but we are ourselves a paradigm to some rather than imitators of others. And as for a name [of our civil society], because our way of living[17] is not for the few but for the many, it is called a democracy; and [while] there is equality according to the laws for all in private disputes, according to the worthiness [of their particular causes], in public affairs, as each is held in good repute for something—not for the most part from rank but from virtue—he is honored, nor again is he hindered by the invisibility of his worthiness on account of poverty, if he has some good thing to do for the polis. And we engage freely in political affairs concerning what is for the common [weal]; and in the suspicion of each other's daily practices, [we are] not angry [at] our neighbor if he should do something for [his own] pleasure, and [we put] on [our] face not punitive but painful and vexing [scowls]. And while we associate without offense in private matters we do not transgress the law in public matters mostly through reverential fear[18] and in obedience to those who are currently in power and to the laws, and especially to as many of the laws as are for the benefit of those who have been treated unjustly and to as many [of the laws] that, [while] being unwritten, bring an agreed [upon] disgrace [to those who break them].   2.37.1   2.37.2   2.37.3

And truly in the interest of our mental activity we have provided very many vacations from toils by our use, throughout the year, of contests and sacrifices and attractive private buildings, the daily pleasure of which shakes off [ordinary] sorrow. And, because of our polis's greatness, all things from the whole earth come here, and it   2.38.1   2.38.2

---

16 The term *emulation* is given a brief history by Socrates in Plato's dialogue *Menexenus* (242a). Socrates says that in the life of the polis first came emulation and then begrudgement (see note 14 above), both consequent on the establishment of peace and prosperity. Once people had attained an orderly civic life, the principle of "degree" or "hierarchy" created ambition and emulation and envy. Aristotle (*Rhetoric* 1388a30) defines emulation thus: "a kind of pain at the visible existence of good things that are held in honor and that are possible for us to attain, possessed by those who are like us in nature; we feel this pain not because the other person has them but because we do not."

17 Most translators suggest that this verb here means "governing," a conclusion they reach because it makes clearer sense than "live" or "inhabit" or "dwell." But perhaps Thucydides is not speaking of government, but of the social life, which is for the many.

18 The meaning of the word that we have translated as "reverential fear" lies somewhere in between "reverence," which seems inspired by goodness, and "fear," which is an expectation of harm. While obedience to those in power and dread of disgrace support fear, obedience to laws that benefit those treated unjustly weighs the balance on the side of reverence.

happens that we don't enjoy the fruit from our own goods with a pleasure any the more familiar than [we enjoy the fruit from the goods] of other human beings.

2.39.1 And we differ from our enemies in the concerns of military matters in the following ways. You see, we offer our polis as common [to all], and there is never [a time] when, by expulsions of foreigners,[19] we keep anyone from a fact to be learned or a sight to be seen, a [fact or sight] that, unless it be hidden, someone of our enemies who saw it might be benefited, [and we do all this] trusting not in devices and deceits more than in the pluckiness we have in deeds. And in all their education, [the Lacedaemonians], when they are young, by painful exercise immediately chase after the [virtue of] manliness, but we,

2.39.2 living in a relaxed way no less go to equivalent dangers. And [here is the] evidence: you see, [the] Lacedaemonians do not campaign on our land by themselves but [do so along] with all [their allies], but we ourselves—[when we] attack the [land] of our neighbors; fighting not with difficulty against those defending their homes—for the

2.39.3 most part prevail. And no one of the enemy has yet happened upon our concentrated power, because of [our] attention to the fleet and [our] deployment of our [forces] on land to many [places]. And if somewhere they mix it up with a part [of our forces], after conquering *some* of us, they boast that *all* [of our forces] have been driven away, but when they are defeated [they boast that they] were worsted by

2.39.4 *all* [of our forces]. And if we are willing to run risks from a light heart rather than from a practice of military exercises and [if we are willing to run risks] not from laws more than from our courageous ways, it results for us not to grow weary ahead of time before future pains and, when we come to them, not to appear more spiritless than those who are always laboring hard, and in these things the city is worthy to be wondered at, and in other things as well.

2.40.1 You see, we love the beautiful with economy[20] and we love

19 This expulsion refers to a specifically Spartan practice. The xenophobic Spartans seem regularly to have engaged in the expulsion of foreigners (Xenophon, *Constitution of the Lacedaemonians* 14.4).

20 The adjective we have translated as "with economy" is one of those words for which several species exist in English for one generic word in Greek. Meanings of the Greek word run the spectrum from economy, frugal, inexpensive, to cheap, and one must rely on context for the most likely equivalent. Here, perhaps, since Pericles is complimenting Athens, parallel uses might be found in Book 8; 8.1.3, where, after the debacle in Sicily, the Athenians decide to re-organize their city on principles of economy; 8.4, where they decide to cut down on unnecessary expenses for reason of "economy"; and 8.86.6, where, for the sake of "economy," they retrench unnecessary expenses.

wisdom[21] without softness. And wealth we use more to get the work done at the critical moment than to vaunt [ourselves] in speech,[22] and it is not a shameful thing for someone to admit that he is poor, but not to escape [being poor] by work is rather ugly. And in the same people there is a care of their own and of the polis's things, and [even] to the others, [who have] devoted [themselves] to [their] works, there is not a deficient knowledge of the affairs of the polis. You see, we alone think that the individual who does not share at all in any of these [matters] is not a quiet-living person but a useless one, and we ourselves judge or at least rightly take to heart [such] matters, thinking not that speeches are harmful to works [that need to be done], but [that what is harmful is] not to be instructed ahead of time by an argument before coming to the work that is necessary to do. You see, indeed, we are different in this too: in what we are about to undertake we are daring and most of all we reason out [the project] to the fullest. To other people, ignorance [is] boldness, and calculation brings a shrinking [from activity]. But the ones who know both what is terrible and what is pleasant and who on account of these things do not turn away from dangers are justly judged strongest in soul. And with respect to the things [that aim at] excellence we have always been opposite to the many; you see, we obtain friends not by being treated well but by treating others well,[23] and surer is the one who has done the favor so as to preserve the [gratitude] owed through the good will [of the one] to whom he has given [the favor.][24] But the one who owes a favor in return is a duller

2.40.2

2.40.3

2.40.4

---

21   Pericles seems to be addressing a worry that must have been in the air in the fifth century—that philosophy and music, the softer subjects, would render a man unsuitable for the manly public life required in the polis. Plato's Callicles expresses the fear about grown men engaging in philosophy (*Gorgias* 485d), and Plato has Socrates worry about the softening effects of too much music in the *Republic* (410d–421a).

22   Here Pericles is including a speech-deed antithesis. In Thucydides' versions of Pericles' speeches, antitheses are quite a marked feature of the rhetor's style. Perhaps Thucydides is exaggerating what was a characteristic of Pericles' oratory even to the point of obscurity. It is possible, of course, that Pericles himself was obscure in his contrasts and that Thucydides is actually imitating this quality of obscurity. It is also possible that Thucydides intended to revise his work into greater clarity. As it is, he has produced, as well as a "possession for always" a "puzzle for always."

23   Perhaps, as for many spy movies, we are not expected to examine the logic too closely. How do the others obtain friends by being treated well? Do they seek friends by asking for favors? This certainly does not seem to be the case in international affairs. But perhaps Thucydides is portraying Pericles as subordinating meaning to the rhetoric of an antithesis, that is, meaning is less important than resplendent phrasing.

24   This is surely a calculating way to think of doing favors! This perhaps *is* closer to the way that international affairs take place than the idea just expressed, that one wins friends by letting the friends treat one well.

[friend], knowing [himself to be acting] not [to confer] a favor, but
2.40.5   to return the goodness for a benefit [that he has received]. And we
alone fearlessly benefit someone not from a calculation of advantage
more than from our confidence in freedom.[25]

2.41.1   Putting [everything] together, I say both that our whole polis is the
schooling of the Greek world and [that] it seems to me that for each
man among us there is provided a body [that is] self-sufficient for
most forms [of action] and [is filled] with most dexterous graces.[26]

2.41.2   And [to understand] how [this statement] is not a vaunt of words in
the present [occasion] rather than a truth of deeds [consider] this,[27]
[that] the polis's very power, which we have obtained from these

2.41.3   ways [of ours] shows [my statement to be true]. You see, she alone of
those [poleis that exist] now comes to a test greater than [any] report
[about her], and [our polis] alone neither is vexed with an attacking
enemy because of the sort [of men by whom] she suffers nor [is she]
blamed by a subject [because he feels that he is] not being ruled by

2.41.4   worthy [men].[28] Since we have provided, along with great signs,[29] a
not-unwitnessed power,[30] we shall be marveled at by people of the
present and future—having no need at all either of a Homer's praise,
or [of the praise of] someone who will please for the immediate
moment with his words but [then be discredited when] the truth of
[our] deeds will harm [his account], but compelling every sea and
land to be a path for our daring, as we plant everywhere everlasting

2.41.5   memorials of our evil and good deeds.[31] And so, concerning such a

---

25   Another set of antitheses. We may observe that while Pericles here denies calculation
in conferring benefits, he has just made remarks in the previous sentences replete with
calculation.

26   This is a puzzling sentence, and the reader should be warned that this particular
rendering interprets the sentence differently from other translators. We see that Pericles
as usual is drawing an antithesis, here between intellectual culture of the polis and the
physical bodies of the individual citizens. He has already spoken of how Athens is an
education for the rest of the Greek world; now he is saying that it is also responsible for
the physical excellence of its citizens (an excellence normally associated with Sparta's
intense training of its citizens). What Pericles means when he says that the Athenian
body is self-sufficient for most forms of action is that it is healthy, well-fed, and strong.

27   Another word-deed antithesis.

28   The contrasts here are triple: (1) Athens' (2) vexation at an (3) enemy; (1a) the subjects'
(2a) blame of (3a) Athens: we Athenians don't resent those who attack us because they
are not worthy; our subjects don't blame us for ruling over them because we are worthy.

29   Perhaps he has in mind the great building projects on the Acropolis.

30   This appears to be a repetition for the sake of emphasis.

31   Reading the ms. But for *kakon* perhaps we should read, as commentators suggest, *kalon*
and translate: *memorials of our evil and noble deeds*.

polis, these men met their end fighting, nobly judging [it] right not to be deprived of [their polis], and it is fitting that every man of those who are left be willing to toil on her behalf.

On account of this I have expanded on these [characteristics] of the polis, making as my lesson [the point] that for *us* the contest is not about a [matter] equal [in value for *those* to whom] none of these [characteristics] similarly applies, and, at the same time, [I have been] setting down with evidence this clear eulogy for those [for whom] I am now speaking. And the greatest [points] of the eulogy have been spoken; you see, the virtues of these men [whom we are burying] and others [like them] have adorned the polis with the qualities for which I have hymned it, and of not many Greeks would their story be in equal proportion to their deeds, as it is for these men. And the sudden destruction of these men here—first revealing and last confirming—seems to me to show the excellence of a man.[32] You see, for those who are somewhat bad in other ways it is just that their manly goodness against their enemies for the sake of their country be placed in the forefront; you see, they have benefited the common good more than they have harmed [it by] their private [deeds], making [their] bad [ways] invisible by [their] good [actions]. And of these men [I can say] that not one man of wealth has grown soft preferring its enjoyment. Nor has any poor man made a postponement of the terrible thing, from the hope that upon escaping [it] he would become rich.[33] But thinking vengeance against enemies more desirable than [wealth or escaping from poverty] and considering [vengeance] the finest of risks, they were determined, with this risk, to take vengeance and to let go of these things, trusting from hope to make the [matters that were still] invisible [come out successfully], but in the action that was already visible they were thinking it right to be confident, thinking it appropriate to engage in defense and to suffer rather than to surrender and be saved. While they ran from the shame of the *speech*, concerning their *deed*,[34] they stayed [at their posts] with their bodies, and through the briefest moment's chance, at the height of their reputation rather than [at the height] of fear, they departed.

2.42.1

2.42.2

2.42.3

2.42.4

---

32   Perhaps Pericles means that for the young men dying, the fight was the first chance they had to show their excellence; how a man faces death is the truest indicator of his virtue.

33   A rich-poor antithesis.

34   The phrase here seems to have a double contrast: the antithesis of running away in battle and sticking to one's post and the antithesis of word and deed.

2.43.1   And these men were as befits such a city; and it is necessary for the survivors to pray to be worthy of having a cast of mind that, while safer, is in no way more cowardly towards our enemies, looking at the benefit not in words alone—[a benefit] that someone might explain at length to you [who] know [it] no worse [than I do], saying how many good things there are in warding off the enemy—but rather seeing the polis's power daily in actions and becoming its ardent lovers and, whenever [the polis] seems great to you, taking to heart that men [who] were daring and knew what things are necessary [to do], even when they had felt shame in their [private] actions, obtained these [benefits], and whenever, even in an attempt, they failed, not on that account did they think it right to deprive the polis of their virtue, but [they] bestowed their most lovely service

2.43.2   on it.[35] You see, those who for the common [good] gave their living bodies, for their [own] private [good] have gotten the praise that is ageless and the tomb that is most notable[36]—not [the literal tomb] in which they are lying, but rather [that figurative tomb] [in which], for [whoever] happens [to pass] by [it], their reputation for word and deed in the critical moment is left always to be remembered.

2.43.3   You see, the whole earth is a tomb of famous men, and the writing on the tombstone not only in [one's own land] stands as a sign, but also an unwritten memorial for each—of his judgment even more than of his deed— stays in the open air in the unrelated [lands of

2.43.4   the earth].[37] Now emulating these men, *you,* judging the happy [to be] the free and the free [to be those with] a stout heart, do not

2.43.5   overlook the dangers of war. You see, the men who fare ill [in their enterprises] would not [be the ones] who are rather justly careless of [their] life—[I speak of] men to whom there is no expectation of good— but [the ones who are rather justly careless of their life are] those to whom a change of fortune to the opposite [of that] in which they live is still a risk and whose [circumstances], if they make

---

35   Pericles' point here—a strange one, perhaps, for a funeral oration—is that even deeply flawed men are redeemed by service to the state.

36   This sentence has notable contrasts: common good and private good, word and deed, literal tomb and figurative tomb. For Pericles, what is more important is the figurative tomb.

37   We interpret the unwritten memorial as celebrating the judgment of the soldiers about dying for Athens rather than preserving their wealth or escaping poverty. Even if a particular soldier died in the first instance of battle, without having accomplished anything of note, he would still deserve the remembrance for having made the right decision to fight for Athens. This sentence too has notable contrasts: one's own land, and unrelated land, written and unwritten, judgment and deed.

some misstep, [would] differ very greatly.[38] You see, to a man who   2.43.6
has sense, of course, mistreatment associated with being soft is more
painful than an unperceived death[39] that comes with strength and a
common hope.

Therefore, even now, I do not wail with as many of you who are   2.44.1
present as the parents of these men, but rather I shall offer [you]
condolence.[40] You see, parents know that they rear [sons] among
varied misfortunes; but the fortunate thing [for sons would be to]
take hold of a most fitting end, as *these* men [have] now [done]
[and the fortunate thing for parents would be to take hold of a
most fitting] grief, as *you* [have done],[41] you for whom life has been
equally measured out both to be happy in and to end.[42] And so I   2.44.2
know that it is difficult to persuade [you about these fallen men],
about whom you will often have reminders in the fortunate times
of others, [the sort of times] in which you yourselves once rejoiced,

---

38   Perhaps the sentence would make more sense if Thucydides had written, "You see, the
men who fare ill [in their enterprises] would not [be the ones] who are regarded as rather
more justly careless of [their] life—[I speak of] men to whom there is no expectation of
good— but [the ones who are regarded as rather justly careless of their life are] those to
whom a change of fortune to the opposite [of that] in which they live is still at risk and
[the ones] whose [circumstances], if they make some misstep, [would] [43.6] differ very
greatly."

39   The phrase "unperceived death" contains the only use of the word "death" in the Funeral
Oration. At other points in the speech, Pericles employs circumlocutions to refer to the
death of the men he is honoring, as at 2.41, where he refers to them as having "met their
end fighting," or as at 2.44, where he refers to them as having taken hold of "a most
fitting end." Here he softens death by describing it as "unperceived"—a claim that could
hardly seem to be the case for the men who died in brutal hand-to-hand combat.

   The palliation of death is, perhaps, consistent with the purpose of the rhetoric in
the speech—to motivate the Athenians to sacrifice everything, including their lives, if
necessary, in service to their polis. In return for this sacrifice, Pericles promises that
Athens will give the people what they most yearn for: the immortality of everlasting
remembrance. Athens can give its citizens this prize only if she herself is eternal. And
such an eternity can be achieved only if the gods (whom Pericles does not invoke in
the speech) and nature, with its eternal cycle of birth, growth, decay, and death, refrain
from bringing her to destruction. While Pericles does not deny the existence of such
transcendent powers, his rhetoric tries to induce the Athenians to forget about them for
a while.

40   Another Periclean contrast.

41   The part of this sentence that begins "the fortunate thing" is unclear in the Greek. Whose
fortunate thing is Pericles speaking about? We take the antecedent to be the sons implied
in the previous clause; that is, we take the implied antecedent of the previous clause as
the antecedent here.

42   The last clause seems to mean that the parents of the dead should rejoice in the time that
their sons were alive, which was a happy time, until it ended with their death.

too. And grief [is] not [felt] for those goods [that] someone is deprived of not having experienced them, but for that [of which
2.44.3   one] is deprived after having become accustomed to it.[43] But it is necessary for those who are still of an age to become parents to be strong also in the hope of other children. You see, [in your lives as] private [citizens] those [children] who are born will be a forgetting of those who no longer exist, and to the polis [those who are born] will bring benefit in two ways—both from its not being emptied and [for its] safety; you see, those who would not similarly risk staking [the lives of] their children would not equally or justly be members
2.44.4   who deliberate in the Boulé.[44] All of you, in turn, who have passed [the age of becoming parents], consider the life [in which] you had good fortune as a complete profit and [consider too] that this your life [now] will be brief and that you will [bear it] more lightly because of the good fame of these [men who have met their end]. You see, the love of honor alone is ageless, and to grow rich with profit in the useless [part] of life,[45] as some say, does not bring much pleasure, but being honored [does].

2.45.1   [2.45] And I see a great challenge, in turn, for the sons and brothers of these men, as many of you as are present. You see, everyone is accustomed to praise a man who is not living—[and so] even for the surpassing [quality] of your virtue you will scarcely be judged their equal but a little worse. You see, the living feel a resentment[46] towards their rival, but what is not in our way is honored by a
2.45.2   good will that involves no antagonism. And if I need to make some

---

43   Still another contrast.

44   The verb that we have translated as *deliberate in the Boulé* can also mean "be resolved," "deliberate," or "counsel." The Boulé is the counsel that prepared matters for action before the Assembly of all the citizens (Aristotle, *Athenian Constitution* 45.4). The idea seems to be that citizens who have children who are at stake in the war and citizens who don't have children will not deliberate with equal seriousness about the issues. Those with children might be more cautious; those without children might take more risks. *In extremis*, the tendencies might be reversed. Perhaps there is a criticism implied of those who don't have children. This view is in sharp contrast to that of the modern West, where today we consider the matter of having children to be private and not one that much concerns the state. In some ancient religions, celibacy was celebrated, but by the principle enunciated here, celibacy would be very much antithetical to a political community. In this section of his speech, Pericles is offering condolence to the parents of fallen sons. Perhaps the condolence comes from recalling that in the polis the family exists for the sake of the polis and that children exist primarily for the good of the polis.

45   Pericles seems to be referring to the age at which one is past having children and thus can no longer usefully provide children to the polis. Earlier (2.36.3) he had spoken of the "established part of life."

46   On "resentment" see the Glossary.

mention of a woman's excellence—for as many women as now will be in widowhood—I shall indicate everything in a brief advice.[47] You see, you will have a great reputation if you do not become worse than your underlying nature, [and she will also have a great reputation] whose fame among males for excellence or blame is very small.[48]

In *word*, a speech has been made by me according to the custom, and I have said as many fitting things as I had to say; and in *deed* those who have been buried have already adorned themselves, and with respect to their [personal affairs], the polis will from this time publicly bring up [their] children until manhood, having placed a beneficial garland from such contests on these men and their survivors: you see, the greatest prizes of virtue lie in these contests, and for these [prizes] the best men engage in the affairs of the polis. And now, having lamented him [whom it] is fitting for each [to lament], go away.

2.46.1

2.46.2

3. Cleon's Speech in the Debate on Mytilene

Athens was sorely taxed in 430, the second year of the war, not so much by the Spartans, who continued to do exactly what they were expected to do, but by a plague that devastated the populace, shut within the city walls in compliance with Pericles' defensive policy. Pericles himself died of the plague in the third year of the war. His death had a profound effect on Athenian politics. According to Thucydides, Pericles' preeminence and acknowledged integrity gave him the authority to tell the Athenians the truth, but those who followed him felt that to compete for the favor of the people they had to tell them what they wanted to hear—to pander to them. Demagogues took over. The "most violent" and "by far the most persuasive among the people" of the new generation of leaders—perhaps for the very reason of his violence—was Cleon.

A great danger for Athens was that her allies—really, her subjects— would rebel against her, depriving her of the resources of men and

---

47   Pericles addresses parents, sons, and brothers of the deceased directly, in the second person. The widows he speaks of in the third person. In the next sentence he will use the pronoun "you" in reference to the widows, before shifting to the third person singular.

48   Praise and blame is a traditional antithesis as well as the principal subject matter of epideictic oratory (see *Gorgias* note 2). A second, more interesting antithesis, also appears in this sentence, where Pericles says that for women the real "fame" is in being known as little as possible. Here the antithesis is between the whole point of fame, which is to be as well known as possible and the so-called "fame" of women, which Pericles says is not to be known at all. Pericles' female companion, Aspasia, was famous—or notorious—among the Athenians.

money that she needed to prosecute the war. One of the most important of these allies was the polis of Mytilene on the island of Lesbos, which did rebel in 428. After putting down the revolt at great cost, Athens had to decide what to do with the Mytileneans. The first decision, impulsively made under the influence of Cleon, was to kill all the Mytileneans—not only the oligarchs who had led the revolt, but also the demos—despite the fact that most of the demos had not supported the revolt. On the day after this decision, even as an Athenian trireme was already on its way with orders to the Athenian commander to carry out the sentence of death, the Athenians had second thoughts and reopened the issue. The renewed debate focused on the relationship between justice and self-interest in the conduct of the affairs of the empire. Cleon, whose argument is reminiscent of Callicles' in the Gorgias—that justice is the advantage of the stronger—urged the execution of all the Mytileneans as at appropriate punishment for their crimes and as a useful warning to Athens' other subject peoples. Thucydides introduces and then presents Cleon's speech:

3.36.6   An assembly was called straightaway, and various opinions were spoken by each [of the participants]. Then Cleon, the son of Cleainetus, who had on the previous day prevailed [in the assembly in persuading the people] to kill—and in other respects the most violent of the citizens, and in the demos far the most persuasive in that time—came forward again and spoke the following:

3.37.1   Often already, even at other times,[49] I, of course, have known about democracy that it is incapable of ruling others, and [I know it]

3.37.2   now especially in your afterthought about the Mytileneans. You see, because [you enjoy] a daily security and an absence of intrigue towards each other, you believe the [situation is the] same also for your allies, and [in] whatever you err because you are persuaded by [their] argument, or [in whatever] you would yield from pity, you don't think [that they are a risk] to you nor that you are weakened [when you aim at] the favor of the allies, not considering that the empire you have is a tyranny[50]—[a tyranny over] both those who plot [against you] and those who are ruled unwillingly, who obey you not from the things that you grace [them with] while you [yourselves are harmed], but [obey you] more because of [the fact] that you are

3.37.3   superior [to them] in strength than by their goodwill. And the most terrible thing of all for us [is] if nothing at all will stand as a sure

---

49   A rather redundant expression. Perhaps redundancy was a feature of Cleon's style, or perhaps Thucydides is using it as a form of characterization.

50   Thucydides' Pericles made a similar claim in 2.63.2.

thing about what is best [to do] and [if] we shall not at all recognize
that a polis that uses worse [but] unchanging laws is stronger than
[one that uses laws that] are good [but] without authority, and
[further] that ignorance with moderation is more beneficial than
cleverness with intemperance, and [finally] that the more ordinary
of people, as against the more intelligent, for the greater part govern
poleis better. You see, [the more intelligent people] wish to appear   3.37.4
wiser than the laws and [wish] to be superior to the things that are
always said for the common [good], as though they could not show
their judgment in other, greater things, and from such [behavior]
they fail their poleis in many ways; but the [ordinary people], not
putting their trust in their own intelligence, judge that they are more
unlearned than the laws and more incapable of finding fault in the
argument than someone speaking well, and since they are impartial
judges rather than competitors, for the greater part they deal rightly.
And it is necessary for us thus to act [when] giving advice, not [as   3.37.5
people aroused] by cleverness and [by] a contest of intelligence to give
advice to the multitude of you that is contrary to [your] opinion.

And so, *I* myself am in the [same] judgment [as before], and I   3.38.1
wonder, on the one hand, at [the judgment] of those advocating [that
we] speak again about [the] Mytileneans and [who are] making a
delay of time, [a delay] that is more [for the advantage] of those who
have acted unjustly; you see, [as a result of such delay] the one who
has suffered makes an attack with a duller anger on the one who
has acted [against him], but a payback, when it comes right after
the suffering, most brings vengeance on the adversary; and, and I
wonder at anyone who will speak against [my view] and will think
it right to show that the wrongs of the Mytileaneans are beneficial
to us and that our misfortunes have been injuries to the allies. And   3.38.2
it is clear that, trusting in [his skill at] speaking he would contend
to show how what is perfectly obvious is *not* known, or, aroused by
profit, having worked out to perfection the sheen of his argument
he will try to lead you astray. But from such contests [of oratory]   3.38.3
the polis gives prizes to others, but she herself bears the dangers.
And *you*, who have wickedly established [these talk] contests, are   3.38.4
the ones responsible—[you], who are accustomed to be viewers of
speeches and hearers of deeds,[51] considering deeds that will happen
in the future as possible because of [what has been said by] those who
speak well, but, concerning what has already been done, [you] don't

---

51   This is Cleon's variant on Homer's "doer of deeds and speaker of words." It is an insult,
      saying that his audience is not at all heroic.

3.38.5 accept an [action that has been] done in your [own] sight as more persuasive than a thing [you have] heard [about] from those who have done a good job of censuring in speech;[52] and [you are] heroic at being deceived by the novelty of a speech, but [you] do not wish to follow what has been thought out, [for you are] slaves of things that

3.38.6 are out of place and [you are] scorners of things customary, and each man [of you] very much wishes to be able to speak [well] himself, but if [he is] not [able to speak well], he contends with those who say such things in order not to seem to [lag] behind them in judgment, and [you] praise a person who says something cleverly, ahead of time—being eager to *perceive* ahead of time what is said but being slow to *understand* ahead of time the consequences that follow from

3.38.7 speeches; and seeking something different, so to speak, from [what we find in the world] in which we live, [you] don't think adequately about the present [circumstances]; reduced simply by the pleasure of hearing, [you] resemble the seated spectators of sophists[53] rather than men who deliberate about the polis.

3.39.1 I, making an attempt to turn you away from these things, declare that the Mytileneans are indeed one polis that especially has treated you

3.39.2 unjustly. You see, I—[towards any] who are unable to bear your empire or [towards any who] have revolted because they were compelled by our enemies—extend a pardon. But when they have an island with walls and it is only by sea that they fear our enemies, a [situation] in which they also were not unguarded by a force of triremes against [these enemies], and when they live under their own laws and are honored by us in the foremost matters, [and] they did such things, what else did these people do but plot [against us] and rise up against [us]—rather than revolt [from us, since] a revolt is in fact from those who suffer some violence—and seek to destroy us, standing with our greatest enemies? And it is more terrible than if, seeking to acquire

3.39.3 power for themselves, they had made war against [us]. And they had as a paradigm neither the misfortunes of their neighbors, many of whom, having revolted from us, had been defeated, nor did their present happiness make them hesitate [about] not coming to terrible

---

52   This is similar to what the Athenians say at Melos (5.111), when they say that the Melians' strongest arguments have to do with what they hope.

53   On the sophists and the sophistic movement, see Introduction pp. 7-8. One of the anonymous reviewers of Focus Publishing has pointed out to us (and a word search in the *Thesaurus Linguae Graecae* has confirmed) that the use of the word "sophist" appears only here in all of Thucydides. Cleon's disdain of the sophists was probably matched by that of Thucydides, who, by avoiding all other references to them, may be indicating (indirectly, of course) how little their views mattered in the actual conduct of affairs.

[outcomes];[54] but becoming bold towards what was in the future and hoping for things greater than [their] power while less than their wishes, they raised a war, thinking it right to put strength before justice; you see, while they thought they would be superior, they attacked us, though they were not treated unjustly. But it is habitual for the poleis to which unexpected prosperity comes in the least amount of time to turn to hubris. And many lucky things that [that occur] in accordance with reason are safer for people [than such things that occur] contrary to expectation, and, as they say, [people] thrust off bad times more easily than they preserve happiness. It was necessary, even long ago, for the Mytileneans to have been esteemed by us no differently at all from the others, and [if we had done so] they would not have engaged in this hubris; it is natural, you see, for a person vainly to look down on what is conciliatory but to marvel at what does not yield. Let them be rightly punished even now for their injustice, and do not let the responsibility [for their crimes] be placed on the oligarchs, as you let off their demos. You see, *all* similarly attacked you, [all], in fact, to whom it was possible to have turned toward us and now be [safely] in their polis again; but after considering the danger from the oligarchs safer [than turning toward us] they joined [with them] in revolt. Consider [what will happen] if you deal out the same [lenient] punishments both to our allies who are compelled by our enemies [to revolt] and to those [allies] who revolt willingly; do you think that any [of them] whatsoever will *not* revolt on a thin pretext when success results in freedom, or, [should the revolt] fail, [when the failure] brings no unbearable suffering at all? But we shall have risked money and souls against each polis, and, on the one hand, even [should we] happen to get back a destroyed polis, you will be deprived in the future of the revenue of an earlier time, through which [revenue] we had our strength; and, on the other hand, should we fail, we shall have [new] enemies added to our existing ones, and we shall make war with our own allies during the time [when] it is necessary to stand against our present established enemies.

And so it is necessary not to put forth hope, either [in the form of] a confidence [generated] by a speech, or a [confidence] purchased by money, that [the Mytileneans] will be pardoned as having made a human mistake. You see, they did not do harm unwillingly, but

3.39.4

3.39.5

3.39.6

3.39.7

3.39.8

3.40.1

---

54   The beginning of the sentence leads us to expect two elements of the paradigm, but Cleon changes his syntax mid-sentence. Perhaps the loss of syntactical regularity is Thucydides' way of portraying him.

they knowingly plotted. And what deserves pardon is the [action
3.40.2   that is] involuntary. And so, *I*, both then for the first time and now,
thoroughly oppose your changing your mind about what seemed
best before and [I oppose your] making a mistake [because of]
the three things most inexpedient to empire—compassion and the
3.40.3   pleasure of speeches and fairness. You see, pity is justly given back
to those [people who are] similar[55] and not to those established as
eternal enemies who necessarily do not pity in return; and those
rhetors who delight [people] by [their] speech will have a contest in
other, lesser [matters], and not [a contest] in which the polis, after
being given [a brief] pleasure about trivia will be punished greatly,
while the [rhetors] themselves, from speaking well, will in return lay
claim to being well treated,[56] and fairness is given to those who will
be trusty [allies] in the future rather than to those who will remain
3.40.4   as they have been and no less our enemies. Putting [everything]
together, I have one thing to say: [if you are] persuaded by me, you
will perform actions to the Mytileneans both just and, at the same
time, advantageous [to us], but judging differently, while you will
not gratify them, you will rather reap the justice you yourselves
deserve. You see, if *they* rightly revolted, *you* would not rightly rule.
But if indeed you think it right to [rule], even if it is not proper, then
it is necessary for you to punish them for your advantage, [even]
contrary to what is fair, or [else it is necessary for you] to quit your
3.40.5   empire and act the good man from a risk-free [situation]. Think it
right to punish with the same penalty [that we have already decided
upon], and [think it right that you,] who are the ones escaping [those
plotting], appear not more insensitive to the pain [inflicted on *you*]
than the plotters [are to the pain they perceive to have been inflicted
on *them*], taking to heart what it is likely that they would have done
3.40.6   had they prevailed over you, especially since they were the ones who
initiated the injustice. The people who, with no [proffered] excuse, act
badly towards someone are very much those who will proceed even
to destroy him, for they observe the danger of someone who would
[henceforth always] remain an enemy; you see, the one who has
suffered something when there was no need and escapes is harsher

---

55   I.e., to those who are not subject-allies, but who are equals. Aristotle has a different view
of pity: he says that it is a feeling of pain for those who are suffering unjustly. One can pity
a dog.

56   The term translated as "being well treated" is—literally—"suffering well." It is a
euphemism and carries the implication of bribery.

than [one who has suffered] from an enemy's equal [injustice].[57]

Do not become traitors of your very own selves, but becoming most   3.40.7
near to your judgment [made from] your suffering and [recalling]
how before everything [else] you valued reducing them, pay them
back now, not softened towards the present immediate [situation]
nor forgetful of the terrible [danger] that once hung over [you].
Punish them rightly, and establish as a clear paradigm to the rest of
the allies [that] he who would rebel will be punished with death. If
they know this, you, careless [of your allies], will fight your allies less
than [you will fight] your enemies themselves.

4. Diodotus' Speech

*Thucydides reports that Cleon was followed in the debate by a certain
Diodotus, who urges Athens to exercise moderation in its punishment of
Mytilene by executing the oligarchical leaders of the revolt but sparing the
demos. Though he claims to argue exclusively on the basis of expediency,
underlying his argument is the same premise that is advanced by the
Platonic Socrates in the Gorgias—that it is better to suffer than to perform
an injustice.*

Cleon said such things. After him, Diodotus, the son of Eukrates,[58]   3.41.1
who in the prior meeting especially had spoken against killing the
Mytileneans, came forward [and] spoke the following.

Neither do I blame those who have again brought forward their   3.42.1
resolution concerning the Mytileneans, nor do I praise those [who
are] reproachfully warning us not to deliberate often about the
greatest [matters], but I consider speed and anger to be the two
[circumstances] most opposed to good counsel, [and] of these
[circumstances], the one loves to come into being along with
mindlessness, the other with a lack of education and narrowness
of judgment. Whoever combats [the idea] that arguments arise   3.42.2

---

57   Perhaps Cleon means this: if you have been wronged by someone who felt no necessity
to wrong you but wronged you for some other motive—greed or meanness—and you
manage to live, you will cause the person who wronged you more trouble than if he
wronged you with some "necessary" motive. For example, if a person comes into your
house and kills your brother for no reason, you will be a more difficult enemy to the
murderer than if he came into your house and killed your brother in revenge for some
evil your brother had done to him.

58   Diodotus is probably an imaginary figure. His and his father's names are symbolic.
Diodotus means "gift of God". The name of his father, *Eukrates*, means "good-ruler."

as teachers of the business at hand is either stupid or he has some private interest. He is stupid if he thinks it is possible to ponder by some [means] other [than argument] something that is future and not apparent, and he bears [some private interest] for himself if, wishing to persuade us about a shameful thing, he thinks that he could not speak well about a thing that is not noble [but] that by delivering slander well he could bully both those speaking against

3.42.3   him and those hearing him. Most difficult also are those who, in addition, charge someone with [making] a display-speech for money. You see, if they blamed [someone] for ignorance, the one who was not persuasive [in speaking] would depart seeming stupider rather than more unjust. When injustice is brought in, the one who has been persuasive becomes suspected, and when he fails to hit [his

3.42.4   goal], [he] is accused, along with stupidity, of being] unjust. And the polis is not benefited in such a [situation]: you see, it is deprived of her counselors because of fear. And it would be most right that [if] the polis had such citizens, they would be unable to speak: you see, [in this way] they would least persuade [the polis] to make mistakes.

3.42.5   And it is necessary that the good citizen not frighten those who speak on the other side but that from an equal [playing field] he appear to be speaking better, and [it is necessary that] a prudent polis not pile on honors to the one advising most things well but also [that it] not lessen [the honor] he already has, and [it is also necessary] that it not

3.42.6   fine or dishonor the one who is not successful with his view. You see, in this way, the one who is successful would least speak contrary to his view, [aiming at] being esteemed for greater things and for favor, and the one who is not successful [would least] reach out to win over the multitude, courting favor for himself.

3.43.1   We do the opposite of these things, and, besides, if someone be suspected of saying the best things [but saying them] nevertheless for the sake of profit, we, begrudging [him] because of the unproved

3.43.2   suspicion of gains, deprive the polis of an obvious benefit. And it has come to pass that good things spoken openly are not at all more unsuspected than bad things, so that it is equally necessary for the one who wishes to win over the multitude [towards] the most terrible things to persuade [them] by deceit, and for the one

3.43.3   who says the better things to become persuasive by lying. And only with respect to [this] polis is it impossible that a person who is not openly deceiving [it] treat [it] well, on account of its over-wiseness; you see, the one who gives some good [advice] openly is suspected

3.43.4   of intending somehow to make a grab secretly. And in reference to the greatest [issues] even in such [a matter as this], we must think it right [for *us*] to speak taking thought a bit more deeply [into the matter]—since *you* are examining [the situation] briefly—and [it is right for us to speak] especially as having advice that is accountable as against [your] unaccountable listening. You see, if the one who has persuaded and the one who follows [the persuasion] suffered equally, you would judge more prudently; but as it is, into whatever temper you happen to fall, when now and then you make a mistake, you blame the single view of the [person] who has persuaded [you] and not your own [views], if many have been mistaken along with [his].   3.43.5

But *I* have come before [you] neither intending to speak against [other speakers] concerning the Mytileneans nor to accuse [them]. You see, our contest is not about *their* injustice—if we are prudent—but about *our* planning well. You see, if I declare that [the Mytileneans] are acting wholly unjustly, not even on account of this [fact] do I bid [you] kill them, unless [it be] advantageous [to us], and if [I declare that] they deserve a bit of pardon, I [I bid you] let [the pardon go] if it should not appear as a good thing for our polis. And I think we are planning about the future rather than about the present. And Cleon strongly insists most of all on this, [that] for the future, for there to be fewer rebellions against you, it will be advantageous [for you] to provide death as punishment, and I myself insist strongly the contrary, and I judge the opposite about what will be good concerning the future. And I do not think it right that you, because of the attractiveness of that speech, reject the useful [point] of my [speech]. You see, his speech, being juster [from the point of view of] your present anger towards the Mytileneans, might immediately be alluring; but *we* are not dealing with them in court so as to need [to do] just things, but we are deliberating [in council] about them— how they will be useful [to us].[59]   3.44.1   3.44.2   3.44.3   3.44.4

And so, among the poleis, punishments of death are put forth for many mistakes, and [not just for mistakes] equal to this one, but [also] for smaller [ones]; nevertheless, lifted by hope, people take risks, and no one yet, having determined that he would not survive in the plot, has come to the terrible [course of action]. And what city, rebelling, has undertaken this while having, in its opinion, too few resources, its own or from its allies? And all people by nature   3.45.1   3.45.2   3.45.3

---

59   Diodotus, like the Athenian ambassadors at Sparta, is talking about the *rhetoric* of the debate. Diodotus says that the rules of forensic oratory and of the courtroom do not apply, for this is an occasion for deliberative oratory, the kind that takes place in the assembly.

make mistakes both in private and in public, and there is not any law [that] will prevent this, since people have, in fact, gone through all the penalties, adding to them, if somehow [they might bring it about that] they be less treated unjustly by the evil doers. And it is likely that long ago [the penalties] were softer for the greatest acts of injustice, but, as transgressions occurred over time, many [penalties] were extended to death; even in this [circumstance], transgressions

3.45.4   occur. Let me tell you, then: either some fear more terrible than [the fear of death as punishment] must be found, or, [we must admit that] this [fear] in fact does not at all restrain [people from wrongdoing]; but poverty, providing boldness [because of] necessity, and wealth, [providing] greed [because of] hubris and spirit, and the other conditions of life, as each is controlled by some invincible stronger [circumstance], drive [people] to dangers [because of] the temper

3.45.5   [engendered]. And in every [situation], hope and erotic desire,[60] the one leading, the other following, the one thinking out a plot, the other assuming the good outcome of luck, harm the most things,

3.45.6   and things unseen are greater than the terrible things seen.[61] Besides [hope and erotic desire], luck tosses in no less [a contribution to] the lifting [of spirits]. You see, when [luck] unexpectedly is present, [she] leads on a person, and no less the poleis, even from rather inadequate resources, to take risks—because [the risks] concern the greatest matters—freedom or the rule over others[62]—and each man, along with all [of his polis] has, without reason, reckoned himself

3.45.7   [capable of] something rather great. It is simply impossible and quite simplistic—whoever thinks that by strength of laws or by some other terrible [power] he can brush aside human nature when it rises passionately.[63]

---

60   This is an echo of the striking use of a cognate ("ardent lovers") in Pericles' Funeral Oration (2.43.1). Perhaps Diodotus rejects these emotions because they are conspicuously irrational.

61   The Athenian ambassadors to Melos will make this same argument (5.93).

62   What we have translated as "rule over others" can be, and usually is, translated as "empire." Our translation preserves the more literal meaning, makes Diodotus' point starker in its moral significance, and also foreshadows the conversation of Socrates and Callicles in the *Gorgias*, where Socrates asserts that what matters is rule over oneself, not rule over others.

63   Diodotus seems to be suggesting that human nature has irrational elements that take over and cannot be resisted. An example of this phenomenon occurs, perhaps, in the *Iliad*, when Achilles tells Patroclus to return to camp after having warded off Hector and the Trojans from the ships. It would be contrary to human nature, as it rises passionately, to expect him to follow the advice. It would be like asking an arrow which is on its way to a bull's eye to stop in its course and return to the archer.

And so it is necessary [for us], having put our confidence in the   3.46.1
punishment of death as a sure thing, neither to make plans in a
worse way nor to make [the situation] hopeless for those who revolt
so that there will not be a change [of their] minds and a very quick
ending of their error. You see, consider whether some polis that is   3.46.2
revolting—one still able to pay back [our] expense [of suppressing it]
and to pay tribute in the future—and knows it will not survive would
come to an agreement. In that case do you think that anyone would
not, on the one hand, prepare himself better than [he does] now, and,
on the other, would not suffer himself to be reduced by siege to the
last extremity, if agreeing at length and [agreeing] quickly have the
same efficacy? And how is it not a harm for us, as we settle down [in   3.46.3
a siege], to undergo expense because of the absence of an agreement,
and, if we do take [the revolting polis, how is not a harm to us] to
receive a destroyed polis and [thus] to be deprived of income from it
in the future? And we are strong from this [income]. So it is necessary   3.46.4
for us [not to be] strict judges of those making mistakes [and thus for
us] to be harmed rather than to see how in the future, as we punish
moderately, we shall be able to use the poleis that are strong in the
account of their money and and think it right to construct a defense,
not from the terribleness of our laws but from our care [of our own]
deeds. Now, doing the opposite of this, we think it useful to punish   3.46.5
[a polis] severely if we shall overpower [one] that is free and ruled
by force and appropriately rebelling for [its] autonomy[64]. But it is   3.46.6
necessary [for us] not to *punish* the free cities exceedingly [when
they] are revolting, but, before they revolt, to *guard* them exceedingly
and to take care in advance that they do not come to an intention of
this, and [after] we have prevailed [over them, it is necessary for us]
to bring the blame to as few as possible.

And *you,* examine how much you would be erring, if you are   3.47.1
persuaded by Cleon. You see, now, the demos in all the poleis is well-   3.47.2
minded towards you, and either does not revolt [along] with the
oligarchs, or, if forced, begins to be hostile straightaway to those who
are revolting, and you go towards war having as an ally the multitude
of the polis that opposes [you because of its oligarchical rulers]. But   3.47.3
if you destroy the demos of the Mytileneans, which has not had a

---

64   It is difficult to understand what poleis Diodotus is referring to when he speaks of those
      that are "free" but are "ruled by force" and are "rebelling" for their freedom. Perhaps
      they are the poleis in the Athenian Empire that maintained something of the character of
      allies in the original Delian League; that is, they supplied ships and men to the Athenians
      rather than pay tribute.

part in the revolt and [which,] when it took control over weapons, willingly surrendered the city, first you will be acting unjustly [in] killing those whose have done good actions, and second, you will do for the powerful people what they most want; you see, upon stirring their poleis to revolt, they will at once have the demos as an ally, since you are showing that the same punishment is set for those acting

3.47.4   unjustly and those not [acting unjustly]. And it is necessary, even if they *have* acted unjustly, to make as if it were not so, so what alone is

3.47.5   still allied to us does not become hostile. And I think that this—that we willingly be treated unjustly—is much more advantageous to the maintenance of empire than [for us] justly to destroy whom it is necessary not to [destroy].[65] And Cleon's claim about "the identity of justice and advantage in vengeance" is not found to be possible at the same time in the same thing.

3.48.1   And *you,* knowing that these things are better, and granting too much neither to pity nor to fairness—[principles] from which *I* do not allow us to act—from what I have advised, be persuaded by me calmly to judge [those] of the Mytileneans whom Paches[66] has sent back as acting unjustly but to allow the others to live [in their homes]. You see, these [actions will be] good for the future and [will

3.48.2   be] fearsome presently to our enemies. You see, whoever plans well is stronger against his enemies than a [person] who goes forward mindlessly with a [brute] strength of actions.

5. The Melian Dialogue

Diodotus carried the day by a few votes and the demos of Mytilene was spared. Cleon nevertheless remained popular in Athens. When, in 425, there was an opportunity for a peace treaty after Athens' victory over Sparta in the battle at Pylos, Cleon, the leader of the war party, succeeded in persuading the Athenians to continue the war. But when Cleon was killed 421, Nicias, the leader of the peace party, was able to negotiate a peace treaty with Sparta. The treaty, which was supposed to last for fifty years, turned out to be not a true peace but merely an armistice, for, after a cessation of fighting, both sides failed to comply with the rest of the terms of the treaty and continued to attempt to expand their power.

---

65   Diodotus is putting the argument in terms of pure expediency, having shown that it is not advantageous to kill the common people, the demos, lest Athens have a harder time in the war.

66   Paches was the Athenian commander in charge of operations in Mytilene. He sent to Athens the ringleaders of the revolt.

One such effort undertaken by Athens was to consolidate her control of the Aegean Sea by forcing the small island of Melos to become her subject ally. Though Melos traced her ethnic heritage to Sparta and was sympathetic to Sparta, she had remained neutral in the war. In 415, an Athenian army arrived to compel the island to submit. Before undertaking military operations, the Athenians sent envoys to negotiate the surrender of Melos. The Melian leaders refused to let the envoys speak before the demos, and the talks were held in private.

Thucydides presents the talks as a dialogue and records the speeches without connecting prose, in the manner of drama and many of the Platonic dialogues. This section of the History, *known traditionally as the Melian Dialogue, confronts the reality of brute power with all its fearsome immediacy. The dialogue culminates in the argument that by a law of nature the strong everywhere rule over the weak. The nameless envoys to Melos—nameless, perhaps, to show that they represent the views of typical Athenians—speak very differently about the Athenians' motives in founding and expanding their empire from the nameless ambassadors to Sparta in the first speech presented above. Like Callicles in the Gorgias, the envoys to Melos speak only about power, saying nothing about justice or honor. In this way, Thucydides quietly shows how Athens has changed in the decade and a half since the beginning of the conflict. War, says Thucydides, is a "violent teacher" that "assimilates the passions of many people to [their] present circumstances." [3.82.2]*

The Athenians' ambassadors spoke the following: 5.85

Since our arguments are not going to be made before the multitude in order that it not be deceived by our continuous verbiage as it hears all at once from us things seductive and not subject to cross-examination—you see, we know that you have brought us before the few with this intention—you, who are sitting here, you are doing a rather safe thing. You see, for each [matter that comes up], you also [won't respond] in one speech [that you give later, when we have finished], but you will interrupt immediately and determine whether something seems not to have been spoken fittingly. And first tell [us] whether what we say is agreeable.

Those of the Melians who were meeting in session answered: The   5.86
fairness of teaching each other calmly is not blamed, but the present and not-future [circumstances] of the war appear differently [to us] in [this proposal]. You see, we perceive that you have come as judges of what will be said and that the conclusion from this [debate] will likely bring us war [should] we be the ones who prevail in the justice

[of our remarks], and on account of [this] don't give in but [will bring us] slavery [should] we be the ones who are persuaded.

5.87   Athenians: Look here, if you have assembled intending to talk about [your] suspicions of the future or intending to plan about something other than [what arises] from present [circumstances] and [other than] what you see that concerns safety for [your] polis, we would stop [the debate]; but if [you are intending to speak] about the [present circumstances] we would speak.

5.88   Melians: It is reasonable and forgivable that those speaking and thinking in such a situation as this turn to many [topics]; this present meeting, however, is about safety, and let the argument take place in the way you have called for it, if it seems best.

5.89   Athenians: Look here, *we* ourselves won't provide [you with] lots of speeches loaded with pretty words that won't be believed—how having destroyed the Mede[67] we justly rule or how having been unjustly treated [by you] we are now attacking, and we won't deem it worthwhile for you to think to persuade [us by] saying that [though] you are colonists of the Lacedaemonians you did not make war on us or do anything unjust [to us], but [let us converse] about the powers from which each of us thinks that he can truly accomplish [his objectives]—as people who know [speaking] with people who have seen that in the human calculation just things are decided from an equal [power to] compel[68] and that those who possess powers act and the weak yield.

5.90   Melians: In truth, we, indeed, of course, think it useful—you see, you have laid it down as a necessity thus to speak about what is advantageous [even though it is] contrary to justice—that you not destroy the common good, but [we think that] someone who, in continuously arising danger, makes persuasive arguments [about] things that are fitting and just and somewhat within [the bounds of] what is accurate, should be benefited. And to you this [common good] is not less [important], since if you should fail you would be a paradigm[69] to others for a very great punishment.

5.91.1   Athenians: We won't lose heart about the end of our rule, if it should stop; you see, those who rule over others, like the Lacedaemonians— they are not terrible to those who have been defeated (and we don't

---

67   See the Speech of the Athenian Travelers, Appendix A, note 5.

68   Like an agreement not to use poison gas, or to engage in MAD (mutually assured destruction).

69   On *paradigm*, see *Gorgias* note 229 and Glossary.

have a contest with the Lacedaemonians [on this policy])—but we suppose [we and the Lacedaemonians *are* terrible] if our subjects themselves, while making an attack, prevail over [us], who rule [over them]. And it must be left to us to run a risk concerning this [matter]. We shall now address our words [to the proposition] that we are present as a benefit to our rule and a source of safety to your polis, and we shall show these [two] things: that we wish to rule over you without toil and that [we wish] you to be saved [so as to be] useful to both of us.   5.91.2

Melians: How do these two converge—that it is useful for us to be slaves and for you to rule?   5.92

Athenians: Because you will [have the chance] to obey before suffering the most terrible things, and we would gain by not destroying you.   5.93

Melians: So you would not accept our living in peace, being friends instead of enemies, [with us as] allies of neither [of the two opposing parties]?   5.94

Athenians: [No]; you see, your hatred of us will not harm us so much as your friendship—your friendship [showing a paradigm] of weakness, your hatred showing a paradigm of power to those we rule.   5.95

Melians: Do your subjects look at what is fitting in this way—that they put into the same category as those having nothing to do [with you] those many who are colonists and some who, after rebelling, have been defeated?   5.96

Athenians: They think that neither of the two lacks a plea of doing what's right, but that [it is] by [their] power [that] some survive and [that] from fear we don't attack [them]; so that apart from [our] ruling even more [peoples] you would provide us safety by our overthrowing you—especially since you are islanders, weaker than others, and you would not prevail over those who are shipmasters.   5.97

Melians: But don't you think that there is safety in what [we said]? You see, it is necessary in turn even there—as you keep us from just arguments and persuade us to be obedient to your advantage—for us to try to persuade [you and to] teach what is useful for us, if the same thing happens to converge [as useful] to you. You see, concerning the many who are now allies to neither of the two of you, how will you not become an enemy to them, when they observe what is going on [here] and think that one day you will come after them? And what else would you increase by this [action] than [the number of   5.98

your] enemies, and [by this action you will] have induced even those who would never have intended to do so on their own [to become your enemies].

5.99   Athenians: We do not think that they [will be] excessively fearsome to us—all, we suppose, who, while they [live] in freedom on the mainland, [will long put off] protecting themselves from us—but [we think] that [the ones who will be excessively fearsome] are islanders like you, [who are] not ruled [by us], and those already vexed by the necessity of our rule. You see, these, trusting in some irrational [calculation], would most put themselves and us into a manifest danger.

5.100   Melians: Truly we suppose, then—if you [put yourselves at] so great a risk in order not to be [deprived of] your rule and those who are slaves [to you put themselves at so great a risk] in turn in order to be released [from your rule]—for us, of course, who are still free it [would be] a great evil and cowardice not to do everything we could before living as slaves.

5.101   Athenians: Not, of course, if you plan prudently. You see, you are not engaged in an equal contest about manly virtue, [about] not deserving shame; rather, the deliberation is about safety, [about] not making a stand against those who are much stronger.

5.102   Melians: But we know the [circumstances] of war, that there are times when one encounters rather more common fortunes than the different number [of forces would lead one to expect]; and for us to yield is to become immediately hopeless, but [when] a person acts there is still hope to stand upright.

5.103   Athenians: Hope, being a calming [balm in a time of] danger, does not destroy, even if it should harm, those who use it from [a condition of] abundance; but for those staking their whole [fortune] on a throw of dice—you see, hope is extravagant by nature—it is recognized [for what it is] when people are failing, and, in the time when someone may still find protection, he does not leave hope behind, [though it is] recognized [in its true nature]. Do not wish to experience this [ignorant condition], you who are weak and [whose lives depend on the smallest weight to cause a] tip in the balance to the other side, and do not be like the many who—when it is possible in all human probability still to be saved,when clearly visible hopes abandon them as they are distressed—entrust themselves to invisible [hopes]—to prophecy and oracles and as much other [nonsense] that, along with hopes, cause ruin.

Melians: We too consider [it] a difficult thing—know [it] well—to 5.104
contend with your power and fortune, if [the contending] will not be
from an equal condition; nevertheless, we trust in our fortune from
the god not to be defeated because we stand as holy people against
those who are not just, and [we trust that in compensation for our]
lack of power we shall have the alliance of the Lacedaemonians, [an
alliance] that has a necessity [for them], if for no other reasons than
to come to the aid of their kinsmen and [to act because of a sense of]
shame. And in this way we are not irrationally bold.

Athenians: Look here, in reference to the proper spirit toward the 5.105.1
divine, we do not think that we have come up short at all; you see,
we consider nothing just and do nothing [that is] outside of human
convention concerning divine matters, and [we consider nothing
just and do nothing] outside of [all peoples'] wishes for themselves.
You see, with respect to the divine we think by opinion and with 5.105.2
respect to the human [we think] clearly [that] it[70] rules everything by
a necessary nature where it is strong; and *we*, neither having made
this convention[71] nor having been the first to use it [once it was]
established but taking it up as it [already] existed and will exist into
always, we, [who will] leave it behind, use it, knowing that you and
others, being in the same power as we, would be doing the same
thing. Thus, from what is likely with respect to the divine, we do 5.105.3
not fear that we will be worsted. Of your conjecture concerning
the Lacedaemonians, which [leads you] to trust that on account of
shame they will help you, while we pronounce your inexperience
of evil divinely blessed, we do not envy your thoughtlessness. The
Lacedaemonians, you see, when it comes to themselves and most
of their native traditional customs employ excellence; but towards
others, someone, having many things to say, [might say] how
they behave, putting it briefly that they especially show that most
apparently of those we know they believe the pleasant to be the noble
and the advantageous to be the just. And such a cast of mind is not
fitting for your current irrational [notion of] safety.

Melians: *We* for this very reason now especially do trust what is 5.106
advantageous to them—not to wish to become distrusted by their
well-wishers among the Greeks [by] betraying the Melians who are
their colonists and [thus] to be beneficial to their enemies.

---

70   The antecedent is unclear. It probably refers to both the human and the divine.
71   This is *nomos*. But see *Gorgias* notes 88, 90, 92, and 160.

5.107   Athenians: Then you do not think that the advantageous is accompanied with safety, but [you think] that the just and noble are done with danger—which is what the Lacedaemonians are, for the most part, least bold about.

5.108   Melians: But we think that they would the more undertake dangers for our sake than for others and would consider [undertaking the dangers to be] safer in proportion to our proximity to the fields of the Peloponnese, and, because of the kinship of our mental attitude, we are more trusted [by them] than others.

5.109   Athenians: But, of course, for those who are going to cooperate [with others] in a contest what is trusted does not appear [to be] the good will of those calling on them [to fight] but whether someone is very eminent in the power of deeds: this the Lacedaemonians examine more than others [do]—and so, in fact, from a lack of trust in their own preparedness [it is] with many allies that they make an attack on their neighbors—and so it is not likely, in fact, that, with us [Athenians] as masters of the sea, they will cross over to an island.

5.110.1   Melians: But they would be able to send others. And the Cretan Sea is big, on account of which the seizure [of ships by] those controlling [it] is more perplexing than the safety of those wishing to elude

5.110.2   [seizure]. And if they should fail in eluding seizure, they would turn on your land and on the rest of your allies, on all whom Brasidas[72] did not attack; and you will have a contest not for land that doesn't belong to you but for your own and your allies' land.

5.111.1   Athenians: [Yes, right, sure:] one of these things [that you have said] would happen to those who've tried [it] and to you and to those who don't know anything—because not even once have the Athenians

5.111.2   through fear of others departed from a siege.[73] But we are taking to heart that after saying that you would plan about safety,[74] you have said nothing in all this talk of yours that would make people who have believed [what you have said] think that they would be saved,

---

72   Brasidas was the most energetic and successful Spartan general of the first decade of the Peloponnesian War. He captured numerous cities allied with or subject to Athens in the northern part of Greece. He and Cleon are both killed at the Battle of Amphipolis. Thucydides gives Brasidas full honors in the description of his death but buries Cleon's death ignominiously in a subordinate clause (5.10–11).

73   We are interpreting this sentence as sarcastic. To read it literally and straightforwardly is full of problems. The sarcasm is enhanced by the climax—to those who've tried us, to you, and to the totally ignorant.

74   We interpret this sentence as repeating the brutal sarcasm of the first. It begins with the kindly "we take to heart" and ends with a threat.

but your strongest [points] have to do with things hoped for, and
your present resources [are too] few to survive the forces already
arrayed against you. You are exhibiting much unreasonableness   5.111.3
of thought, unless after removing us from your presence you will
know some other thing more prudent than these [things that you are
thinking]. [If you come to this prudential determination] indeed,
you will not turn to the disgrace that most destroys people in
shameful and foreseeable dangers. For many who still do foresee are
carried to this sort of thing—the thing called shame—by the power
of a tempting name. Shame, by the work of a phrase, has seduced
those who are weaker to fall willingly into irremediable disasters
and to accept a shame more shameful [because it comes along] with
mindlessness. If you are counseled well, you will guard against this,   5.111.4
and you will not think it unfitting to be worsted by the greatest polis
when it is bringing forward moderate [proposals]— to become allies
while holding your own [land]— tribute-paying, to be sure—and,
when you are given a choice about war and safety [you will] not be
so eager for strife as to choose the worse. Those prosper most who
do not yield to their equals but bear themselves well towards the
stronger and are moderate towards their inferiors. And so, when we   5.111.5
have gone elsewhere, examine and often take to heart that you are
planning for your fatherland—and the future will depend on one
deliberation aiming at one plan that [either] succeeds or does not
prosper.

And the Athenians went away from the talks; and when the Melians   5.112.1
were by themselves, since [the situation] seemed to them the same
as they had responded [to the Athenians earlier], they answered the
following:

It does not seem different to us, Athenians, from the way it seemed at   5.112.2
first, nor in a short time will we deprive of its freedom a city that we
have inhabited for seven hundred years; but trusting in the fortune
from the divine that has saved it until this time, and [trusting] in the
assistance from people, even the Lacedaemonians, we shall try to
save ourselves. We call on you as witnesses that we are friends and   5.112.3
enemies to neither of you, and [we call on you] to go away from our
land having made a treaty that seems fitting to both of us.

The Melians answered with such [words]. But the Athenians,   5.113
breaking up the talks, said, "And so you alone, as you seem to us
from these plans, judge that future things are clearer than the things
that are [actually] seen, and you see—because you wish for them—
that things invisible are already happening, and having hazarded

most and most having put trust in the Lacedaemonians and luck and hopes, you will be undone."

The Athenians then laid siege to Melos and eventually captured it. They took a terrible revenge on it, killing all the men and selling the women and children into slavery, their actions partaking more of Cleon's brutal justice than Diodotus' humane self-interestedness in the earlier Mytilenean affair.

6. Alcibiades' Speech to the Spartan Assembly (6.88–93)

Thucydides, a master of artful juxtaposition, immediately follows the destruction of Melos with an account of Athens' Sicilian Expedition, when Athens, ignorant of the size and resources of Sicily, attempted the same kind of aggression, this time with far different results. The Athenian army and its generals were entirely vanquished in a staggering reversal of fortune.

Among the many episodes in Thucydides' account is the description of the arrest and flight of Alcibiades. Alcibiades was a gifted politician and a brilliant general, but he was also ambitious, extravagant in his tastes and expenditures, and licentious in his private conduct. When Athens decided to attack Sicily, she put the huge invasion force—100 triremes, 5,000 hoplites, and a proportionate number of archers—under the command of Alcibiades and two other generals. Just before the force was about to sail an extremely unsettling crime occurred: throughout Athens, statues of Hermes that stood in the doorways of homes and temples were mutilated. Suspicion immediately fastened onto Alcibiades, who was also charged with having participated in mock celebrations of the Eleusinian Mysteries. These events were somehow tied in the public mind to a plot to overthrow the democratic government. Alcibiades sailed with the fleet, but before it arrived in Sicily, he was ordered to return to Athens to stand trial. Knowing that others had already been put to death for the same alleged crimes, he fled to the only place he could go to receive protection—Athens' enemy Sparta. To win Spartan protection, he revealed information about the Sicilian invasion and gave advice about crippling Athens by the seizure of Decelea, a key fortification on the road to Athens' food supply in Euboea.

The following is Alcibiades' speech to the Spartans. In it we can see an artful use of rhetoric, by which Alcibiades explains away his previous hawkish war policies towards Sparta and his betrayal of his native city. As Socrates was closely linked in the Athenian mind to Alcibiades as his teacher and mentor—an association that Plato has Socrates himself bring up more than once in the Gorgias—the following speech will shed light on the Athenians' attitudes towards Socrates, attitudes that perhaps help explain why he was executed.

It is necessary to speak to you first about the slander [concerning]   6.89.1
me so that you won't, because of suspicion, listen too dismissively to
me [as I speak on] public matters. [Though] some of my ancestors,   6.89.2
on some complaint about you, rejected the official friendship[75] they
[had established with you], I myself took [it] up again and took care of
you and your interests, especially in your bad fortune at Pylos. While
I continued to be eager [to maintain] our official friendship], you,
when you were reconciled with the Athenians, bestowed power on
my enemies, after you had acted through them, but [you bestowed]
disgrace on me. On account of these things you were justly harmed   6.89.3
by me as I turned to the [affairs] of the Mantineans and the Argives
and did as many other things [as I could] in opposition to you; and
now, if someone, in experiencing then [what I did against you], was
angry with me [even though] not appropriately, afterwards, looking
at the truth, let him be persuaded. Or if someone, also because I
somewhat favored the [side of] the people, was thinking the worse of
me, he too is not right in thinking that he is annoyed. You see, we are   6.89.4
always at odds with tyrants (and the whole [tribe] that is opposed to
those who act like group-tyrants is called the "people"), and from this
[opposition to tyranny] there continued our leadership of the many.
And, at the same time, since the polis was ruled by the people, it
was necessary to follow [the circumstances] that were present [at the
time]. And we were trying to be more moderate than the prevailing   6.89.5
licentiousness in political affairs. But there were others both long
ago and now who were leading the mob to more wicked things—and
they were the very men who drove me out. And we were the leader of   6.89.6
the whole [society], judging it right to preserve this—the manner in
which our polis happened to be greatest and freest and [the manner]
and in which it had come down to us, since we—the ones who were
a bit thoughtful—recognized it as a democracy, and [I] myself worse
than no one [else recognized it as such], by as much as I reviled [it].
But concerning this agreed-upon mindlessness nothing new should
be said. And to change [the mindlessness of democracy] did not
seem to us safe when, as enemies, you were laying siege [on us].

And such things have come to pass as far as the slanders about me   6.90.1
are concerned. But concerning the things that you must plan and
that I must explain—if I know something more [than you do]—

---

75   The word we have translated as *official friendship* is, in Greek, *proxenia*. It refers to a
friendship between a polis and a private individual. A proxenos, as a citizen of one polis,
might be appointed by a different polis as a consul to the polis of which he is a citizen. It
would be as if the United States appointed a Frenchman to be its consul in France.

6.90.2   learn [it] now. We sailed to Sicily, first, if we were able, to crush
the Sicilians, and after them, in turn, the Italians, and then also to
make an attempt on the empire of the Carthaginians and [on the
6.90.3   Carthaginians] themselves. And if all or the greater part of these
[plans] went forward [successfully], we were already intending
to make an attempt on the Peloponnese, [and] after bringing the
whole power of the Greeks added from there[76] and after hiring many
barbarians—Iberians and others from there who are agreed to be
the most warlike today of the barbarians—and [after] building many
triremes in addition to ours—Italy having an unsparing [supply of]
wood—[and] laying siege to the Peloponnese by means of [these
triremes] and at the same time, by means of land attacks by our
infantry, taking some of the cities by storm, and taking others [of
the cities] after [having built] walls of circumvallation, we hoped
that we would easily reduce [the Peloponnese] by war and, after
6.90.4   these [events], rule all of the Greek world. And so that any of these
matters would be rather easy to carry out— the places added from
there would provide a sufficiency of money and food without [any
additional] income from [our empire here in Greece].

6.91.1   You have heard such things about the current expedition that has
departed [from Athens] from the person who knows most accurately
how we planned it; and all the generals who are left [in Sicily], if
they can, will carry out these things in the same way. But how the
[affairs] there won't come out successfully [for you]—unless you
6.91.2   help—learn [from me] now. You see, though the Sicilians are more
inexperienced [than the Athenians], nevertheless, if all of them unite
together, even now they might survive; but the Syracusans alone,
defeated in a battle with their whole people and at the same time
blockaded by [our] ships, will be unable to hold out against the force
6.91.3   of the Athenians now there. But if the polis [of the Syracusans] is
6.91.4   taken, all Sicily will be possessed and straightaway all Italy. And the
danger from there that I was just predicting won't be long falling on
you—and so let [each of you] think that he is deliberating not about
Sicily alone but also about the Peloponnese—unless you do quickly
the things [that I recommend], that is, send on ships the kind of
army that [once it has been] brought to [Sicily] is immediately [ready
to fight as] foot soldiers, and—what I think is still more useful than

---

76   There is perhaps a deliberate lack of clarity in the antecedent of "from there." Is Alcibiades
referring just to Sicily, or is he including also the rest of Italy and the Carthaginian world?
The lack of clarity makes the threat seem more ominous to the Lacedaemonians.

the army—send a man of the Spartiate class[77] to be in charge and put in order the existing [forces] and compel the ones not willing [to serve]. You see, in this way both your friends who are already there for you will be more confident, and those who are hesitating will more fearlessly join you. And [finally,] it is necessary to expand the war more openly in [the situation] here, both so that the Syracusans, thinking that you care about them, resist more [aggressively], and so that the Athenians send less additional help to their own or their allies' forces. And it is necessary to wall in Decelea [as a fort]—a [prospect] that the Athenians always most fear and the only one of the [evils that] they have not experienced in the war. Most safely would one thus harm his enemy, if he should perceive what they fear most of all, and, when he learns it clearly, should attack [it]; you see, it is fitting that all people know for themselves most accurately what [they have to] fear. Concerning the ways in which you will benefit yourselves by walling in [the stronghold at Decelea], while you hinder the enemy [from being benefited], I shall pass over many [of the ways] and sum up the most important. You see, many of the things with which the land is furnished will be taken by you, and the rest you will have spontaneously. And they will immediately be deprived of the revenues from the silver mines of Laurium, and [they will be deprived] of as many things from the land and from the courts by which they are now benefited, and especially of the less regularly paid-in revenue from their allies, who, judging from your [actions that] you are already going to war with [all] your strength, will take lightly [the levies placed on them by the Athenians].

6.91.5

6.91.6

6.91.7

And it depends on you for any of these things to happen quickly and more to your heart's desire, since of course I am completely confident [that they can be carried out]—and I don't think I've made a mistake in judgment. And I think it right that I seem to none of you to be a worse [man], if, once seeming to be a lover of my polis, now, along with those who are its greatest enemies, I strongly attack my own [polis]; and I don't [think it right] that my speech be suspected for its [expressing] the zeal of an exile. You see, I am an exile from the wickedness of the people driving me out, and not because, if you are persuaded by me, from any benefit [I've provided to you]; and you who harm your enemies are not, I suppose, more hostile [to a polis] than those who compel their friends to become enemies [to it]. And I do not have love of my polis in [those situations in which]

6.92.1

6.92.2

6.92.3

6.92.4

---

77   The Spartiates were the ruling class in Sparta. The class was devoted wholly to war, boys being taken from their mothers at age seven and then disciplined in the military arts.

I am treated unjustly, but in [those in which] I was living safely as a citizen. Nor is it against my fatherland that I think that I am going, but it is much more [a land] that isn't [mine] that [I think I am] trying to recover. And he who is rightly a lover of his polis is not he who after he has lost it unjustly does not attack it but he who from every resource tries to take it back on account of his desire [for it]. Thus I think it right that you fearlessly use me in danger and every distress, Lacedaemonians, knowing this, the argument urged on by everyone, that if I, as an enemy, harmed you exceedingly, so also as a friend I would benefit you sufficiently, in proportion, on the one hand, to my knowledge of the affairs of the Athenians, and, on the other, to my conjecture about your affairs. [And I think it right that you] yourselves—having determined that you are now deliberating about [your] greatest interests—not hold back the army [from going] to Sicily and Attica so that, concerning the [situation] in those places], you may, [by] assisting with a small part [of your military], bring about safety in the greatest matters and destroy the present and future power of the Athenians, and after these [actions] you will live safely and you will hold hegemony over all the Greek world—[and they shall be] held willingly!—by good will and not by force.

6.92.5

Appendix B

Rules of Socratic Dialectic Derivable from the *Gorgias*

From the *Gorgias* of Plato it is possible to extrapolate a set of rules for Socratic dialectic as it is used in the *Gorgias* and in the dialogues generally. The rules are a combination of the universal ways in which philosophers go about reasoning and of the idiosyncratic ways particular to the Platonic Socrates. The term *Platonic* is essential, for the rules laid out here are not in evidence in the other surviving ancient portrayals of Socrates' conversational methods. A compendium of the rules derivable from the *Gorgias* follows.

- The answers must be short. When Socrates asks Gorgias a question, he answers with a long speech; Socrates requests that he keep his answers short (448e).

- Both participants must desire to understand what the argument is about; in this way they will advance the argument (453b).

- Both parties in the dialogue must understand that the one who asks the questions is speaking on behalf of the audience, many of whom are too shy to speak. In short, the questioner is interested not only for his own sake but also for that of people in general (455d).

- Both speakers must have good will and must be consistent. If both parties are not alike in this respect, the conversation must be ended. If the answerer gets caught in a contradiction—an *aporia* (the Greek word means "a place of no exit")—he must not become angry. To be caught in a contradiction is not a disgrace, if one's answers were sincere; in fact, it is a blessing, for now he knows that what he thought was in error. And surely, Socrates says, no person wants to be in error (457d).

- Each interlocutor aims at getting the other to be a witness to what the interlocutor has said: what the other is to be a witness to is the truth of what has been said, for such agreement means that the arguments square with reality. If such agreement is not reached, nothing will have been accomplished (472b, 474a, and 475).

- When such agreement is achieved, we have friendship. Truth has the power to unite human beings in friendship, but error and falsehoods do not (473a).

- The dialogue must be between two people only. The practitioner of dialectic must speak with only one person at a time (474b).

- Contradiction guarantees that what has been said is not true; if there is a choice between what is contradictory and what is not contradictory, what is not contradictory, however absurd, must be true (480e).

- There are three prerequisites of intellectual character for engaging in dialogue (487a): (1) *knowledge*: each participant must know something and recognize knowledge when he sees it; that is, he must recognize when words square with reality; (2) *good will*: that is, each participant must have his opponent's welfare at heart; he must be arguing for truth, not victory; (3) *that each must speak freely*; that is, each must say what is on his mind and not hedge or equivocate or hold back (487a).

- Each participant must be aware that repetition does not invalidate truth. No matter how familiar a truth may be to the participant, no matter how trite a truism may sound, he must acknowledge its truth and not turn away out of boredom, looking for something different out of a desire for novelty (490e).

- Sincerity is essential in each interlocutor: each must say what he believes or the implied contract in the dialectical conversation is broken (495a).

- Engaging in such dialogue is the greatest good in and for life, for this is to engage in philosophy (500c).

- All people should compete in the pursuit of truth through this dialectic, for only from such sincere, prolonged competition will truth emerge. And truth is a common good for humankind (505e).

- If an argument is true, one must see what follows from it. In other words, the dialogue must go on, no matter where it leads (508b).

Why it is important to understand these rules of dialectic may be illustrated by an analogy. As to an observer of a person sneezing it is not apparent whether the sneeze be from a head-cold or an allergy—two radically different causes of the same effect—so to an observer of two people wrangling in a debate it is not clear whether the wrangling be caused by a desire for victory or for truth. Whether the aim be victory or truth, we observe the same signs—stirred emotions, complex arguments, intense concentration. In the dynamic situation of two people, moreover, it may be that one is aiming at truth, the other at victory, and, of course, the goal might shift even in the same individual as he loses or gains self-control. The rules we have extracted from Socrates' comments in the *Gorgias* are ideal rules, and, as we have occasionally pointed out in the notes, even Socrates doesn't seem always to follow them. But, again, *Plato's* purpose, at least in part, as we have said,[1] is different from that of the *character* Socrates. Plato's purpose is to draw his readers into the debate and have them say, "*I* could have done better here. What Socrates—or Polus or Callicles— *should* have said is…."

An essential rule that deserves to be emphasized is that the dialectical engagement be one-on-one. In this respect alone, dialectic—where one person wishes to discover truth with one other person—is quite different from politics, where a speaker wishes to move a crowd. In dialectic, there is much less room than in speeches for sleights of argument, for every claim is assessed as it is made, the interlocutors focused solely on the claim and not distracted by emotional appeals or other forms of rhetorical pandering. Finally, it should perhaps be observed that teaching by dialectic is radically different from most of the teaching that goes on in high schools, colleges and universities, even that in tutorials and seminars. Socratic teaching is exceptionally rare, and when it does occur, it seems to embroil its practitioners in many of the same problems as it did Socrates, principally the attribution of a bad motive—that the dialectician is not pursuing truth but is deliberately trying to humiliate his interlocutor by driving him into perplexity (*aporia*) .

---

1   See Introduction, pp. 6-7.

Appendix C

Mythos and Logos

In *Gorgias* 523a, Socrates says:

> Hear a very fine account [*logos*] indeed, as the saying goes, one you'll consider a tale [*mythos*], as I think, but I an account [*logos*].

With these words Socrates introduces his "myth" of the afterlife, in which he describes the underworld and the three judges who judge the souls of human beings. A brief history of the use of these words in Plato's dialogues may help to explain this strange use of the words *logos* and *mythos*, which we have translated as "account" and "tale."

In the *Theaetetus* (155d9 ff.), Socrates uses *mythos* to introduce a summary of a metaphysical theory that he gives without any fictive detail at all and then rejects the theory as false. Here the word is used both of exposition, in a sense that would seem to require *logos* (argument), and of falsehood, in a sense appropriate to one of the usual meanings of *mythos*. In the *Laws* (719c), the Athenian Stranger says that there is an ancient *mythos*, which he refers to frequently and which all men can accept, to the effect that poets, when they sit on the tripod of the Muses and are inspired, gush forth like fountains with a mixture of the true and the false, which they cannot distinguish. Later in the *Laws* (872c1), he speaks of "the *mythos* or *logos* or whatever you wish to call it . . ." and, at the very end of the *Republic* (621b8–c1), Socrates says:

> And thus, Glaucon, a *mythos* has been saved and is not lost, and it would save us, if we would be persuaded by it, and we shall cross the river Lethe well and shall not be stained in soul.

Here Socrates uses *mythos* in the same way that he uses *logos* in the *Gorgias*.

From this evidence, one might conclude that the two words are interchangeable. Each word can signify either a real or a fictive world; and whichever world Plato has in mind, he can use either term to show that the account he is giving is either true or false. Thus in the *Theaetetus*, *mythos* signifies an account of reality that is false. In the *Laws*, *mythos* signifies an account of fictive reality that expresses truth. In the *Republic*, *mythos* hovers between these two meanings. In other words, even if the *mythos* should not be fully accurate, and hence false to some extent, it presupposes a reality about which truth can be expressed.

In the *Gorgias*, Socrates says that Callicles may call the account a *mythos* in the sense of being a description of a fictive world and a false one at that. Presumably Callicles would deny that any true account of a fictive world could be given. To Socrates, however, *mythos* signifies either an account of reality that is true or an account of a fictive world that still expresses truth. The term *logos*, which Socrates says here that he prefers, will also signify these two alternatives (i.e., either an account of reality that is true or an account of a fictive world that still expresses truth). Whichever we choose, the operative word will be "true": as Socrates says immediately, "The things that I shall say, you see, are [things] I intend to say as truth."[1]

---

1   On such truth in fiction, see *Gorgias* note 221.

Glossary

aim (σκοπὸς *[skopos]*: 507d)

We have translated this word somewhat cumbersomely as "what we must set our eyes on in order to live properly." While its meaning is essentially the same as *telos* ["goal" or "end"], its etymology is quite different, containing a metaphor of looking or gazing—images related to vision.

choice of life (βίου αἵρεσις *[biou hairesis]*: 521a)

Socrates says that he is trying to persuade Callicles to reject a life that is greedy and intemperate and instead to choose "a life [that is] orderly and adequate and content with the things it happens to have." When Cicero said that Socrates took philosophy out of the sky and put it in the cities and houses of human beings (*Tusculum Disputations* 5.4.10) he was referring to this emphasis on making the choice of the best possible life. The idea that one has a choice of life—that one's life is not based solely on a fixed fate determined by a divine source—is a permanent feature of the Greek mind from the very first surviving work of literature, Homer's *Iliad*, in which Achilles has the choice of a long and undistinguished life or a short and glorious life; to the famous choice of Heracles between Virtue and Vice; to the choice alluded to in the *Gorgias*, in Euripides' *Antiope*, and discussed in later philosophical writing on the relative merits of the contemplative and practical lives; to the choice, also debated in the *Gorgias*, on the relative merits of the tyrannical and the law-abiding lives. From the fourth century on there are numerous stories about conversion-experiences that result in the choice of a philosophical way of life. Among such converts are Plato, who converted from drama; Polemon, who converted from a playboy-life of drunken debauchery; Antisthenes, a disciple of Gorgias, who converted from rhetoric; Zeno, who converted from a business life; and Crates, who converted from a life of affluence. In the New Testament, the choice of life often results from a miraculous conversion experience, as, for example, the experiences of Peter, Andrew, James, John, and Paul.

convention (νόμος *[nomos]*: 482e)

Convention comes from the Latin word meaning *to come together*. It indicates a pre-arranged agreement to act in a certain way, even when any given individual has no personal conviction that such action is especially good. For example, members of a certain fraternity may be expected to shake hands in a certain way on particular occasions. Because human beings become so habituated to their environment (with its conventions) that everything in it seems natural, they sometimes have difficulty distinguishing between its actually natural and conventional features. The ancients discussed this matter

221

in the fifth century B.C.E., in what is known as the debate about convention and nature (*nomos* and *physis*). The term "convention" differs from "custom" in that with "convention" there is a pre-arrangement, though the distinction is thin and not always observed. For example, while it is a convention for a fraternity to shake hands in a certain way, it is a custom to shake hands. The Greek word *nomos* can also mean "law," and it regularly does so in compounds, such as law-making and law-giving. We have typically not used "law" in this translation even where its use might seem to be called for (e.g., at 474e, 488d, and 523a) in order to emphasize the sense that conventions are established by the decisions of human beings. In 488e, Socrates introduces a variant with overlapping meanings—*nomima*—perhaps in an attempt to preserve some of the relevant distinctions. We have translated *nomima* as "rules."

demos (δῆμος *[demos]*: 451b)

Demos refers to what is in the public domain, sometimes specifically to public lands or townships. Sometimes it refers to the populace, as distinct from the nobility (*aristoi* in Greek, from which we derive "aristocracy") or from the well-off few (*oligoi* in Greek, from which we derive "oligarchy"). In some cases, as here, it may refer to the popular assembly. *Demos* is part of the word *democracy*, which means "rule by the public at large"—not representative rule (as, say, in the United States; in fact, Aristotle seems to suggest that elections for representatives are undemocratic, for they take political power away from the public and put in into the hands of the few [*Politics* 130a9-b4]).

engage in dialectic (διαλέγεσθαι *[dialegesthai]*: 448)

The verb translated as "engage in dialectic," the method of question and answer that Socrates uses, is also the verb for "engage in conversation." Since Socrates enunciates the various rules for dialectic throughout the dialogue, we have chosen the more technical meaning for this translation, for it was probably the sense that would resonate within Plato's group, which very likely constituted the original audience of the dialogue. For those outside Plato's group, the meaning "engage in conversation" would have been more natural. Since, alas, we have no knowledge at all of Plato's actual audience, any assumption is speculative. We should, perhaps, leave open the question of whether for Socrates conversation and dialectic are distinct. Briefly stated, dialectic is a technique of question-and-answer in which the participants debate some issue that is (to them) vitally important. Dialectic rests on the assumptions that (1) truth exists; (2) truth is the agreement of two human beings following the rules of reason; (3) inconsistency, that is, contradiction, is the surest sign available that the conclusion reached is not true; and (4) both people must be willing to "stay at their posts" and argue until consistency is reached. When consistency is achieved, the participants enjoy the certainty and the calmness of soul that results from it. See also Appendix B.

excellence (ἀρετή *[arête]*: 479b)

The Greek word that we have translated as *excellence* basically refers to an ability to do something well. The ability differs according to the nature of the particular thing that possesses the ability. Achilles speaks of the "excellence" of horses he will offer in the funeral games for Patroclus (*Iliad* 276); Socrates speaks of the "excellence" of eyes (*Republic* 353b) and in the *Gorgias* (479b) of the "excellence" of a body—and in each of these cases it refers to the special ability of the object—the running of horses, the seeing of eyes, and the numerous functions of bodies. Because the word is used of human excellence, it is often translated as "virtue," but we have elected the more general sense. What actually comprises human excellence is a matter that underwent various changes in Greek culture, from warlike prowess in Homeric times to rational activity in Aristotle; it is a matter that continues to engage scientists, humanists, and social scientists—indeed, trying to discover just what constitutes the particular excellence of human beings may be one of their defining characteristics. For a splendid history of the word and the concept in ancient Greece, see Werner Jaeger, *Paideia: The Ideals of Greek,* tr. Gilbert Highet (New York: Oxford University Press, 1945) Volume 1, 4–14.

experience (ἐμπειρία *[empeiria]*: 448c)

Aristotle explains that the starting points for each science come from experience (*Prior Analytics* 46a). Thus, to use Aristotle's example, one experiences the celestial phenomena and, once they are adequately apprehended, applies reason to create the logical demonstration that turns the collection of observations into the science of astronomy. One of the differences between rhetoricians of the fifth century and the poets who preceded them was that the rhetoricians gave examples from contemporary affairs, whereas the poets told tales from mythology. In the *Gorgias,* for example, Gorgias discusses his helping his physician brother convince a patient to take his prescribed medicine, while Polus supports his argument by bringing up the example of the contemporary tyrant Archelaus. What vexes Polus when Socrates calls rhetoric at most "an experience" is that Socrates appears to rank experience very low in the intellectual hierarchy. Surely, in Polus' opinion, experience is to rhetoric as stargazing was to the science of astronomy.

graspingness (πλεονεξία *[pleonexia]*: 508a)

The term we have translated as "graspingness" is, in Greek, *pleonexia*. It indicates a desire to have more than one's proper share and, obviously, is opposed to having an equal or proper share. (The last logical possibility—a desire to have less than a proper share—is never addressed.) In mythology "graspingness" is what characterizes those who would aggrandize themselves against the gods. Callicles, however, praises grasping for more than one's equal share, at *Gorgias* 483c. While ancient morality generally deplored graspingness among private individuals (e.g., Herodotus, *History of the Persian Wars* 8.112, where Themistocles' greed is disparaged), it seems to have been an acceptable motive for one sovereign power to attack another. Throughout the histories of Herodotus and Thucydides the aims of conquering the good things of others or of acquiring still more power are adduced as motives for aggression. (See, for example, Herodotus 1.71, 9.122; Thucydides *History of the Peloponnesian Wars* 5.105, 6.18).

moderation (μετριότης *[metriotes]*: 484c)

Where self-restraint is control exercised over one's passions or appetites, "moderation" is an actively calculated seeking of the mean. *Moderation*, derived from *measure* (μετρον), first determines and then seeks the right quantity. Because self-restraint and moderation are closely related and often accompany one another, they are often confused. The difference is perhaps one of nuance: *self-restraint* is control exercised in repressing a desire for too much of a good thing; moderation is the activity of aiming at the mean or, in the case of a moderate person, a settled disposition to aim at the mean. For example, a person might say he exercised *self-restraint* at the dessert buffet when he took only one piece of blueberry pie but that he aimed at *moderation* when he deliberately chose a low-fat main course from the menu. As has been observed (Helen North, *Sophrosyne: Self-Knowledge and Self-Restraint in Greek Literature* [Ithaca: Cornell University Press, 1966] 113 and Michael Palmer, *Love of Glory and the Common Good* [Savage, MD: Rowman and Littlefield, 1992] 130 n. 31), Thucydides uses terms related to *moderation* (μετριότης) of Athenians rather than of Spartans, for whom he uses words related to self-restraint (σωφροσύνη). Perhaps Thucydides did not think his fellow citizens capable of self-restraint but of a calculated political moderation.

nature (φύσις *[physis]*: 465c)

Nature is what art imitates, what science analyzes. Most uses of nature can be resolved into one of these three propositions: (1) nature is whatever happens; (2) nature is the statistical majority; (3) nature is what ought to be. The famous line in *Hamlet*—that art holds a mirror up to nature—rests on the assumption that nature has reality and form; contemporary relativistic notions assume that reality consists of a series of imposed viewpoints, the sum total of which will, at any given time, constitute reality, and this totality increases with each new scientific theory or observation, with each new artistic vision. Human nature is that part of nature in which we find the operations of the human psyche—reason, free will, emotion, thought. When Stoics speak of a "life according to nature," they often mean "according to human nature," i.e., "in accordance with reason."

out-of-place (ἄτοπος *[atopos]*: 465e)

Underlying the term is the idea of a *cosmos,* an ordered whole—either of a *polis* or the universe—where things have a proper place. The term generally carries more negative connotations than our word "eccentric." Nevertheless, Plato seems fond of the term *out-of-place* and uses it often of Socrates (*Gorgias* 494d, *Symposium* 221d). Perhaps Plato is suggesting that Socrates is out-of-place in *this* world of practical affairs and that his proper place is in the world of ideas. Thomas More uses the root *-top* in the equivocal title of his *Utopia,* where the "U" can come either from *eu*—"good"—or from *ou*—" no"—yielding "Goodplace" or "Noplace."

pandering (κολακεία *[kolakeia]*: 463b)

The term we have translated as "pandering" is usually translated as "flattery." Both translations are somewhat problematic. "Pandering" strictly refers to acting as a sexual go-between or pimp. In contemporary informal usage, especially in political discourse, it refers to telling voters what they want to hear in order to win their support. Such pandering may compliment voters or play to their fears or seduce their hopes, and it is exactly this political sense, with its moral repugnance but without any sexual connotation that we are stressing. The term "flattery" refers to winning the favor of a hearer by compliments and, at least in contemporary American English, does not carry the distaste and contempt of "pandering."

paradigm (παράδειγμα *[paradeigma]*: 525b)

A paradigm is one of Aristotle's three classes of imitation (*Poetics* 1460b). The three kinds of imitation are (1) things as they were or are; (2) things as they are said or seem to be; (3) things as they ought to be. The last is the paradigm (1461a13), of which Aristotle says, "The paradigm ought to excel." The paradigm is not the model that the artist imitates, but the imitation itself, as an electric eye is a ""paradigm" of the human eye that, for the purposes for which it was designed, is superior to the human eye. In the *Rhetoric* (1393a), Aristotle says that since the paradigm resembles an induction, it is a starting point of knowledge. He goes on to point out that paradigms may be either the invented kind found in fables or the historical kind.

persuasion (πειθώ *[peitho]*: 453a)

Persuasion is the process of inducing a desired response in other individuals. In general, though there are many forms of persuasion, including torture, bribery, extortion, and threats, the term refers to inducing the response by *logos.* In rhetoric, the *logos* generally takes the form of an appeal to the emotions; in philosophy it takes the form of argument. Civilized society allows both forms. Since it is easier to give a semblance of truth rather than formulate a comprehensible and consistent argument, rhetoric has enjoyed a greater success than philosophy. In antiquity hundreds of manuals were written to teach the arts of persuasion by rhetorical means. For Plato, however, such rhetoric was the enemy of philosophy; for Aristotle, rhetoric was a subject of philosophical inquiry and could serve philosophy. It is perhaps ironic therefore that the dialogues of Plato are emotionally inspirational on account of their rhetoric, while the surviving works of Aristotle, rhetorically dull, are far less stirring.

pleonexia (πλεονεξία [pleonexia]: 508a)

See "graspingness."

polis (πόλις [polis] 452d)

The usual translation, "city-state"—conjuring up images of Vatican City or the principality of Monaco—does not adequately convey a sense of what a *polis* was. In brief, a polis embraced the entire life of a human being; in the ancient world it was to a human being what a herd is to cattle, but, of course, with all the characteristics that define humanity. Each polis was its own culture, with its own linguistic features, music, literature, history, religious rituals and local deities, weights and measures, calendar, constitution, and manner of life. To suffer exile from one's polis was to be deprived of everything and everyone that was meaningful in life—and perhaps this fact helps us to understand why Socrates (in both the *Apology* and *Crito*) chooses death rather than separation from Athens. For us, the term "city-state" is, ironically, too "political" in the modern sense of the word—focusing too much on government and bureaucracy and too little on culture.

power (δύναμις [dynamis]: 452e)

The term "power" usually refers to power in the physical sense, as distinct from *kratos*—power in the legal sense. But for Socrates in the *Gorgias* there is no power without mind (466e). Thus, says Socrates, even though rhetors may be in charge of their *poleis*, they have the least power in them.

resentment (φθόνος [phthonos]: 2.35.2])

There are a number of words that show pain at the good fortune or success of others: covetousness, envy, resentment, indignation, emulation, and begrudging. These words differ in meaning in subtle but significant ways. We shall try to distinguish these in English and indicate which exist in Greek. *Covetousness* is the pain one feels at another's material good combined with a desire to possess *that very* good, not a material good like it, but that very good. For example, one might covet his neighbor's Ferrari: he does not want one like it, but that very Ferrari (this is the sin God forbids in the Ten Commandments in the Bible). *Envy* is the pain one feel at another's advantage combined with a desire for the same advantage. For example, one may envy his neighbor his academically successful children and desire that one's own children be similarly successful. There do not seem to have been words for covetousness and envy in the ancient Greek vocabulary. *Resentment* (φθόνος) is the pain one feels at another's success when the success is deserved, and it is felt when the success is achieved by persons similar to oneself and one is displeased that the other individual has achieved it. It is not accompanied by a desire to achieve that same success; it is merely a pain at *the other's* having achieved it. For example, if one's neighbor has won praise for saving a child from a burning building, one might resent the praise the neighbor has received without wishing to obtain it for oneself. Resentment may be accompanied by begrudging (a term explained below in this entry). Resentment is not virtuous and bespeaks a bad character. *Emulation* (ζῆλος) is the activity resulting from the pain felt at another's good that it is possible for one to obtain. The activity involves trying to surpass the good the other has achieved. For example, in emulating a neighbor's garden, one seeks to have a garden better than his. Emulation is virtuous and characteristic of virtuous people. *Indignation* (νέμεσις) is the pain felt both at the undeserved fortune of a bad person and at the failure of a good person to achieve what he deserves. For example, if a neighbor, a member of organized crime, inherits a fortune from the estate of a man his crime organization has murdered, or if a courageous man goes unrecognized for his courage, one feels the pain of indignation. Indignation is characteristic of virtuous individuals. These distinctions are not always observed, especially in English, where "envy"—the usual translation of the Greek φθόνος—is often confused with "resentment"—our translation of φθόνος. A related word, *begrudging,* refers not to the pain felt at another's good, but to the pain felt because one does not have some good—a pain joined with the desire that another not have that good either. For example, if one cannot grow roses in his garden, he does not want his neighbor, or anyone else, to grow roses either—he begrudges his neighbor the growing of roses. Begrudging also bespeaks a bad character. Yet another related word, *jealousy,* refers to the possession of something and a desire that no one else have it. For example, a man who is jealous of his wife possesses her and does not wish to share her with others; in the Ten Commandments, when God says that he is a jealous God, he means that he does not wish to share the devotion of his people with other gods. A child who is jealous of his toys does not wish to share them with other children. Whether jealousy is good or bad depends on the nature of the possession and the correctness of sharing it.

The sympathetic reader will understand that distinguishing all these words, and then trying to ascertain which Greek word goes with which in English (if any) is a matter complicated and ripe with opportunities for error. This comment may be applied to the entire glossary and translation.

rhetoric (ῥητορική *[rhetorike]*: 448d)

Rhetoric is the use of language to work on the emotions. One starts with certain aims and intentions, certain ideas, and then seeks ways to make them persuasive. The set of techniques for doing so leaves the user of rhetoric open to the charge of insincerity, of a lack of organic connection with his subject and position; hence the sustained attack by Plato on rhetoric. Inquiry into the techniques of persuasion was a sustained focus of study in antiquity, and a great many treatises were written. Perhaps the best was Aristotle's *Rhetoric*.

self-restraint (σωφροσύνη *[sophrosyne]*: 492a)

Self-restraint refers to the Delphic injunction "know thyself"—as it is reflected primarily in knowing one's limitations—both as a man and as a citizen. It goes beyond what we would call "moderation," the usual translation of the Greek word, for the emphasis is not so much on seeking the mean as on repressing one's appetite for pleasures. Self-restraint is also manifested in repressing *pleonexia*, the grasping for more than one's proper share. Self-restraint restrains the tendency of people to think that they are mightier than they are—whether in the myths about the men and women foolish enough to challenge the gods to contests or in the politics of the real world where polis challenges polis to war. The opposite of self-restraint is wantonness (ἀκολασία). For a brilliant and thorough account of *sophrosyne* in Greek thought (including the use of the term in Plato's *Gorgias*), see Helen North, *Sophrosyne: Self-Knowledge and Self-Restraint in Greek Literature* (Ithaca: Cornell University Press, 1966).

serious (σπουδή *[spoude]*: 501b)

The Greek noun and its congener verb show a range of mental focus that can be rendered by such English words as "serious," "eager," and "enthusiastic" and their substantival forms ("seriousness," "eagerness," "enthusiasm"). Opposed to seriousness is playfulness, and clearly, for many, including Callicles in the *Gorgias* (481b–c), the two are opposites. Thus Callicles asks Chaerephon whether Socrates is being serious or playing and a bit later (484c) says that philosophy, presumably a non-serious activity, is suitable for young people in moderation but not for mature persons (484c). Plato, however, seems to have held a different view. In the Sixth Letter, speaking in his own person, Plato writes that seriousness is the sister of play (323d). And one might read a good many of the dialogues as play, with their comic reversals, puns, and silliness, while at the same time serious points emerge. Aristotle taught that opposites fall under the same genus (*Topics* 111a), a point Plato anticipated when at the end of the *Symposium* (223d) he has Socrates forcing the tragedian Agathon and the comedian Aristophanes, to admit that the same person who can write tragedy can also write comedy. And, as if to give divine authority to a sense of humor, Plato has Socrates declare in the *Cratylus* (a dialogue rich in humor) that the gods love play (*Cratylus* 406c).

technical skill (τεχνη *[techne]*: 500a)

The Greek word refers to a skill that requires the specialized knowledge of a set of rules and procedures. Lyre-playing, medicine, horsemanship would be examples of such "technical skills." See below, 500e–501a, where Socrates talks about what it is to be a "technical skill." The word can also be translated as "art," where it is understood that a set of rules applies. In the *Protagoras* (318d), Plato has his character Protagoras include number theory, astronomy, geometry, and music among the technical skills.

wantonness (ἀκολασία *[akolasia]*: 492c)

The Greek word that we translate as "wantonness" and in its adjectival form as "wanton" is derived from the verb that means "to prune" or "cut back" "keep within proper bounds and limits." Behavior that is not "pruned," "cut back," or "kept within its proper bounds" is wanton, i.e., not governed by self-restraint. As the term in the dialogue refers to an absence of restraint in the matter of pleasures, the English term does a good job of translating the notion. The Greek word is often translated as "immoderate" or "intemperate," and while these translations are adequate, they do not fully reflect that the line has been crossed into lewdness. For example, a person who drinks too much at a dinner with friends is *intemperate*; if he then goes around the table finishing off the half-empty wine glasses of his companions, he becomes *wanton*: this is the point at which the lack of moderation or temperance crosses the boundary into the territory covered by wantonness. In an older era, *intemperance* would have carried a devastating stigma; today, alas, we do not normally look upon a person who is intemperate as bathed in the moral disgrace that still accompanies *wanton*. If one reads Callicles' praise of vice in 490e–492c and substitutes "intemperance" for "wantonness," he will miss the radically shocking assertion Callicles is proclaiming. Another problem with "intemperance" is that it tends to refer in contemporary English to overindulgence in alcohol (perhaps because of the nineteenth century Temperance Movement), whereas the Greek word refers to a lack of restraint not merely in alcohol and food but (and perhaps especially) in sex—again, a meaning still present in "wantonness."

Bibliography

Editions

Dodds, E.R. (ed.), *Plato. Gorgias: A Revised Text with Introduction and Commentary*. Oxford: Clarendon Press, 1959.

Burnet, John (ed.), *Platonis Opera* vol. 3. Oxford: Oxford University Press, 1903.

Lodge, Gonzalez (ed.), *Plato. Gorgias*. Boston: Ginn & Co., 1891.

Translations

Helmbold, W.C. (tr.), *Plato. Gorgias*. Upper Saddle River, NJ: Prentice Hall, 1952.

Irwin, Terence (tr.), *Plato. Gorgias*. Oxford: Clarendon Press, 1979.

Lamb, W.R.M. (tr.), *Plato: Lysis, Symposium, Gorgias*. Cambridge, MA: Harvard University Press, 1925.

Nichols, James H., Jr. (tr.), *Plato: Gorgias*. Ithaca and London: Cornell University Press, 1998.

General Books on Rhetoric

Guthrie, W.K.C., *The Sophists*. Cambridge: Cambridge University Press, 1971.

Kennedy, George A., *A New History of Classical Rhetoric*. Princeton: Princeton University Press, 1994.

Wardy, Robert, *The Birth of Rhetoric. Gorgias, Plato and Their Successors*, London (Routledge) 1998.

Recent Studies in English on Plato's *Gorgias*

Arieti, James A., "Plato's Philosophical *Antiope*: The *Gorgias*," in *Plato's Dialogues: New Studies and Interpretations*. G. Press (ed.), Lanham, MD: Rownan and Littlefield, (1993): 197-214.

Benardete, Seth, *The Rhetoric of Morality and Philosophy. Plato's Gorgias and Phaedrus*. Chicago: University of Chicago Press, 1991.

Blank, David L., "The Fate of the Ignorant in Plato's *Gorgias*." *Hermes* 119 (1991): 22–36.

231

Consigny, Scott, "Gorgias' Use of Epideictic." *Philosophy and Rhetoric* 25 (1992): 281–297.

Daniels, Charles B., "The Afterlife Myth in Plato's *Gorgias*." *The Journal of Value Inquiry* 26 (1992): 271–279.

Demos, M., "Callicles' Quotation of Pindar in the *Gorgias*." *Harvard Studies in Classical Philology* 96 (1994): 85–107.

Fussi, Alessandra, "Callicles' Examples of *nomos tes phuseos* in Plato's *Gorgias*." *Graduate Faculty Philosophy Journal* 19 (1996): 119–149.

Gentzler, Jyl, "The Sophistic Cross-examination of Callicles in the *Gorgias*." *Ancient Philosophy* 15 (1995): 17–43.

Haden, James, "Two Types of Power in Plato's *Gorgias*." *Classical Journal* 87 (1991–92): 313–326.

Kastely, James, "In Defense of Plato's *Gorgias*." Publication of the Modern Language Association 106 (1991): 96–109.

Kerferd G. B. "Plato's Treatment of Callicles in the Gorgias." *Proceedings of the Cambridge Philological Society* 20 (1974): 48–52.

Michelini, A.N., " Pollè agroikía. Rudeness and Irony in Plato's *Gorgias*." *Classical Philology* 93 (1998): 50–59.

Nightingale, Andrea Wilson, "Plato's *Gorgias* and Euripides' *Antiope*: A Study in Generic Transformation." *Classical Antiquity* 11 (1992): 121–141.

Pangle, Thomas L., "Plato's *Gorgias* as a Vindication of Socratic Education." *Polis* 10 (1991): 3–21.

Plastira-Valkanou, Maria, "Medicine and Fine Cuisine in Plato's *Gorgias*." *L'Antiquité Classique* 67 (1998): 195–201.

Rocco, Chris, "Liberating Discourse: The Politics of Truth in Plato's *Gorgias*." *Interpretation* 23 (1996): 361–385.

Saxonhouse, Arlene W., "An Unspoken Theme in Plato's *Gorgias*." *Interpretation* 23 (1983): 139-169.

Turner, Jeffrey S., "*Atopia* and Plato's *Gorgias*." *International Studies in Philosophy* 25 (1993): 69–77.

Weiss, Roslyn, "Killing, Confiscating, and Banishing at Gorgias 466–468." *Ancient Philosophy* 12 (1992): 299–315.

Index

Page numbers are those of this edition. Where a number is in italics, the reference is to a footnote on the indicated page. A number in boldface indicates a quotation. A number in both boldface and italics indicates a quotation in a footnote. Finally, a word in boldface is entered in the Glossary.